YOUR KNOWLEDGE HAS ~~VALUE~~

Bibliographic information published by the German National Library:

The German National Library lists this publication in the National Bibliography; detailed bibliographic data are available on the Internet at http://dnb.dnb.de .

Cover image: Marina Zakharova @Shutterstock.com

Imprint:

Copyright © 2017 GRIN Verlag
Print and binding: Books on Demand GmbH, Norderstedt Germany
ISBN: 9783668891531

This book at GRIN:

https://www.grin.com/document/460986

Barry Grossman

Metaphoric self-awareness in reflexive constructions

GRIN Verlag

GRIN - Your knowledge has value

Since its foundation in 1998, GRIN has specialized in publishing academic texts by students, college teachers and other academics as e-book and printed book. The website www.grin.com is an ideal platform for presenting term papers, final papers, scientific essays, dissertations and specialist books.

Visit us on the internet:

http://www.grin.com/

http://www.facebook.com/grincom

http://www.twitter.com/grin_com

METAPHORIC SELF-AWARENESS IN REFLEXIVE CONSTRUCTIONS

by Dr. Barry H. Grossman

Contents

List of Tables

4

<u>List of Figures</u>

List of Appendices

Part I: Self-Aware Events and Reflexives

Chapter 1: Reflexives and Self-Awareness

1.1   Introduction

Dave Dahl, the owner and creator of Dave's Killer Bread, spent some time in prison where he did a fair amount of self-contemplation. In the quotation below, taken from the bread package label, Dave uses reflexive pronouns to convey his introspection and the insights he's gained from it.

> …15 years in prison is a pretty tough way to find oneself, but I have no regrets. This time around, I took advantage of all those long and lonely days by practicing my guitar, exercising, and getting to know myself - without drugs... It's been said adversity introduces a man to himself and I found this to be true... A whole lot of suffering has transformed an ex-con into an honest man who is doing his best to make the world a better place… One loaf of bread at a time (Dave Dahl, label on "Dave's Killer Bread").

What does the phrase *find oneself* mean and how do we know this? Does a person *find oneself* in the same way one finds a coin on the sidewalk? Why is the metaphor of *find* used and not some other verb, as in the next sentence, *…getting to know myself*, an expression famously used by Socrates for introspection, "Oh man, know thyself and thou shall know the Universe of the Gods!" Furthermore, the abstract noun *adversity* in the final example takes the place of a human agent that can perform introductions, i.e., *introduce a man to himself.* This phrase is used metaphorically, but how do the individual components of the phrase allow for a Self-Aware[1] meaning? Does the meaning of *found* in the conjoined clause in line four have the same meaning as *find* in line one?

In the investigation that follows, it will be seen that the underlying conceptual commonality of these instances is Self-Awareness, not simply in reference to a speaker's self-knowledge, but an acute meta-awareness of one's state or situation. Although phrases such as *know myself* have been around for a long time, there are other verbs which, when used

---

[1] I will be using the capitals 'S, A' in Self-Awareness to refer to the deeper, mainly subconscious aspect of the human psyche.

metaphorically within in a reflexive construction, also refer to this type of Self-Awareness. Previous syntactic and semantic descriptions of English reflexivity have failed to adequately account for this conception, predicated by way of a metaphorically extended verb + reflexive 'x-self'[2].

The following discussion focuses on examples such as:

1. *I found myself* missing her more every day.
2. *They lost themselves* in the music.
3. *Tom caught himself* giggling during the meeting.

Particularly conspicuous is the metaphoricity which will be shown to be the result of an underlying conception of the 'emergence or loss of Self-Awareness' (hereafter SA). Examples such as those above are marked reflexive and contain transitive verbs but will be shown to differ in fundamental ways from prototypical transitive and reflexive events. Furthermore, these examples differ from other metaphorical senses of reflexives such as:

4. *He asked himself* a question.
5. *Jenny made herself* finish the workout.
6. *Jack baked himself* on the beach.

In the above examples, there are salient, identifiable Objects (differing in their semantic roles, see Chapter 2). In (4), one part of the mind asks another part of the mind a question (this may also be literally acceptable, as one may actually hear a question formed in the mind), in (5), one part of the mind forces or assumes control over another part, and in (6), the reflexive event refers to a meronymous relationship, understood as part of Jack's body (the part of skin that was exposed to the sun) undergoing sunburn. Compared to examples (4-6), the concreteness of the Objects in the SA events (1-3) seem ambiguous. An attempt is made below to show that these events refer to the realization of some mental or physical meta-perception that can be uniquely identified, i.e., Self-Awareness. Specifically, this research addresses the following questions: 1) How is Self-Awareness expressed through the reflexive-metaphorical constructions? and 2) Can the construal and predication of SA events be semantically delineated and categorized?

---

[2] 'x-self' refers generically to the English reflexive pronouns; myself, yourself, herself, etc. used specifically with reflexive meaning.

Discussion of these questions will bring to light a previously neglected phenomenon and show that SA events are a nontrivial semantic subcategory of reflexive events in English. The following discussion in Part I proceeds in Section 1.2 by investigating lexical issues related to defining the meaning of three verbs appearing in SA events. In Section 1.3, various definitions of reflexivity will be discussed. It will be shown that in addition to a syntactic interpretation, a semantic component is necessary to account for SA events.

Dealing specifically with the semantic representation of the reflexive event, Chapter 2 explores the notions of expectation, valency and transitivity. In section 2.1, a semantic description of reflexivity in terms of the expectation of a distinct Object Participant will be seen beneficial when delineating the general function of the reflexive event. Verbs that license two separate and unique participants are prototypical and expected. When two participants are the same entity however (contrary to expectation), the need for clarification arises. The reflexive pronoun functions as such a clarification marker.

In section 2.2 the concept of valency will be discussed and also shown to have explanatory value for SA events. Viewing reflexive events from a valency perspective provides leeway for semantic idiosyncracies of reflexive events, SA events being one example of this. Section 2.3 explores the notion of transitivity as a non-binary phenomenon. Although structurally transitive, SA events will be shown to be conceived and construed as less transitive than prototypical reflexives but more transitive than prototypical middle and intransitive events, based on the inherent components of emergence of event action and the degree of participant distinction.

Chapter 3 presents a summary of the discussion of SA events and charts future steps in the research.

1.2   Lexical and Grammatical Definitions

It is common knowledge that meanings of individual lexical items vary and may function differently in different environments, "...we need only to glance at a good grammar or dictionary of a language or think about the languages we know to see that this is the way languages operate. Polysemy is a pervasive property of human language, not just in the lexical domain but also in grammar" (Kemmer 1993:5). In this section, the verbs occurring in reflexive events will be delineated and shown to vary greatly in their description and meaning. It is only when SA is proposed as a unifying conception that semantic anomalies can be uniformly explained.

1.2.1 Find x-self

The present discussion begins with the verb *find* in the corpus-based Longman Dictionary of Contemporary English Online[3]. Twenty-one different instances were listed. The verb *find* is categorized as a transitive verb (see Chapter 2 for a discussion of transitivity). The first definition is: 'get by searching - to discover, see, or get something that you have been searching for'. The first two examples for this definition are:

> 7. I can't find the car keys.
> 8. Hold on while I find a pen.   (Longman Dictionary of Contemporary English 2014)

Particularly noticeable is the semantic incongruence between the definition and the examples. In both (7) and (8), *the car keys* and *a pen* have not yet been obtained by the act of searching, and therefore the definition, 'get something by searching' does not accurately describe this conception. The definition could be changed to fit the examples, i.e. to search for something, or vice-versa, i.e., choosing appropriate examples to fit the definition, i.e., *I found the car keys* or *I found a pen*. Two more examples in the LDOCE are listed under this definition and properly account for the conception of 'get by searching':

> 9. Her body was later found hidden in the bushes.
> 10. She had almost given up hope of finding a husband. (ibid.)

In (9-10), the sought-after items had been obtained, and therefore the definition is supported. It might also be noticed that there is a tense/aspect difference in the two sets of examples. Because variation in meaning here is based on a predictable grammatical pattern, it is plausible that this definition be distinguished from the first; 1) the atelic (uncompleted) sense of searching for, i.e., the present tense in examples (7-8) or future, e.g., *I'll find it later*, and 2) the sense of get by searching for telic (completed) events, as in (9-10). The present motivation of this research is not to make a final determination for these cases but to direct attention to the complexity involved when such decisions need to be made.

---

[3] A corpus-based dictionary was used to exemplify language usage in society.

The second definition in the LDOCE states: 'see by chance - to discover something by chance, especially something useful or interesting'. Two example sentences are given:

11. I found a purse in the street.
12. We found a nice pub near the hotel. (ibid.)

Example (11) supports the definition, but (12) may not, depending on whether the people who had *found the pub* were actually searching for a pub or just happened upon it as they strolled through the streets. This is conceptually ambiguous in this example. The key concept discerning these two possibilities is intent. In (11), *finding a purse in the street* is typically a happenstance event, not something that one exerts effort to make occur, thus there is no intent on the part of the Agent/Experiencer. This same lack of intent accounts for the sense of accidentally *finding a pub* in (12), but not if the Agents/Experiencers *went searching for a pub and subsequently arrived at one*, the conception from the first description of 'get by searching'.

Definition number four of the LDOCE is: 'do something without meaning to - to be in a particular state or do a particular thing, or to realize that this is happening, especially when you did not expect or intend it'. The example provided is:

13. After wandering around, *we found ourselves* back at the hotel. (ibid.)

In definition two above, it was shown that the ambiguity of *find* was based on the concept of lack of intent. Examining the sub-category listed under definition four here may help clarify this issue: 'find yourself/your mind etc. doing something'. Two examples are provided:

14. When he left, *Karen found herself* heaving a huge sigh of relief.
15. *She* tried to concentrate, but *found her mind* drifting back to Alex. (ibid.)

We see again here a lack of intent semantically motivating the definition. In (14-15), something that was not intended or expected had occurred, *sighing in relief* and *thinking of Alex*, respectively. The conception of intent/expectation can be seen more clearly when compared with examples that do not include *find* but other sensory perception verbs such as:

16. When he left, Karen *felt (saw, heard) herself* heaving a huge sigh of relief.

Comparing the above, example (16) expresses no conceived intent or expectation. There is a complete absence of this conception even if metaphorically extending the senses of *see* and *hear*. In other words, *Karen* was simply aware of her physical or mental sensations in response to the stimulus of *his leaving*. In example (14), however, lack of intent or expectation seems to motivate the construal and choice of the verb *find*, which includes these qualities in its underlying semantics. In other words, *Karen* was not only aware of the physical sensations brought about by the stimulus of *his leaving* but was surprised by her own response to that sensation, in other words, there was an emergence of meta-perceptual Self-Awareness.

There is one more SA-related definition of *find* in the LDOCE that requires consideration. This is description number 16: 'find yourself, 'informal' - to discover what you are really like and what you want to do – often used humorously'. The solitary example is:

17. She went to India *to find herself.*

Here, the discovery of some deep self-knowledge is evident. This sense is different from those above and there is no concept correlating to intent/expectation. Intention/expectation may or may not be subsumed under the concept of discovery. One can intend to discover something and succeed (or fail), or one can discover something by accident without having had that specific intent. These examples are, therefore, conceptually ambiguous. If the above definitions of *find* are semantically related (and it may be assumed they are, see 1.2.1 below), we must look elsewhere for some unifying concept. Returning to the first definition given above (repeated here), a different concept contained within the definition may help to unify the definitions:

"do something without meaning to - to be in a particular state or do a particular thing, or to realize that this is happening, especially when you did not expect or intend it" (ibid.)

If a fundamental Self-Awareness is proposed as the unifying concept for *find*, all reflexive examples above can be accounted for, seen below by comparing all of the reflexive examples so far:

18. [13] After wandering around, *we found ourselves* back at the hotel.
19. [14] When he left, *Karen found herself* heaving a huge sigh of relief.

20. [17] *She* went to India to *find herself.*

In (18), there is the realization/awareness of some spatial perception, in (19) a realization/awareness of some sensory perception, and in (20) the (possibility of) realization/awareness of one's deeper Self. The consolidating notion here is not based on the perceptions themselves (physical/mental responses to stimuli) nor some intent/expectation to act, but a Self-Awareness of one's state or experience brought about by some kind of perception.

In the online version of the Oxford English Dictionary (2008), a focus on self-aware perception is found in definition 5b: 'To perceive oneself to be in a specified place or position, or condition of body or mind'. One fairly recent example from the 19th century is:

21. *"We found ourselves* opposed by a parapet of congealed snow."

(1823 F. Clissold, Narr. Ascent Mont Blanc 21) (ibid.)

In (21), it was not the actual wall of snow or the fact that their path was blocked by it that is the conceptual focus of *found*, but the awareness of that perceived situation. If the experience itself were the focus, more pragmatically and semantically economical examples such as (22) and (23) below would best suit that conception:

22. We were opposed by a parapet of congealed snow.
23. A parapet of congealed snow blocked our way.

The construal of this situation through the metaphorical extension of *find* within a reflexive construction points to the author's motivation to convey the Agent/Experiencer's Self-Awareness of the experience as the prominent conception.

The underlying conception of realization/awareness is further confirmed in the Collins English Dictionary Online (2014) under the definition *find oneself* (British English): "to realize and accept one's real character; discover one's true vocation". Besides the seemingly ad hoc pairing of these definitions under the same heading, the examples below represent a different sense of the *find oneself* construal, again creating non-congruence between definition and examples. Only (25) displays congruency between definition and example:

24. "*One* is rather surprised *to find oneself* marginally on the outside of society.

(Times, Sunday Times (2002))

25. A dark forest, as Dante noted, is a good place to get lost and *to find oneself* again. (Begg, Ean & Rich, Deike On the Trail of Merlin - a guide to the Celtic mystery tradition)

26. After an evening of Richard's company, it was easy *to find oneself* talking like him.
(Thomas, Rosie The White Dove)

27. In a way, an ability to remember only good things about one's past seems rather a benign state in which *to find oneself*. (Times, Sunday Times (2002)) (ibid.)

1.2.2 Lose x-self

If Self-Awareness is the conceptual motivation for SA events, it must be tested with other SA candidate verbs. Examining the verb lose in the LDOCE (2014), the only definition directly related to reflexive use is 15: 'lose yourself in something--to be paying so much attention to something that you do not notice anything else':

28. *She* listened intently to the music, *losing herself* in its beauty.

As with *find* above, the meaning of *lose* is metaphorical, i.e., *lose oneself in the music* does not have the same meaning as the literal 'lose oneself in a forest'. The central concept in (28) can be identified as 'not notice anything else'. To 'not notice' is to have no perception of it, i.e., to be *unaware* of it. But what does it mean to be unaware of oneself? It is proposed here that the metaphorical sense of *lose* refers to the (temporary) loss of Self-Awareness, i.e., the loss of the perception of one's physical and mental sensations. In some cases, the terms 'consciousness' and 'awareness' may be (nearly) synonymous, for example, *I found myself knocking on her door* (i.e., *I was aware/conscious of my knuckles rapping on her door*). However, this synonymy is incongruous with the metaphorical construal of *lose oneself*. To 'lose awareness' is not synonymous with 'lose consciousness' for SA events. The former is a typically psychological state and the latter a physiological one, as seen by the LDOCE example: "By the time the ambulance arrived, Douglas had lost consciousness"[4] This loss of awareness of perceptual states can be clarified further by comparing other metaphorical entries for *lose* in the

---

[4] Listed under the first definition of lose: "stop having attitude/quality etc [transitive] to stop having a particular attitude, quality, ability, etc. or to gradually have less of it, with the subheading: lose your touch." ("Longman Dictionary of Contemporary English," 2014)

LDOCE: "lose one's appetite, lose heart, lose face, lose your mind", etc. (ibid.) Each of these refers to the loss of some particular sensory or mental/psychological perception. SA events, on the other hand, refer to an independent meta-perception, distinct from any particular physical sensory or mental/psychological perception. SA events refer to the awareness of sensations, not the sensations themselves. Loss of that awareness can then be construed and predicated through sentences such as (28).

In the OEDO, definition 10 contains two related sub-entries: 'To lose one's (or its) identity; to become merged (in something else)', and 'To become deeply absorbed or engrossed (in thought, etc.); to be bewildered, overwhelmed (in wonder); to be distracted, lose one's wits (from emotion or excitement)' (2008). The only reflexive example from the first sense with a human[5] Agent/Experiencer is:

> 29. *I* love to *lose myself* in other men's minds.
>
> (1822   C. LAMB Detached Thoughts on Bks. in Elia 2nd Ser.)

And four examples under the second sense:

> 30. These strong Egyptian Fetters *I* must breake, Or *loose my selfe* in dotage.
>
> (a1616 Shakespeare Antony & Cleopatra (1623) I.ii.110)
>
> 31. *I* almost *lose my selfe* In joy to meete him.
>
> (1639 J. Shirley Maides Revenge IV.sig.G2ᵛ)
>
> 32. As *I* pace the darkened chamber and *lose myself* in melancholy musings…
>
> (1809 'D. Knickerbocker' Hist.N.Y.I.II.V.109)
>
> 33. Her voice was low at first, but *she* soon *lost herself*, and then it rose above the other voices.   (1890 T.H. Hall Caine Bondman III.vi)   (ibid.)

We can recover the focal concept of Self-Awareness from all examples. The loss of the Self-Awareness drives the conception and subsequently its construal and predication. It is the perceived objects (i.e., *other men's minds, dotage, joy, melancholy, bashfulness*) of which the Agent/Experiencers are completely and totally aware. The Agent/Experiencers' meta-perception of these things have been temporarily suspended, i.e., loss of Self-Awareness. This can be tested by comparing minimal pairs:

---

[5] Non-human Agent/Experiencers are possible, for example, *The company lost itself in the merger,* but examples are rare. This will be dealt with in detailed in the corpus-related chapters in Part III.

34. a. *I lost myself* in the music. (non-meronymous, loss of SA)

 [?]b. I lost my dotage/joy/melancholy/bashfulness in the music. (meronymous, non-SA)

35. a. *Jack lost himself* in thoughts of her. (non-meronymous, loss of SA)

 [?]b. Jack lost his thoughts of her. (meronymous, non-SA)

The (a) and (b) examples above have very different conceptions. Only the (a) examples reflect the SA conception while the admittedly borderline (b) examples refer to some part-whole relationship with the perceptual physical-mental Self. As stated above, Self-Awareness as a meta-perceptive state is proposed to be the core, focal conception and construal of SA events.

1.2.3 Catch x-self

Another verb that appears in SA events, *catch x-self*, is discussed below. Definition 24 of the LDOCE (2014) states: 'catch yourself doing something, to suddenly realize you are doing something':

36. Standing there listening to the song, *he caught himself* smiling from ear to ear.

The meta-perception of one's experience is consistent with that of the definition of SA described above. The physical act of *smiling ear to ear* is not itself the conceptual focus here; it is the awareness of that large smile. This can be compared to an example where direct perception is the focus, as below:

37. Standing there listening to the song, *he felt himself* smiling from ear to ear.

Another definition concerning SA is: 'To check, interrupt in speaking'. Two examples are given:

38. Not that I do (*he* presently *caught himself*) in the least confess, etc.
     (1670, C Cotton tr. G. Girard Hist. Life Duke of Espernon III.xii.623)

39. Saying on Day thus…*he* immediately *catch'd himself*, and fell into this Reflection.
     (a1726 W. Penn WKS.I.App.233) (ibid.)

Examples (40) and (41) also demonstrate SA events, employing the metaphorical sense of the verb catch to express meta-perceptive Self-Awareness that is gained in the middle of a speech act. Not only speech acts but other vocalizations such as laughing, giggling, etc. and certain physical, mainly involuntary movements such as twitching, wincing, cringing, etc. are used for SA construal.

40. *Shelly caught herself* laughing even on this sad day.
41. *Sam caught himself* cringing at the notion of another transfer.
42. *The lawyer caught herself* snickering in front of the judge.

In all cases, Awareness of a vocalization or physicality is construed and expressed by way of the metaphorical sense of the verb *catch* and used within a reflexive event. This type of event, as explained for *find, lose* and *catch* is coined *Self-Aware (SA) event.*

1.3   Grammatical Definitions

The complexities of delineating lexical senses in relation to SA events have been considered above. Defining the immediate grammatical environment of SA events, i.e., the reflexive construction, is just as complex. The functions of the reflexive construction, according to the Longman Grammar of Spoken and Written English, are fourfold: "marking co-reference with the subject, alternating with personal pronouns, marking emphatic identity, and empty reflexives" (1999:342-345). 'Marking coreference' is the only function considered here as it is the only environment in which proposed SA events occur. The others, although bundled together under the reflexive category, will not be examined except when necessary to contrast syntactic and semantic environments of SA events (see Section 1.4 below).

Considered first are descriptions of the reflexive pronoun. "In their purely reflexive use, these pronouns mark identity with the referent of the preceding noun phrase within the same clause, usually in subject position. The reflexive pronoun carries a different syntactic role; it is typically an object or complement in a prepositional phrase" (Biber et al. 1999: 342). In this description, reflexive antecedents relate and mark coreference with another noun and reflexive pronouns hold an object (or complement) relation in the phrase. Various descriptions in which the reflexive pronoun is 'used as object' appear in the literature. "You use a reflexive pronoun to make it clear that the object of a verb is the same person or thing as the subject of the verb, or to emphasize this…(Collins Cobuild English Grammar 2011) This explanation is similar to that given below by Faltz:

> The subject and object noun phrases are coreferent if and only if the object noun phrase consists of one of the words myself, ourselves, yourself, yourselves, himself, herself, itself, oneself, or themselves. The presence of these reflexive pronouns in object position to mark coreference with the subject constitutes the primary reflexive strategy for English (1985: 4).

Thus, there is a syntactic entity called *subject* and a syntactic entity called *object*. Reflexive pronouns signal that these are the same entity. This seems straightforward; however, the semantics of the predicate often affect the nominals with which they are aligned. These cases have revealed the necessity to account for the semantics of the verb together with its nominals in descriptions of reflexivization. Following this, Gast and Siemund define reflexivity as, "…the co-indexation of two argument positions of a transitive predicate..." (2006: 346). As stated above, syntactic definitions traditionally tethered the coreferent nominals to each other without regard for the verb. But Gast and Siemund's definition considers the function of the verb in relation to its nominals, or more precisely, the whole predicate.

The restriction on the transitivity of the verb seems logical enough given that two nominals are needed to co-refer. König and Gast suggest the following definition: "Reflexive pronouns (anaphors) are self-forms used in order to indicate that a semantic or syntactic argument of a predicate is co-referenced with another argument of the same predicate (co-argument), typically with the subject. This co-argument is called the antecedent of the reflexive pronoun" (2002: 4). They make a careful and detailed argument for incorporating a semantic component into the definition of reflexivity, mainly to distinguish 'true' reflexives from polysemous intensifying and logophoric -self meanings.

Thus, in order to distinguish the different functions and environments in which reflexive pronouns occur, a definition that covers its semantic function is necessary. Without this semantic aspect, it is very difficult to account for predications where the semantics of the verb directly affects the whole structure of a phrase. Lange helps clarify and strengthen this claim:

> …by extending the definition of reflexivity to include both syntactic and semantic arguments of predicates, examples like the following are also covered: (3.16) John

considers himself to be the perfect candidate. (3.17) Suddenly I found myself in a large cave. Excluded from the class of reflexive anaphors are then all intensifying uses of x-SELF as well as 'logophoric' or 'untriggered' SELF-forms... (2007: 37).

Although Lange uses sentence (3.17) to make an argument for the necessity of a semantic definition of x-self to differentiate the various functions of the reflexive, it is also necessary in order to distinguish SA events from other reflexive sense types. A strictly syntactic definition cannot account for the different meanings (3.17) could assume, shown below in (a-c):

(3.17) Suddenly *I found myself* in a large cave.
    a. I suddenly realized that I was in a cave. (SA event)
    b. I suddenly realized my true, deeper self in a cave. (True-Self event (Lakoff 1992))
    c. I found a mannequin (or other physical entity made to look like me) of myself in a cave.

Accounting for SA events necessitates a precise definition of reflexive argument relations and their semantic functions. At the risk of repetitiveness, simply stating that (3.17) above and examples 43-45 below are reflexive (inasmuch as they fulfill the syntactic requirements for such) does not address their different functions and meanings.

    43. John made himself a tuna sandwich.
    44. John made himself go to the gym.
    45. John made himself completely invisible.

In (43-45), the reflexive pronouns, or semantic Object Pronouns (Geniusiene 1987) represent three different semantic roles; in (43), Recipient or Beneficiary (the 'receiver' of an action or event), in (44), Content ("the second role in verbs of perception and mental activity" or Patient (the affected entity of a caused event), and in (45), Patient (ibid.: 40). These distinctions are crucial for an accurate description of SA events as contrasted to other literal and metaphorical reflexive events and are discussed in more detail in the next chapter.

Ambiguity within the reflexive construction may be due to polysemous morphological components representing differing semantic conceptions and functions. The ramification of this is to understand that boundaries (if any) between conception and formal representation are malleable. Dictionary definitions provide clues to lexical conception but may contain descriptive inconsistencies and gaps in data, especially when *meaning in use* is a consideration. The SA event verbs *find*, *lose*, and *catch* were shown to be such instances.

Chapter 2: Valency and Transitivity

2.1 Introduction

In Chapter 1, Self-Awareness was proposed as the unifying concept for the metaphorical senses of *find*, *lose* and *catch* when used in the reflexive construction. In Chapter 2, focus on the semantics of the predicate will show that two factors play a crucial role in understanding reflexivity and the construal of SA events. The first, considered in section 2.1, is the distinction between 'other-directed' and 'non-other-directed' situations. Incorporated into the meaning of some verbs is whether or not its action is typically directed towards a Patient/Object. This will be seen to be a major determinant for choosing the reflexive strategy.

The second factor, considered in section 2.2, is that *valency* needs to be carefully identified and categorized and that *transitivity* is necessarily viewed as a gradient phenomenon. Working with notions of valency and transitivity entail examining the relationship of verbs along with their associated *participants*. Reflexive events in English are shown to be prototypically transitive but may also occur non-prototypically, closer to intransitive and middle events. It is within this non-prototypical environment that SA events are to be found.

Section 2.3 includes a discussion of middle events and their relation to reflexive and SA events. *Participant distinguishability* and *quality of action* are two precise semantic sub-components that are delineated and revealed to be the main components that help in the accurate description of SA events.

The conclusion drawn in Chapter 2 is that SA events are construed as low-transitive reflexive events occurring between middle and reflexive events on the transitivity continuum. Furthermore, distinction of participants and quality of action of SA events are especially critical in demarcating SA events from other reflexive and middle events.

2.2 Other-directed vs. non-other-directed events

The notion of 'other-directedness' has been proposed as the underlying motivation for prototypical transitive events because the interlocuter expects the action of the verb to affect a Patient that is a separate entity from the Agent (Hopper & Thompson 1980; Kemmer 1993; König & Gast 2002; König & Siemund 2000a; König & Vezzosi 2004; Lange 2007). The definition of 'prototypical transitive event' used in this discussion concurs with that of Rice:

Two entities, which are usually conceived of as being asymmetrically related, are involved in some activity; the interaction between them is unidirectional; because there is movement and effect, contact between the two entities is presumed to take place, with the second entity being directly affected by the contact instigated by the first; finally, the entities are taken to be distinct from each other, from their locale or setting, and from the speaker/observer/conceptualizer (2011:423).

The reflexive event, on the other hand, is used to signal that the action of the typically unidirectional (i.e., other-directed) event is directed towards the same originating entity of the action, contrary to expectation. This non-prototypicality and unexpectedness has been described as the motivation for the use of the English reflexive pronoun (Beck 2006; Faltz 1985; Kemmer 1993; König & Siemund 2000b; König & Vezzosi 2004; Lange 2007, 2011; Peitsara 1997) "Non-other-directed" (i.e., self-directed), on the other hand, refers to events that are expected to have only one participant (semantic Subject), such as intransitive events. Only one participant is involved in the action, and the same entity that causes the action is also the affected entity of that action.

> 46. Sally squashed the cockroach under her heel.
> 47. The doctors swam for charity.
> 48. *The doctors swam themselves for charity.
> 49. Ted forced himself to finish the tea.

In (46), the verb *squash* is prototypically transitive, requiring an entity that initiates the 'squashing' and a separate entity that receives the 'squashing'. In (47), a prototypically intransitive event, there is only one entity involved in the action, with the origination and goal of the action being congruent. As such, the reflexive, which also signals this congruency, is unnecessary and inappropriate, as in (48). In (49), as in (46), the prototypically affected entity of the action is expected to be a separate entity, however, it is not. The reflexive pronoun signals coreference of the initiating and affected entities. Use of the simple personal pronoun results in an inappropriate reference to some other second entity, i.e., *Ted$_x$ squashed him$_y$ between the walls*. The reflexive pronoun is used to mark the unexpected coreferentiality of the participants in the event, i.e., *Ted$_x$ squashed himself$_x$ between the walls*. This notion of 'expectedness' was the motivation for the morphological merger of 'personal pronoun + self':

Without SELF, the more likely interpretation of the sentence would be that subject NP and pronouns are disjoint. By intensifying the pronoun, SELF indicates that the referent designated by the pronoun is central, thereby reversing the expected prototypical transitive structure with two participants where an agent acts upon a patient...SELF signals that subject and object have the same referent.. (Lange, 2007:57).

Whether verbs instantiate two separate participants of an event or one is illustrated in Table 1. The sub-categories listed under the non-other-directed situations generally include intransitive verbs and those verbs that take the middle voice. Examples for each of these categories are; grooming, e.g. *John shaved*; preparing & protecting, e.g. *Jack was ready*; defending & liberating, e.g. *Jane was free*; and pride/shame, e.g. *Jessica was proud/ashamed*. Examples for other-directed situations are: violent actions, e.g. *John killed him*; emotions, e.g. *John loves Mary*; communicating, e.g. *John told him to write*; and jealousy/anger/pleasure, e.g. *Mary was jealous of John, John was angry with Mary*, and *John was pleased with Mary*.

Table 1. Non-other-directed and other-directed verbs (König & Siemund, 2000: 61)

Non-other-directed	Other-directed
Grooming	Violent actions (killing, destroying)
Preparing, protecting	Emotions (love, hate)
Defending, liberating	Communicating
Be proud/ashamed of	Be jealous of/angry with/pleased with

If we apply the concept of 'unexpectedness of the coreferent entities' onto the sub-category of verbs listed under other-directed situations in Table 1, sentences such as those below are predicated:

50. John$_x$ killed him$_y$(self$_x$).
51. John$_x$ loves him$_y$(self$_x$).
52. ? John$_x$ told him$_y$(self$_{x,y}$) to write.
53. *? Mary$_x$ is jealous of her$_y$(self$_{x,y}$).
54. John$_x$ is angry with him$_y$(self$_x$).
55. John$_x$ is pleased with him$_y$(self$_y$).

Two sentences raise questions of well-formedness when the reflexive test is performed. Examples (52) and (53) are acceptable if the events are construed metaphorically, but the reflexive pronoun in (53) is only acceptable in cases where someone or something (an actress or wax figure) is representing *Mary* and the 'real Mary' is jealous of that representation. However, even though the reflexive pronoun is employed, it can be argued that this is not a true case of coreferentiality because two separate physical entities are manifest and therefore the direction of the action is unidirectional, i.e., a prototypical transitive event. Nevertheless, in all cases the reflexive marker signals events that are prototypically expected to be other-directed but have that expectation quashed by being construed as non-other-directed.

'Non-other-directed' events are those in which the verbs usually occur with only the affected semantic Subject (which is semantically indistinguishable from the Agent in English but may be aligned with the Patient in Ergative languages (Bowers 2002; Comrie 1989; Dixon & Aĭkhenval'd 2000)). So, for example, grooming verbs include sentences such as:

56. Eric shaved.
57. Ryan washed.
58. Jessica bathed.

In these cases, the Agent and (unrealized) Patient are expected to be one and the same entity; therefore, no reflexive strategy (nor overt Object/Patient) is required. Logically, if we expect these verbs to be non-other-directed, the contrary unexpected situation should be that which is other-directed. This is the case, seen in the following:

59. Eric shaved his brother.
60. Ryan washed his sister's face.
61. Jessica bathed her little brothers.

Although in English these are not marked (i.e., zero-marking), they are semantically and pragmatically atypical, construing events in which the Object/Patient has very little control over his/her own actions and in which their typically pragmatic Agency has been essentially undone. Another unexpected, non-other-directed event may also take place, i.e., the reflexive event:

62. Eric shaved himself.
63. Ryan washed himself.

64. Jessica bathed herself.

In these examples, due to some pragmatically extraordinary circumstances (such as incapacity, unwillingness, social inconformity, etc.), the Subject could not or did not previously perform the action, thus, its sudden performance is unexpected.

There are difficulties in English when applying this broad non-other-directed category to many verbs, however. Many of the grooming verbs are meronymous and require a body-part Object to be overtly realized:

      65. a. Cathy brushed her hair/teeth.

            b. *Cathy brushed.

      66. a. Leslie combed his hair/moustache/beard.

            b. *Leslie combed.

Difficulties also arise with other subcategories:

      67. preparing and protecting:

          a. Henry prepared (for) dinner.

          b. *Henry prepared.

          c. Henry protected (the children, himself).

          d. *Henry protected.

      68. defending and liberating:

          a. They defended (their house, themselves) against their enemies.

          b. *They defended.

          c. The prisoners liberated (themselves) from their captives.

          d. *The prisoners liberated.

Examples (65-68) are subsumed under the non-other-directed category and therefore prototypical predications should be zero-marked (in English) when the action refers to the Subject. Contrarily, some type of Object is necessary to form acceptable sentences. Resolution of this particular issue is adjunct to the present discussion (see section 2.3); however, a focus on SA events in (69-71) shows that the other-directed vs. non-other-directed conception accurately accounts for typical reflexive events. In other words, use of the reflexive pronoun signals an unexpected, non-other-directed action of the verb from the initiator to the recipient and that these are one and the same entity:

69. *I found myself* craving more and more chocolate.

70. *Frank lost himself* in the drama of Amy's love life.

71. *I caught myself* daydreaming again.

The semantics of prototypical reflexive events is preserved here, i.e., the reflexive pronoun marks an unexpected, non-other-directed construal. Being so, they fall under the prototypical transitive construction licensing two participants, an Agent and a Patient; atypically, however, these are the same entity. The simplicity of the theory of unexpectedness and other-directed events is appealing; however, SA events will be shown below to be much subtler than this notion alone can handle.

2.3 Valency & Transitivity

In section 2.1, the unexpectedness of coreference of an inherently other-directed verb was a significant motivating factor for the reflexive event. There is a different facet to this verb-participant relationship, however, that necessitates investigation. Focusing specific attention on a predicate's participant number(s) and semantic role(s) uncovers important insights into reflexive (including SA) events. A verb's inherent ability to license a certain number of participants is termed *valency*. The term *transitivity* refers to the descriptive categories to which those participants lend themselves. This section will investigate how the reflexive event is described with respect to these notions.

2.3.1 Valency

Defining the parameters of valency, Martin concisely summarizes:

> A verb like rain, which has no referential noun phrases associated with it, is said to
> be zero-place or avalent; a verb like disappear, which takes only a subject argument,
> is said to be one-place or monovalent; verbs like devour and give are said to be two-
> place (bivalent) and three-place (trivalent), respectively (2000: 375).

The description above is the widely accepted notion of linguistic valency, albeit expressed in various ways in the literature (Comrie 1989; Herbst 2007; Herbst & Götz-Votteler 2007; Kalinina, Kolomatsky, & Sudobina 2006; Matthews 2007; Quirk, Greenbaum, Leech, & Svartvik 1985). Their affinity lies in the inherent lexical property of each verb to license a specific, limited number of participants. This lexical idiosyncrasy creates difficulties for minimalist and typology researchers hoping to reveal over-arching mechanisms that account for syntactic and/or semantic data. Because the valency of each individual verb is different, it is difficult to generalize over a wide syntactic or semantic arena. Herbst states, "...valency is definitely one of the more messy aspects of language. Although nobody will deny that certain general tendencies are also at work... The amount of idiosyncratic word specific knowledge that is involved is considerable" (2007: 27). One of the most ambitious projects that attempted to record this vast amount of information for practical use is A Valency Dictionary of English (VDE) (Herbst, Heath, Roe, & Götz 2004), a corpus-based dictionary[6] providing information about participant numbers, collocations and the patterning of semantic roles of verbs.[7]

2.3.1.1 Valency and SA event verbs

The VDE entry for *find* lists four separate senses: 'discover', 'judge', 'consider' and 'unexpected situation'. The reflexive pattern appears only with Sense D, UNEXPECTED SITUATION, noted as, "A person can find themselves doing something or being in a particular situation, i.e., doing something they had not expected" (ibid: 314). This independent, corpus-based result strengthens the claim above (section 2.1) that the notion of unexpectedness is a pragmatic/semantic motivator for the reflexive marker. Considering specific coverage of reflexive events in Table 2, the verb *find* used with the reflexive object pronoun is described as having one Sense (D, UNEXPECTED SITUATION) occurring with four different valency patterns (T1, T2, T4, T6). The item's Sense is further delineated as to whether the constructions are active or passive as well as the number of minimum/maximum valency complements the verb can license (in this case, 3/3). The obligatory (obl) complement sense categorization (II) precedes the specific use (REFL PRON). The reflexive pronoun is shown in four different

---

[6] The University of Birmingham's COBUILD corpus was utilized for this dictionary.
[7] The condensed web version, named Erlangen Valency Patternbank_BETA (Thomas Herbst 2014) is a freely available resource for public use.

patterns: two with a noun (+ N), one with a verb in its -ing form (+ V-ing), and one with an adverbial (+ ADV). Specific corpus examples are provided for each pattern.

Table 2. find + the reflexive construction in the VDE (Herbst et al. 2004: 312-314)

find verb	
D UNEXPECTED SITUATION Active: 3/3	
II obl [REFL PRON] T1-2.4.6	
<u>T1:</u>	+ REFL PRON + N D Durell found himself an exile amongst exiles.
<u>T2:</u>	+ REFL PRON + N D Susan, about to refuse, found herself tempted.
<u>T4:</u>	+ REFL PRON + V-ing DI found myself, inexplicably, liking him.
	•[8] Their lack of education compared to men limits their opportunities, and they most often find themselves holding marginal jobs.
<u>T6:</u>	+ REFL PRON + ADV D Alderson found himself out of a job.
	• We followed his directions to find ourselves on the steps of one of the royal palaces.

The insight that can be drawn from this data is the transparency to which reflexive events with the verb *find* are predicated through distinct patterns and are construed under one main sense, UNEXPECTED SITUATION. However insightful and useful this data is for a variety of research avenues, it is not without drawbacks for the present discussion. Besides the given Sense UNEXPECTED SITUATION applying to all reflexive pronouns (seen above in section 2.1), the two example sentences in Table 2 (T4 and T6), determined extraneous to the Sense, need to be accounted for. This can be provided by proposing Self-Awareness as the main Sense for all examples, i.e., [find + REFL PRON + N/ V-ing/ ADV]. All data may then be considered inclusive of the defining Sense. Taking the VDE examples from Table 2 above:

72. *Durell found himself* an exile amongst exiles.

73. *Susan*, about to refuse, *found herself* tempted.

74. *I found myself*, inexplicably, liking him.

---

[8] • indicates use not covered in the identified sense.

75. Their lack of education compared to men limits their opportunities, and
    they most often *find themselves* holding marginal jobs.

76. *Alderson found himself* out of a job.

77. *We* followed his directions to *find ourselves* on the steps of one of the royal
    palaces.

Instead of establishing the Sense UNEXPECTED SITUATION for these examples to the exclusion of (75) and (77), SA is proposed as the agglutinating conceptual Sense. The meta-perceptive, Self-Aware conception of the SA event is construed and predicated metaphorically as *finding someone, somewhere, who is doing, thinking or feeling something.* In (72), the meaning of *Durell found himself in exile* is 'Durell is aware of himself being in exile'. In (73), *Susan found herself tempted* means that 'Susan is aware of herself being tempted'. *I found myself liking him*, in (74), conveys the meaning 'I am aware of myself liking him'. In (75), *they find themselves holding marginal jobs* can be comparably expressed as 'They are aware of themselves holding marginal jobs'. Example (76) means Alderson is aware of himself not having a job, and finally, (77) can be rephrased as, 'We are aware of ourselves being on the steps…palaces'. Establishing Self-Awareness as the Sense foundation for the metaphorical use of *find* in a reflexive event allows an all-inclusive categorization of the data. Depending on the details of each pragmatic situation, one of the above three valency patterns in Table 2 will then be predicated. This does not mean that UNEXPECTED SITUATION is not a valid conceptual notion. Its validity is attributed to the higher-order semantic category associated with the reflexive event in general (as per section 2.1), not specific to any one verb or its valency. It is, therefore, unable to account for much idiosyncratic data, SA events in particular.

More support for this claim can be seen when considering another SA event, *lose x-self* as (see Table 3). For the reflexive Sense III, the second example is categorized as extraneous to the sense meaning. "The basic meaning of lose can be described as 'no longer having something' or as 'not gaining something'" (ibid: 505). Delineating [lose + REFL PRON + N/ V-ing] as SA event eliminates the need to exclude the second example, thus encompassing more data. In the case of *lose*, however, it is not the emergence of Self-Awareness but the temporary lack of Self-Awareness that is construed. This *loss* may occur for reasons such as intense concentration, intense emotional reaction, illness/injury, chemical toxicity (intentional or not), etc. The two examples from Table 3 may be rephrased as, 'She was unaware of her other sense perceptions when reading literature' and 'I want your help to be unaware of my everyday self when loving you and others'. The SA event as an explicit conception allows for the second, previously excluded example to be included. This evidence[9] lends support to the proposal that SA is a distinct semantic event categorically subsumed within the reflexive event.

Table 3. *lose* with the reflexive construction in the VDE (ibid: 504-505)

lose   verb
Active 1/3   Passive 1/3   General:0
III   [REFL PRON] T3
T3   + REFL PRON + in N/V-ing
She was able to cut herself away from the demands of those around her, to lose herself in literature.
• Help me to lose myself in loving you and in loving others.

The use of corpus data to reveal valency patterns (along with their collocations) has provided a fast and accurate method for finding and analyzing recurring and polysemous complementation patterns previously overlooked. For this reason, as well as the insights gained from Cognitive and Corpus linguistic research, the concept of valency has become a recently rejuvenated topic of discussion (see: (Dixon & Aĭkhenval'd 2000; Herbst 2007; Herbst & Götz-Votteler 2007; Herbst et al. 2004; Kulikov, Malchukov, & de Swart 2006). For the present moment, it can be stated that the reality of valency as a viable categorization strategy may prove valuable for delineating idiosyncracies in individual data while categorizing that same information into analyzable semantic categories.

Valency information reveals that verbs can be categorized by the number of participants they license. Specific focus on the *functions* of those participants is called transitivity. The reason for distinguishing notions of valency from transitivity can be seen below:

78. It rains.

79. *The sky/cloud rains.

---

[9] Unfortunately, there was no REFL PRON data in the VDE for the verb catch.

80. ame ga futte-iru.

rain$_s$ fall$_{v-pres-cont}$

81. *sora/kumo ga ame wo futteiru

sky/cloud$_s$ rain$_{d.o.}$ fall$_{v-pres-cont}$

The verb *rain* in (78) is zero-valent; in other words, no entity is seen to be directly responsible for the *raining* action. The act of rain and similar examples do not, therefore, often appear in discussions of transitivity. Even though English marks for a syntactic Subject, adding a semantic S in (79) renders the construction unacceptable. Example (80) shows the participant-less status of an event like *rain* in Japanese as well. 'Ame' (rain) is a noun subject-marked with the particle ga. The verb 'furu' (fall) is expressed in its present continuous form ($_{verb\ stem}$ + tte-iru). There is no need whatsoever for the presence of an initiator of the action of *rain*, and artificially adding one, as in (81), also renders the sentence unacceptable.

The 'monovalent' *sits* in (82) licenses one participant. This one participant is both the initiator and recipient of the event action or state. This intransitive event can be shown by the unacceptability of inserting another participant into the event action, as in (83).

82. Nancy sits.

83. *Nancy sits Harold/herself.[10]

84. Nancy pinched her(self) on the arm.

85. *Nancy pinched. / *Nancy pinched her the arm.

86. Nancy gave her(self) an injection on the arm.

87. *Nancy gave on the arm. / *Nancy gave her(self) on the arm.

Two participants (bivalent) are licensed for the verb pinch in (84), a causer or initiator of the event action or state (Agent/Experiencer) and a separate recipient of that event action or state (Patient). This type of event is termed 'transitive'. When more/less than two participants are predicated, the sentences are deemed unacceptable, as in (85). Notice in the reflexive account in (84) that the same entity (*Nancy, herself*) is both the Agent and Patient of *pinch*. The two are

---

[10] Interestingly, the construction 'sit oneself down' is admissible, but the role of the x-self pronoun here is intensifying, not reflexive (see section 1.3), and therefore the intransitivity of the clause remains unchanged.

regarded here as (syntactically) separate entities[11] even though this may seem counter-intuitive. The verb *give* in (86) is 'ditransitive', licensing three participants, the action initiator, the recipient of the action and the transferred object. Changing the number of participants is unacceptable, as in (87). Changing the semantic roles of the participants similarly affects the function of the whole argument, rendering the construction unacceptable. Therefore, even though valency and transitivity are related notions, their separation is necessary in order to distinguish subtleties between participant number and function.

2.3.2 Prototypical Transitive Events

The above descriptions of transitivity are broad generalizations and exceptions and idiosyncrasies are present, depending upon usage. Due to space considerations, however, a full account cannot be provided here (see:Allerton 2006; Comrie 1989; Dixon 2005; Faltz 1985; Frajzyngier & Curl 2000; Herbst & Götz-Votteler 2007; Hopper & Thompson 1980; Kemmer 1993; Klaiman 1991; König & Gast 2008; Kulikov et al. 2006; Levin & Hovav 2005; Næss 2007; Rice 2011). Although idiosyncrasies do occur, there are merits in postulating formulaic theories that attempt to capture general tendencies in the data. For transitivity, this has resulted in efforts to find the most common denominators in which to postulate a prototypical transitive event. Researchers have engaged in such an effort to define this 'prototypical transitive' notion (Bowers 2002; Comrie 1989; de Swart 2006; Hopper & Thompson 1980; Kalinina et al.,2006; Kemmer 1993; LaPolla 1996; Næss 2007; Rice 2011; Rozas 2007). One description of the prototypical transitive (two-participant) event is by Kemmer, who states that "a prototypical two-participant event is defined as a verbal event in which a human entity (an Agent) acts volitionally, exerting physical force on an inanimate definite entity (a patient) which is directly and completely affected by that event" (1993: 50). This idea most likely originates from the description proposed by Hopper and Thompson,

> ...transitivity is traditionally understood as a global property of an entire clause, such that an activity is 'carried-over' or 'transferred' from an agent to a patient. Transitivity in the traditional view thus necessarily involves at least two participants... and an action which is typically EFFECTIVE in some way (1980: 251-253).

---

[11] One explanation is that 'pinch' licenses a body-part Patient (see transitive 'middle', section 2.3), a meronymous relationship to the Self, and therefore assumes separate entity status.

The two dimensions, 'transferred action' and 'affectedness of patient' seem to delineate the transitive event in general terms, but there are other dimensions to transitivity that have been proposed, one being 'distinctness of participants', i.e., to what extent each individual/separate participant is construed to be. This is posited by way of 'The Maximally Distinct Arguments Hypothesis': "A Prototypical transitive clause is one where the two participants are maximally semantically distinct in terms of their roles in the event described by the clause" (Næss 2007: 30). This notion of distinctness of participants, whatever the wording, is often cited as a crucial concept of transitivity (Comrie 1989; de Swart 2006; Hopper & Thompson 1980; Kemmer 1993; Levin & Hovav 2005; Rice 2011).

Thus, there are certain semantic properties of a transitive event, i.e., 'distinctness of participants', 'transfer of action' and 'affectedness of patient' that are relevant to the fundamental notion of prototypical transitivity. One interesting quality of these properties is that they are thought to be non-binary, i.e., gradient (Bowers 2002; Comrie 1989; de Swart 2006; Dixon & Aïkhenval'd 2000; Geniusiene 1987; Hopper & Thompson 1980; Kalinina et al. 2006; Kemmer 1993; LaPolla 1996; Næss 2007; Rice 2011; Taylor 2003).

> It has been recognised for quite some time that the concept of "transitivity" behaves like a prototype category...In other words, membership of the category "transitive verb" or "transitive clause" is gradable depending on an item's degree of similarity to a central exemplar – a prototype structure (Næss 2007: 12).

If the notion of gradable transitivity is taken as the modern standard for investigations into the transitiveness of an event, we must delineate the specific measures on which that scale is based. One of these metrics, proposed by Hopper and Thompson (1980), establishes ten distinct components that play a role in the prototypical transitivity of a clause, each component having a 'high' or 'low' quality depending upon use in discourse. These components may be thought of as the semantic building blocks of a prototypical transitive event. The more building blocks a structure has, the more stable and concrete it becomes. The prototypicality of the transitive event is dependent upon the number and level of its semantic components. The more components relevant to the event that are high on the prototypicality scale, the more transitive the event, and vice-versa.

The first component of a transitive event according to this transitivity matrix (ibid.) is an inherent DISTINCTION OF PARTICIPANTS, i.e., the action or state of the verb that affects a definable Patient, and in which a definable Agent (or Experiencer, in the case of perceptual or psychological verbs) is the origin of that action. A prototypical transitive event therefore involves two participants as in (88) below, whereas an intransitive event involves only one participant, seen in (90). "…a transitive clause is one which describes an event which involves two distinct, independent participants, both in the sense that they are physically distinct and independent entities, and in the sense that their roles in the event are clearly distinct: there is only one instigating agent and only one affected "endpoint" (Næss 2007: 46).

The reflexive event, however, presents an interesting situation. Only one entity participates in the event, but that participant is realized as two separate entities, as in (90). Thus, although structurally transitive, it is highly non-prototypical.

88. I asked my boss for a vacation for my birthday.

89. I went on vacation for my birthday.

90. I treated myself royally on my birthday.

Considering the reflexive transitive event when compared to the prototypically highly distinct participants in (88) or to the intransitive event (lowest distinctness) in (89), the participants in (90) are 'less' distinct than (88) but 'more' distinct than (89), emphasizing and clarifying the gradient quality of transitivity mentioned above as well as introducing the status of the reflexive event as occurring as an intermediary construal between these transitivity poles.

Another component directly related to SA events in Hopper and Thompson's transitivity matrix is AFFECTEDNESS OF O, referring to "The degree to which an action is transferred to a patient[12] (and) is a function of how completely that patient is AFFECTED…" (ibid: 252-253). Examples (91) and (92) below display this parameter, showing high and low degrees of transitivity, respectively. In these examples, being *shot* (a physicality) 'affects the O' more than being considered (non-physicality) does. Other types of reflexive events, however, such as the 'causative' in (93) and SA in (94-97) exhibit just how gradient this component can be. The quality of action in SA events can be described as the emergence/lack of Self-Awareness. The action instantiates a low amount of AFFECTEDNESS OF O and therefore its low transitivity.

---

[12] Hopper and Thompson define the term 'patient' as "an O which is in fact the 'receiver' of the action in a cardinal (prototypical) transitive relationship" (1980: 252) (my parenthesis).

91. *The policeman shot himself* in the foot.

92. *The policeman considered himself* a failure.

93. *The policeman made himself* apologize.

94. *The policeman caught himself* reaching for his gun.

95. *The policeman found himself* in prison.[13]

96. *The policeman found himself* in prison.[14]

97. *The policeman lost himself* in thoughts of revenge.

Even though Self-Awareness may be dramatic (it can be so potent as to be life-changing), it is still a relatively non-physical, non-observable action. The quality of emergent/lack of Self-Awareness is not a flow of action from A → P as much as an emergence/lack (however quick) of Self-Awareness within the gestalt co-referent complex. The AFFECTEDNESS OF O for this construal is prototypically lower than that of literal and/or other types of metaphorical reflexive events discussed. Precisely because of its intangibility and the effects on the construal of the AFFECTEDNESS OF O, SA events are construed between the prototypical transitive and intransitive events, i.e., the transitive middle (see section 2.4).

The third component of the transitivity matrix immediately relevant to SA events is the INDIVIDUATION OF O, which "refers both to the distinctness of the patient from the A(gent) and to its distinctness from its own background" (ibid: 253) (my parenthesis). This component has been given central importance to the notion of transitivity. "...the distinctness of participants is at the core of the notion of transitivity, and all lower-level "transitivity properties" can be understood as contributing in some way to this distinctness..." (Næss 2007: 122). Qualities of a more individuated patient are that it is: proper, human/animate, concrete, singular, countable, and referential/definite, whereas a non-individuated patient would have qualities such as: common, inanimate, abstract, plural, mass, and non-referential (Hopper & Thompson 1980). According to this, examples (98-105) demonstrate a high-to-low gradient of transitivity, respectively:

98. Bob killed John.

99. The politician killed the bill.

---

[13] This sense has the meaning of 'He was acutely aware that he was in prison'.

[14] This sense has the meaning, 'He realized his deeper, inner self in prison'.

100. Congressmen killed some bills.

101. Conservationists killed reform.

102. Bob killed himself. (Literally or metaphorically.)

103. The politician killed himself. (Literally, or metaphorically, i.e., 'political suicide'.)

104. Congressmen killed themselves. (Literally or metaphorically.)

105. Conservationists killed themselves. (Literally or metaphorically.)

The senses of (102-104) display examples of meronymy and/or perhaps metonymy, the reflexive pronoun referring to a part of the physical Self, in this case, the physical body (a meronymous relationship). If the physical body were considered a gestalt entity and the pronoun stood for the patient, then the situation would be considered metonymous. Complications arise, however, when metaphorical senses are considered. On one hand, the A and O are pragmatically indistinct from one other (being co-referential), and therefore should rate low in individuation. On the other hand, the A and O are structurally distinct from one another and from their own background and therefore should rate high in 'individuation'. The situation becomes even more interesting when SA events are considered (c.f., examples (96-99)). Due to the quality of the Self-Aware action, there is very little INDIVIDUATION OF O. As mentioned with regard to AFFECTIVENESS OF O, an emergence/lack of Self-Awareness defines the SA event. This emergent quality of action has ramifications for the INDIVIDUATION OF O in that the conception of two distinct participants is minimal. Delineation of the SA event with regard to the INDIVIDUATION OF O is twofold: 1) a non-static, gradable view of INDIVIDUATION OF O is necessary and 2) different types of reflexive events must be distinguished (i.e., literal, metaphorical, causative, SA, etc.), each having their own INDIVIDUATION OF O signatures. Taking both of these parameters into account allows for typological generalizations of prototypicality to be upheld while also accommodating semantic and pragmatic idiosyncrasies within the reflexive paradigm itself.

The components taken together confirm transitivity to be realized along a gradient scale, from those events that are highly prototypically transitive to those that are definitely not, with a number of intermediate positions. These intermediate positions, often called the transitive 'middle' are the subject of the next section.

...The conception of the middle as a verbal category seems to be as old as the tradition of grammatical description in Indo-European (IE) languages. Rules specifying the selection of middle vs. active inflections appear in the Classical Sanskrit grammar attributed to Pāṇini... (Klaiman 1991: 82).

Delineating a specific, cross-linguistic definition of 'middle' has proved a herculean task due to the multiple phonological, morpho-syntactic, semantic, and pragmatic contexts with which it is related. Even within a single language, the number of meanings to which the 'middle' may be related can be numerous. For instance, in some (Tibeto-Burman) Chin languages, "there is a prefix ki- or ng'- (depending on the dialect), the semantics of which covers reflexive, reciprocal, stative, intransitivizer, indirect benefactive, reflexive and passive meanings, all meanings associated with middle marking" (LaPolla 1996: 13). The middle may be expressed by unique phonological markings (Smith 2004) as in Romanian (Calude 2007), by morpho-syntactic marking such as Dutch (Ackema & Schoorlemmer 1994), Greek (Lekakou 2002), Sanskrit, Indo-European, Fula, Tamil (Klaiman 1991), Russian (Faltz 1985) and Spanish (Maldonado 2000). It may also share its marking with the reflexive as in Tibeto-Burman (LaPolla 1996) or passive as in Irish (Doyle 2007) or have no overt marking like English and Dutch (Abraham 1995; Kemmer 1993). Categorizing the structural functions of the middle encounters similar difficulties:

> In a middle construction, the viewpoint is active in that the action notionally devolves from the standpoint of the most dynamic (or Agent-like) participant in the depicted situation. But the same participant has Patient-like characteristics as well, in that it sustains the action's principal effects (Klaiman 1991: 3).

> ...a crucial property of middle semantics...(is) the degree to which a single physico-mental entity is conceptually distinguished into separate participants, whether body vs. mind, or Agent vs. unexpectedly contrasting Patient (Kemmer 1993: 66).

Klaiman addresses the similarities of the Agent-Patient construal; the participants seem to approach each other from opposing action-based positions (initiator and affected) to form a merged Agent-Patient participant. Kemmer focuses on the separateness of Agent-Patient as key to differentiating types of middles. Although superficially distinct, these views may be complementary. In the description of examples such as (106) and (107) below, the 'merged' participants in the action simultaneously initiate and receive the effects of it (as per Klaiman). The participants are also distinct in that there is some concept of separation of the two participants (as per Kemmer), no matter how opaque and even if only one participant is overtly expressed.

106. Randy showered, shaved, and dressed for the dance.
107. Daniel moved (himself) away from the car.

These participants, no matter the degree of separation (as long as they are coreferent), share in the action. English middles, not having a unique marking, share their marking with intransitive and reflexive events depending upon the verb. The difference between these is the distance the participants are conceived of as being from each other in relation to the event action. The participants are deemed closer in example (106) (*Randy* and his body as barely distinct entities), and further in (107) (*Daniel* and his holistic Self as distinct 'other' entities). Furthermore, removal of the reflexive pronoun in (107) brings the participants closer towards a more merged conceptual entity, while inserting it distances them. Thus, a gradient can be established with regard to how participants associated with an event action are construed, in other words, a scalable cline of participant distinction.

The notion of participant distinguishability (Kemmer 1993) has obvious associations with gradient transitivity and therefore with the relationships between reflexive and non-reflexive middle events. Hopper and Thompson (1980: 277) note that "Reflexives in many languages have properties which can be explained by appealing to their intermediate status between one-argument and two-argument clauses: compared with one-argument clauses, they may be more transitive, ...compared with two-argument causes, they typically display features associated with lower transitivity..." If reflexive and middle events are both intermediate between prototypical transitive poles, they must be clarified if they are to be properly delineated. Lange explains, "...while the reflexive personal pronoun serves to indicate coreference with two-place predicates and therefore acts as a detransitivising device, the middle marker has no similar syntactic status...Verbs taking the middle marker are mostly intransitive in the first place" (2007: 89). Lange considers middles intransitive events based on their morpho-syntactic (zero-) marking and valency criteria while Hopper & Thompson (1980) consider reflexives and middles as two functional 'intermediaries' insofar as they represent positions intermediate between the transitive and intransitive prototypes (i.e., the 'traditional' view of middle action based on action initiation and affect (Klaiman 1991)[15].

> 108. Harry placed an apple on the chair.
> 109. Harry placed himself on the chair.
> 110. Harry sat on the chair.
> 111. It's raining.

The two stances can be illustrated by examining (108-111). According to Lange, (108) belongs to the category transitive, (109) to the less transitive group due to the existence of the detransitivizing factor of the reflexive pronoun, and (110-111) are grouped together into intransitive events. Hopper & Thompson view (108-111) as one gradable cline of transitivity based on semantic components, different positions along that axis representing degrees of transitivity. This transitivity matrix might be envisioned as a numerical scale ranging from 1-10[16], where a rating of 1 represents highly prototypical transitive events (i.e., (108)) and a 10 rating represents highly prototypically intransitive events (i.e., (111)). Example (109) might be judged a 4-5 due to lack of differentiation of Agent/Patient (coreference), and (110) might fall near a 6-7 due to the inherent semantic reflexivity of 'middle' verbs. The purpose of comparison here is not to decide which of the theories is more valid nor the exact numerical value for each event, but to emphasize the different approaches to the notion of transitivity when 'grey area' data are found. That being said, examining SA events will lead to a hypothesis more in line with Hopper and Thompson (1980), Kemmer (1993), de Swart (2006) and Næss (2007), i.e., that transitivity is subject to gradable nuances regardless of syntactic representation, the interpretation of which is dependent on semantic and pragmatic information. Kemmer calls these nuances relative elaboration of events:

> …the degree to which the facets in a particular situation, i.e. the participants and conceivable component subevents in the situation, are distinguished…the speaker has a choice of either marking reference to events as undifferentiated wholes or making reference to their

---

[15] Although Klaiman rejects the view of 'middle' as a strictly detransitivizing device, he does admit typological relationships between the middle voice and affectedness, transitivity and reflexivity (with respect to morphological patterning on the verbal lexicon).

[16] These numerical values have not been used in the literature as far as I am aware. They are used here only for descriptive purposes, but are similar in concept to de Swart's Transitivity Continuum (de Swart 2006).

substructures or component parts. Thus, relative elaboration of events is the key property by which reflexive and middle events are distinguished (1993: 208).

It is beyond the scope of this investigation to recount the detailed argument Kemmer makes for reflexive, middle, and prototypical intransitive/intransitive events in relation to the relative elaboration of events. The argument can be summarized as consisting of two main components; *distinguishablility of participants* and *event action initiation and affect* (i.e., the origin of the action and the affected entity of that action, respectively). These components interplay with voice (active vs. passive) and valency/transitivity in the conception, construal and predication of an event (ibid).

The amount of participant distinguishablility conceived for each event has immediate repercussions for the construal and predication of that event. The greatest level of distinction is two completely independent, sentient entities, as in (112) below. At the other end of the spectrum is a single, non-sentient (or empty) entity with no possibility of participant distinction, as in (113 a, b), respectively[17]. And then there is everything in between. Many of these were discussed previously in relation to Hopper and Thompson's transitivity matrix[18]; therefore, only those aspects directly related to the middle and SA events will be discussed below.

112. Marci kissed Brad.

113. a. The tree grew.

b. It snowed.

114. Marci dressed quickly.

115. *The child saw herself* in the still water.

116. a. *Marci considered herself* healthy.

b. *Marci thinks herself* a genius.

117. *Marci found herself* liking the cough medicine.

118. *Marci caught herself* chuckling at the thought.

119. *Marci lost herself* in romantic daydreams.

Examples (114-119) exhibit varying degrees of participant distinguishablility. In (114), the Patient is not and need not be overtly expressed; the inherent semantics of the verb licenses the expectation of coreference. This expectation of coreference is thought to be one factor that

---

[17] See Dowty (1991) for an interesting distinction of semantic 'proto-roles' of Agent and Patient.

[18] See Næss (2007) and Kemmer (1993) for similar yet more concise versions of this matrix.

positions the middle event in (114) closer to one-participant events than the reflexive events in (115) and (116) (Kemmer 1993), even though they are all conceived and construed as intermediate between the prototypical transitive and intransitive poles. The non-metaphorical direct reflexive[19] events in (115) and (116) are construed as two participant events in which the Patient (the entity affected by the event action) happens to be the same entity as the Agent (the starting point of the event action) (ibid). The difference lies in the individuation (Hopper & Thompson 1980) or distinctness (Kemmer 1993) of the Patient related to the Agent. In (115), the *reflection* that is seen is more distinct from the *seer* than the distinctness of the idea of *self* that is considered/thought by the *thinker* in (116 a, b). The notion of distinctness of Patient (from Agent) related to transitivity has been noted within and across languages, although called by various names and described within various theoretical constructs (Comrie 1989; de Swart 2006; Dowty 1991; Frajzyngier 2000; Geniusiene 1987; Hopper & Thompson 1980; Kemmer 1993; Lange 2007; Levin & Hovav 2005; Maldonado 2000; Næss 2007; Onishi 2000; Peitsara 1997; Safir 2004; Stephens 2006; Taylor 2003).

The SA events in (117-119) represent interesting distinction of participant cases. On the one hand, the metaphoricity of the events can be analyzed as synonymous with the non-metaphorical senses and given prototypical reflexive semantics, i.e., the participant distinctions of *find, catch,* and *lose* do not change; they are construed as separate entities (even though in reality they are synonymous). On the other hand (the one developed here), the metaphoricity of SA events involve changes in their inherent semantic senses, thus manifesting unique distinctness of participant signatures. *Marci finding/catching/losing herself* entails minimal conceptual participant distinction, less than non-SA event reflexives but more than other middle events which, noted above, include participant distinction properties within the verb semantics. Furthermore, SA events are also distinguished from mental events occurring with verbs such as *consider* or *think* (116 a, b), which construe independent (albeit non-tangible) senses of Patient. Provisionally, then, with respect to the distinction of participants, SA events are construed as intermediary between non-SA reflexive events and middle events.

The next component concerning middle and SA events is the source of the event action and the affectedness of the action on the participant. Kemmer calls these Initiator and Endpoint (Kemmer 1993), but they have been described in relation to prototypical transitive

---

[19] In contrast, the 'indirect reflexive' is described as an event in which the Patient assumes a Benefactive, Instrumental or other adjunctive role (regardless of syntax), such as "I did it for myself" and 'I did it by myself' etc. Due to the differences in construal with the direct reflexive, however, they will not be discussed here. For further reading, see (Dixon & Aïkhenval'd, 2000; Geniusiene, 1987; Helke, 1979; Kemmer, 1993; Lange, 2007; Lederer, 2013; Næss, 2007).

events as Agency, Volitionality and Affectedness of O (Hopper & Thompson 1980), Volitionality, Concrete/Dynamic Action, and Patient effect (Næss 2007), and Experiencer and Patient (Comrie 1989). For the sake of clarity and economy, I will refer to the initiation of the event action as *initiator* and the affected participant of the event action as *affected*. Sentences (120-125), shown again from (114-119) for convenience, exemplify the participant initiator and affected properties of the event action:

> 120. Marci dressed quickly.
> 121. The child saw herself in the still water.
> 122. Marci considered herself healthy.
> 123. *Marci found herself* liking the cough medicine.
> 124. *Marci caught herself* chuckling at the thought.
> 125. *Marci lost herself* in the wooziness of her fever.

The middle event of sentence (120) includes the verb *dress*, an action that is usually done by oneself to oneself.[20] The action is initiated by *Marci* (initiator) and the affected entity of the action is *Marci* (affected). There is no overt marking to draw attention to this point in English (except for the intransitivity of the verb) and the only way to know this is to know its valency/transitivity. The description just given may be misinterpreted because the phrase by 'oneself to oneself' assumes a flow of action from one participant to another whereas with a middle event, there is only one 'real' participant. Therefore, the description for the action flow can be rephrased as *emergence* of initiator/affected action. This notion can be more fully envisaged by comparing the actions of the events in (121) and (122). In these events, there is a directional flow of action from the initiator to the affected, irrespective of whether the affected is a separate entity or not. In (120), however, the action of *dressing oneself* cannot be given a specific directional flow, either to one body part or another; it is an emergent action derived within the gestalt initiator/affected composite. This can be applied to other similar forms of body action middle events, as in (126-128).

> 126. Henry sat in the chair.
> 127. Scott shaved for the party.
> 128. Charlene laughed wholeheartedly.

---

[20] There are some situations in which one entity dresses another entity due to age, inability, etc., as in *Marci dressed her baby/grandmother/cat*, but these are adjunct to the present discussion.

Although LaPolla (1996) and Kemmer (1993) describe this as a lack of participant differentiation, Kemmer also notes that "...the body action middles are characterized by minimal conceptual differentiation between initiating an endpoint activities" (ibid: 71). Focusing on the event action brings the discussion back to the defining quality presented above, i.e., an emergent gestalt action derived within the initiator/affected composite. The SA events in (123-125) represent this emergence of action, not a directional flow of action.

It was noted in section 1.2 that Self-Awareness was an accurate categorical label for the metaphorical reflexive senses of *find*, *catch*, and *lose*. Examples (123-125) are metaphorical and construe separate senses from non-metaphorical meanings. Metaphorical *find*, *catch*, and *lose* do not involve actual physical or non-physical *finding*, *catching*, or *losing* of an object, which are transitive events and have high participant distinguishability and directional action flow. SA events convey the concept of the 'emergence of awareness of one's experience at a certain moment in time and space'. The SA senses rate much lower on the scale for distinguishablilty of participants (there is only one participant, similar to middle events) and action quality (emergence of action within the single initiator/affected participant). In other words, SA events express a minimal conceptual differentiation of referential entities due to the emergent quality of Self-Aware action. SA events may, however, construe slightly more participant distinction than typical middle events due to the predication of the event by way of reflexive morpho-syntax, suggesting perhaps, some level of conceptual separation of the (initiator/affected) participant. Therefore, the proposal advanced here is that SA events are construed as middle events, more transitive than the body-action middle events but less transitive than literal and non-SA reflexive events.

Figure 1: SA-inclusive transitivity scale

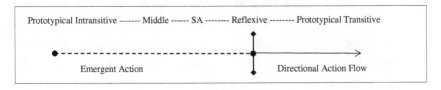

SA events, non-SA reflexive events and middle events can be identified by distinction of participants, but only in relation to the quality of the initiator/affected action. Their proposed locations on the transitivity scale are given in Figure 1. The quality of the actions of (123-125) do not flow directionally; *find oneself, catch one*self and *lose oneself* all construe an emergence of Self-Awareness. The quality of Emergent Action includes middle and SA events.

In contrast, Directional Action Flow begins at non-SA Reflexive Events and continues through two-participant Prototypical Transitive events. At the risk of magniloquence, the difference between these conceptual actions can be imagined as the difference between a river (non-SA reflexive and two-participant transitive events) and a geyser (SA and middle events). The source of a river continuously flows upward from its subterranean source (Directional Action Flow), continuing to flow until its gravitational force has diminished (emptying into a larger body of water). Contrary to this, a geyser erupts upwards, its single burst (Emergent Action) ending abruptly, the water falling to virtually the same place it broke the surface (lack of continued Action Flow). The SA events *find, catch*, and *lose x-self* refer to this Emergence of Self-Awareness within the gestalt initiator/affected composite. In other words, Awareness of one's mind/body sensations materializes in consciousness, where it is acknowledged and (usually) then commented upon by the conscious mind. The expression of this conception is by way of the reflexive construction (which carries the coreferent meaning). The concept of emergence is expressed through the meanings of verbs *find, catch*, and *lose*, judged (unconsciously) by speakers to be pragmatically/semantically similar to the Emergence of Awareness experience. The amalgamation of these two notions results in the SA event described in this discussion.

2.5 Chapter Conclusions

A description of semantic components is vital for the proper categorization and delineation of valency, transitivity and event action with regard to middle and reflexive events. SA events are specific cases of middle events that exemplify the need for such detailed semantic descriptions. Generalizations about transitivity for reflexive and middle events gloss over important differences in their relative elaboration of events, perhaps the reason SA has been described so sparsely in the literature. Classifying SA events simply as reflexive events fails to account for their unique participant distinguishability and event action signatures. SA events were seen to construe an emergence of initiator/affected action predicated by way of the metaphorical senses of the verbs *find, catch*, and *lose* used within reflexive constructions.

3. Part I Conclusions

3.1 Conclusions

Two questions were addressed so far within the traditional linguistic syntactic and semantic paradigm: 1) How is Self-Awareness expressed through metaphorical reflexive constructions? and 2) Can the construal and predication of SA events be delineated and categorized? Chapter 1 outlined difficulties in categorizing various senses of verbs that appear metaphorically. Self-Awareness was proposed as the unifying concept underlying the use of the metaphorical sense of the reflexive pronoun with the verbs *find*, *lose*, and *catch*, in contrast to other categorization labels proposed in the OED online, CEDO and LDOCE. It was also seen that a purely structural description of reflexivity could not account for the polysemy and idiosyncrasies that occur, especially with metaphorical reflexive events. Analysis of verb semantics along with the nominals they license is necessary to appropriately categorize these kinds of events.

Chapter 2 explored the complexities of delineating SA events with respect to notions of expectation, valency and transitivity. Specifically discussed were reflexive events categorized in terms of other-directed vs. non-other-directedness. It was shown that reflexive marking was implemented when the coreferentiality of participants is unexpected. It was concluded that although these categorizations account for reflexivization in general, they are too broad to adequately satisfy the descriptive requirements of SA events in particular.

The inherent property of a verb to license a certain number of participants, i.e., valency, was discussed and considered important for the construal of SA events. The concept of valency allows for idiosyncratic lexical semantic factors to be taken into account, crucial if SA is to be delineated with precision. However, it was also seen that valency alone was not able to account for specific SA traits. To do this, transitivity was explored and shown to provide various conceptual tools for the detailed analysis of SA events. These 'tools' include defining specific semantic components of the verb-participant relationship in a transitive event. Once these subcomponents are made available, participants are seen to differ in their distinctness from each other with respect to an event and its action. Along with components such as affectedness of Patient and quality of event action, transitivity was seen to be gradient, ranging from prototypically intransitive to prototypically transitive. The intermediate range along this cline, i.e., the middle, was shown to be semantically complex as well as subtle. SA is delineated within this middle range when distinction of participants and initiator/affect event action are taken into consideration. Specifically, SA events express an emergence of event action with minimal participant distinction. These factors provide the appropriate backdrop from which SA events are adequately evaluated.

In conclusion, metaphorical construal of Self-Awareness is conceived and predicated by way of the verbs *find*, *catch*, and *lose* when used in reflexive constructions. It is proposed here that SA events are distinct from previous categorizations of either reflexive or middle events. This investigation was an attempt to identify and categorize SA events lexically, structurally and semantically, hoping to provide an accurate account of an opaque and subtle linguistic event in the English language.

Further research in Part II will help clarify the conception, construal, and predication of SA events by way of Cognitive Linguistic theories. Discussed in detail will be the description of Conceptual Metaphor as it relates to SA events. Descriptions of *force dynamics* and *causation* will be described in order to demonstrate how metaphorical reflexives interact with cognitive construal. Subjectivity/Point of View will also be shown to play a dynamic role in the construal of SA events.

Part II: Cognitive Linguistic Analyses

Chapter 4: Cognitive Linguistics and Self-Aware Metaphors

4.1 Introduction

This chapter investigates English metaphorical reflexive expressions of Self-Awareness, i.e., SA events, from a Cognitive Linguistics viewpoint and proposes that these are cases of 'metaphor from metonymy' (Goossens 2002) as well as 'target-in-source metonymy' (Ruiz de Mendoza & Díez 2002). In other words, the reflexive pronoun construes a WHOLE FOR PART metonymic relationship standing for the specific mental function of Self-Awareness. The overall expression, on the other hand, instantiates a metaphorical construal of the emergence (or lack) of Self-Awareness. This is expressed by way of a conceptual cross-domain mapping of the entailments of [FIND] and [LOSE] such that [FINDING ONESELF IS HAVING SELF-AWARENESS] and [LOSING ONESELF IS HAVING HAD SELF-AWARENESS].[21] Examples (129) and (130) exemplify these SA events; the metaphorical senses of *find* and *lose* coupled with the metonymically construed reflexive pronoun in the (a) sentences and their possible paraphrases in the (b) sentences.

129. a. ...*John found himself* in a large, square, tiled hall...
                                                  (COCA:1997.MAG.GoodHousekeeping)
      b. John₁ was aware that he₁ was in a large...hall...

130. a. *Mary lost herself* in a daydream then... (COCA:2015.FIC.AntiochRev)
      b. Mary was totally engrossed in a daydream then...

Within Cognitive Linguistics, specific discussion of SA events is rare, but when it does appear its subtleness and potential for ambiguity with similar construals is glossed over and/or supporting corpus data is scant. This seems enigmatic in that, firstly, Self-Awareness is a prime candidate for the well-entrenched theory of *image schema* (aka *primary domain*) being a thoroughly embodied concept, i.e., entrenched in very early human interrelated developmental patterns of physicality and cognition. Secondly, readily available and user-friendly corpus tools

---

[21] This discussion will follow the conventional cognitive semantic typography as conveyed by Feyaerts (A. Deignan, 2007). Small capitals (TREE) will be used for conceptual structures, italics (*tree*) for linguistic structures, and double quotes ("tree") will be used for semantic structures.

are now commonplace, creating opportunities to examine hypotheses against actual usage, fortifying or invalidating theoretical arguments with vast amounts of data. The following research is an endeavor in this manner.

Section 4.2 presents a definition of Self-Awareness as a specific cognitive function based on perceptions of stimuli. It defines Self-Awareness in precise operational terms so that it may be implemented in linguistic analyses of metaphor.

Section 4.4 defines and delineates conceptual metaphor and metonymy in order to lay the theoretical foundation from which SA expressions can be explicated in full. The verbs *find* and *lose* in the overall predication are first argued to be cases of metaphor, i.e., exemplifying a cross-domain mapping relation between subcomponents of their 'common' meanings and their metaphorical senses. SA predications are then viewed from a metonymic aspect, where the reflexive pronoun and its antecedent are analyzed and concluded as having an intra-domain, WHOLE FOR PART relation.

Section 4.5 discusses SA events specifically with respect to Langacker's Cognitive Grammar (1987b; 2006; 2008), the 'divided self' phenomenon (A. Lakoff & Becker 1992; G. Lakoff 1996b; Talmy 2003) and the Awareness Onset model (Grady 2005). These theories have been used with relative success in cases similar to SA events and can account for many aspects of metaphorical reflexivity. Key to this discussion are the theories of *image schema* and *domains*. Precise delineation of these terms and what they represent will be discussed, a necessary first step for the clarification of ambiguous predications.

Chapter 5 follows with an analysis of SA events that combines metaphor and metonymy and provides evidence that both the metonymical mapping of the object pronoun to the antecedent along with the metaphorical mapping of the 'predication as a whole' depend upon one another. This consequently creates an inseparable, gestalt metaphor. From this, it is concluded that SA events are a instances of 'metaphor from metonymy' and that SA event construals can be explained more clearly and precisely from such an evaluation.

Chapter 6 concludes the discussion and introduces further research.

4.2 Operational Definition of Self-Awareness

For the purposes of this linguistically-oriented discussion, I define Self-Awareness in the following way:

Self-Awareness is the embodied, cognitive function of conscious meta-perception. In other words, the conscious realization of one's own physical, emotional and/or mental reaction(s) to perceptions of interior and/or exterior stimuli.

It is critical here to distinguish between self-awareness and perception, although in folk[22] use these may be used interchangeably. Perception, as it is used here, involves the direct, involuntary reaction(s) to stimuli in/on the body and/or mind. For example, the automatic physical and/or emotional feeling(s) from an injury, the physical and/or emotional feeling(s) brought about by tender words from a loved one, etc. Perceptions therefore, are the brain's way of making sense of internal or external stimuli. Self-Awareness, however, is one step 'removed' from this, as it were. It is the conscious awareness of perception(s) (Damasio 2010b; Ismael 2006; Janzen 2008; Nida-Rümelin 2011; Watson 2006; Williams 2000).

This definition of self-awareness is basically congruent with that of self-awareness in the Oxford Dictionary of English (2015), "Conscious knowledge of one's own character and feelings". SA events in the (a) examples from (129-130) above as well as those presented hereafter are to be understood with this specific definition in mind. For example, in (129 a) it is John's ability to be aware of the physio-psychological experience of hiding in the closet and emergence of conscious awareness that is found. Compare the sentence *John was hiding in the closet*, where John's awareness of his situation is not reported. He could have known he was in the closet or he could have been oblivious to this. The narrator/author gives us no information about John's state of conscious awareness. By specifically expressing *He found himself...*, the narrator/author wants the reader/hearer to know that *John* was aware that of *himself in the closet*. On the other side of the coin, in (130 a), Mary's concentration on *her daydream* was so intense that her awareness of any physio-psychological perception other than *the daydream* was temporarily blocked or absent, i.e., *lost*.

4.3. Definition and delineation of metaphor

Sometimes language is literal. During a basketball game, for example, if the basketball unintentionally slips from a player's hands and the ball hits the floor, the player can say, *I dropped the ball*. However, sometimes the experience of unintentionally dropping a ball is commonly shared within a certain group of people. The literal meaning may then be extended

---

[22] The use of the word *folk* here is used with in the sense of *non-specialist*.

(i.e., mapped) onto another experience that seems to have some relation to dropping a ball.[23] For example, when a salesperson fails to sign a potential client and says to his boss, *I dropped the ball*, he means that he failed to sign the client. *Unintentional dropping of a ball* is related, in the minds of the interlocutors, to *failing*. These metaphors, if firmly established and widely used, can manifest and spread throughout a community and perhaps further across populations and/or conceptual boundaries (if other types of experiences and/or expressions are related with dropping and/or failing). Thus, clarification of the use of the term *metaphor* is a first necessary step towards proper analysis of SA events.

I will begin here with what is not meant by metaphor in this discussion. The term metaphor, as it is used here, is not what is commonly known as literary metaphor, often used in poetry, literature, art and drama. This is the purposeful, ad hoc use of figurative language for dramatic and imagistic purposes.

The meaning of the term *metaphor* utilized here is often called *conceptual metaphor* when referring to the underlying patterns of thought or *linguistic metaphor* when referring to the expression itself (G. Lakoff & Johnson 2008: 7). This type of metaphor occurs in natural language use. It is mainly unconscious, conceptual and grounded in human experience and culture (Deignan 2008; Feldman 2008; Kovecses 2002; G. Lakoff 1993b; G. Lakoff & Johnson 1999; Langacker 2002; Panther, Thornburg, & Barcelona 2009; Yu 2008).

The distinction between literary and conceptual metaphor is not as clear-cut as I have described above, however. The literary metaphors in the passage below by Dante Alighieri are also instances of conceptual metaphors, specifically, LIFE IS A JOURNEY[24] and KNOWING IS SEEING (Deignan 2005, 2008; Yu 2008).

> 131. In the middle of life's road
> *I found myself* in a dark wood.
> (Alighieri, "The Inferno", lines 1-3. In G. Lakoff 1993b: 237)

Lakoff explains that *I found myself in a dark wood* evokes the knowledge that if it's dark you cannot see which way to go. This evokes the image of SEEING and the conceptual metaphor KNOWING IS SEEING...The experiential basis in this case is the fact that most of what non-

---

[23] The word *seems* is pivotal. It is very often 'mapped' only in the minds of those members who share that experience, not in 'reality'.

[24] The conceptual metaphor LIFE IS A JOURNEY as related to Dante's Inferno will not be discussed here due to space constraints, but Lakoff's analysis seems valid.

impaired humans know comes through vision, and in the overwhelming majority of cases, if we see something, then we know it is true" (1993b: 240). Although the KNOWING IS SEEING metaphor as related to the first and second lines of the LIFE IS A JOURNEY metaphor is warranted (for *dark wood*), in this particular case there is an alternative analysis for line two that is just as pertinent to the intended meaning. The use of the metaphor *I found myself* is a key component of the construal here if the translator's note (Alighieri 2008) with regard to *dark wood* is taken into consideration. Dante's world was socially and politically controlled by the Church, where 'passions, vices and perplexities' were considered evil. If SELF-AWARENESS were proposed as the metaphorical meaning for *I found myself...*, with the interpretation of 'I was suddenly aware that I was surrounded by evil', it would certainly convey Dante's well-known contempt for the unethical political situation of Church politics surrounding him at that time (Alighieri 2008). This is further supported by lines 10-12 in example (132):

132. I cannot well repeat how there I entered,
So full was I of slumber at the moment
In which I abandoned the true way (ibid.: 1).

Dante writes metaphorically that he *cannot repeat* (i.e., he doesn't remember) how he *entered* (the *dark wood*) because he was *so full of slumber at the moment* (i.e., metaphorically, unaware). Furthermore, *the true way* in line three most certainly refers to the Catholic righteous path of moral and ethical behavior. Thus, because of Dante's awareness of the unethical state of affairs surrounding him, the expression *I found myself within a dark wood* implies that he was previously unaware of the immoral situation but has now become aware of it. Furthermore, he is now fully aware of this situation and he wants the reader to know this. If Dante had written *I was in a dark wood*, the character might or might have not been aware of his situation (even though the narrator/author is sure to be).

Thus, literary metaphor is often used a tool used for imagistic purposes but conceptual metaphors are used throughout the literature as well (Raymond W Gibbs 1994; Kövecses 2010; G. Lakoff & Turner 2009). The construals SEEING IS KNOWING and FINDING ONESELF IS EMERGENT SELF-AWARENESS are conceptual metaphors that are vital to understanding the deeper meaning of Dante's poem as well as for understanding SA events at large.

4.4. Conceptual Metaphor

Three general questions need to be addressed regarding conceptual metaphor before the specifics of SA events are discussed. 1) What exactly is a conceptual metaphor? 2) How are metaphorical concepts related? 3) Is there more than one type of relation conception between and among concepts?

There are many variations and levels of specificity regarding definitions of metaphor. "A metaphor is a word or expression that is used to talk about an entity or quality other than that referred to by its core, or most basic meaning. This non-core use expresses a perceived relationship with the core meaning of the word, and in many cases between two semantic fields" (Deignan 2005: 34). This definition is accurate in that it captures the function and structure of metaphor, i.e., its non-core use, along with the establishment of a relationship between the meanings of a word along with the concept of semantic field. However, how does one define and delineate what is core and/or basic and what is not? What is a semantic field and what is its composition? The above definition lacks the specificity needed to analyze the precise components of metaphorical expressions. Cameron provides a more precise definition. "Linguistic metaphor is identified through the use of words or phrases that are potentially linked to a vehicle (or source) domain which is distinct from the domain of the surrounding, ongoing talk (a topic or target)" (2008: 198). The term 'linking of domains' is found, in one form or another, in other cognitive linguistic definitions of metaphor as well (Bartsch 2002; Dirven 2002; Gibbs 2008; Kovecses 2002; G. Lakoff & Johnson 1999, 2008; G. Lakoff & Turner 2009; Warren 2002). However, due to the subtleness of the SA event construal and in order to avoid as much ambiguity as possible, an even more specific definition of metaphor is required. The definition utilized in this discussion is the following:

> Metaphor is the cognitive mechanism whereby one experiential domain...is partially mapped onto a different experiential domain, the second domain being partially understood in terms of the first one. The domain that is mapped is called the source or donor domain, and the domain onto which it is mapped, is called the target or recipient domain. Both domains have to belong to different superordinate domains (Barcelona 2002: 211).

The specificity of Barcelona's definition is insightful and useful but questions remain: What is an experiential domain? What is a mapping and why is the mapping only partial? What is a superordinate domain and why do the domains need to be separate? By treating each of these concerns below, a common theoretical foundation can be built from which SA events are delineated and categorized.

4.5. Schematicity and domains

Due to their inherent abstractness, the difficultly of delineating the exact parameters of cognitive domain and/or schemata should not be underestimated. Thus, differing opinions about what these consist of abound. As a starting point, however, "...a schema is a superordinate concept, one which specifies the basic outline common to several, or many, more specific concepts. The specific concepts...fill in that outline in varying, often contrastive ways" (Radden, 2002). Each specific concept (see encyclopaedic knowledge, (Tuggy 2007: 83)) is either conceptually prominent (i.e., 'profile' (Langacker 2002)), or is part of the 'background' from which the prominent components are built. Background information guides the interlocutors towards shared meaning of a predication within its context (Langacker 1987a; Croft 1993; Littlemore 2015). This background is the main idea behind the concept of 'domain'. The definition proposed by Croft is quoted in full:

> Profile and base are conceptually interdependent. On the one hand, profiled concepts cannot be understood except against the background knowledge provided by the base. On the other hand, the base exists as a cognitively unified and delimited "chunk" of knowledge only by virtue of the concept or concepts defined with respect to it... We can now define a domain as a semantic structure that functions as the base for at least one concept profile (typically, many profiles) (1993: 166).

In other words, domain knowledge guides the meaning of every aspect of what we hear, say and think. It is experiential and encyclopaedic, i.e., it is formed from physical and psychological experience and changes with every experience, respectively. In sum, a thing cannot be understood except within the conceptual background upon which it is proposed.

4.6. Image Schema

From this concept of domain come the terms 'base' and 'profile' (Langacker 1987b, 2002, 2006), and are also related to what is termed 'image schema' (G. Lakoff & Johnson 1999, 2008). In general terms, image schemata are the most basic conceptual components that cannot be broken down into smaller conceptual parts. The importance of clearly and precisely defining what this constitutes, however, cannot be stressed enough. Throughout the literature on the subject, there are various definitions and examples of image schema that seem to depart from the original concept based on embodied perception put forth by Lakoff and Johnson (1999) and separately (in other terms) by Langacker (1987a). "Image schemas are among the central pillars of cognitive linguistics…because so many scholars have been drawn to them as intuitive and powerful instruments for analyzing the nature of thought and language…And yet there is still disagreement, and even confusion, about what image-schemas are, and what exactly the term refers to" (Grady 2005: 35-36). Thus, the clarification of what constitutes image schemata remains a challenge.

Grady's call for simplification and precise specification of the definition of image schema is timely. Instead of proposing a new definition that encompasses facets of revised versions of the term, he proposes returning to the original and most fundamental elements of that original definition. In particular, he focuses on *embodied perceptions* as prototypical image schemas for which other, more abstract conceptions may be created, even though they themselves may be ontologically gestalt and basic. "…the most useful way of understanding image schemas is to see them as mental representations of fundamental units of sensory experience…Defining image schemas in this way allows us to refer to a set of mental representations with a special and fundamental status, distinct from the infinite variety of "schematic" images which we can form over a course of a lifetime…" (Grady 2005: 44). For example, from the time we are infants, we physically experience objects being located inside receptacles. The receptacles for the items can be called 'containers'. These containers provide the boundaries that contain the items found within them. Our first experience of this is antenatal; our mothers' uterus provides the container in which we, as fetuses, are 'contained'. Our experience of being inside a container, and then, during birth, being thrust outside a container is one that is physically and psychologically basic, i.e. not based on or built on any other concept. It is an experiential gestalt concept, an 'image schema' based on embodied perception and experience. This image schema is appropriately coined the CONTAINER schema (Croft 1993; Johnson 2013; Kövecses 2003; G. Lakoff & Johnson 2008; G. Lakoff & Kövecses 1987; Matsuki 1995). It is one that is continuously reinforced through life experiences and construed/predicated both literally and metaphorically. Literally, we construe and predicate concepts such as *The cat is in the box*. We use these experiences of CONTAINER to construe other types of expressions as well, as in *I am in love*. The expression *in love* precludes that love is a conceptual CONTAINER, so that one is contained within the 'boundaries' of *love*. Thus, we can also *fall out of love*, where the love 'container' no longer envelops us.

There are various ways in which the CONTAINER schema is used to talk about things, many having seemingly very little in common (from an ontological perspective). Compare the following sentences: *I ran in the race, I followed in the path of my forefathers* and *I'm in big trouble*. These situations do not include physical containers. Use of the preposition *in* for these various situations can be explained through the CONTAINER schema, where metaphorical concepts abstract away from the original, physical concept of what a literal CONTAINER entails (Johnson 2013; Kövecses 2003; G. Lakoff 1990b; G. Lakoff & Johnson 1999).

If non-perceptual concepts are to be included in the definition of image schema, then countless abstract entities are viable to be considered as such and the credibility of the term becomes diffuse, confused and eventually meaningless. The original, embodied concept of image schema was meant to address centuries of dualistic thinking of the body and mind as separate entities with their own logic and structure (Johnson 2005, 2013; G. Lakoff & Johnson 1999, 2008). If this perceptual, embodied sense of the definition is upheld and other more abstract concepts are given other terminology, then the clarity, simplicity and genius of the original definition remains intact. This is, I believe, the spirit in which Grady (2005) writes and one which helps clarify the present discussion.

Through this clarification, the SA event is also made more transparent. The foundation for proposing SELF-AWARENESS as an image schema lies in the embodied physical, sensory-motor experience of the mind-body complex. Each sensory input is assigned meaning by the mind (i.e., perception), and when the mind becomes explicitly conscious of this meaning, it is Self-Aware. When this Self-Aware pattern of thought is repeated often enough, it becomes strengthened and familiar (i.e., a Self-Awareness image schema), and can then be utilized as a 'base' or 'background' in which other concepts can be related and built. In this way, the logic of Self-Awareness as an event can be put to use (i.e., construed and predicated) in situations deemed relevant to the interlocutors.

> 133. *I found myself* blushing. (BNC:CEX 623)
> 134. *...she loses herself* in the cracks in the ceiling... (COCA:1998.MAG.PsychToday)

Taking into account the specific definition of image schema as described above along with the definition of self-awareness given in section 4.2, it is proposed that in example (133), *I found myself blushing* expresses SELF-AWARENESS of the perception(s) of *blushing*, while in (134) ...*she loses herself...*, expresses temporary lack of SELF-AWARENESS of mental perceptions of anything *but the cracks in the ceiling*. SELF-AWARENESS is a primary, embodied conceptual notion used as the base of metaphorical expressions, thus passing the requirements for image schema as defined in its original sense.

4.7. Abstract Domains and Metaphor

In general, a *domain* is usually made up of many smaller parts but may sometimes be itself a gestalt-type category (Gärdenfors & Löhndorf 2013; G. Lakoff 1993b; Langacker 1987a; Radden 2002; Ruiz de Mendoza & Díez 2002). Langacker defines a domain as "a context for the characterization of a semantic unit. Domains are necessarily cognitive entities: mental experiences, representational spaces, concepts, or conceptual complexes" (1987a: 91). He establishes two types of domains, "basic" and "abstract". A basic domain is one that is directly rooted in experience, is an experiential gestalt concept (i.e., it cannot be broken down further into smaller conceptual parts (i.e., image schema)), and acts as the base for any given profile (i.e., foregrounded concept). An abstract domain, on the other hand, is made up of two or more basic domains, and can be used as the profile for another domain.

Metaphors rely on these conceptual contexts and the logic abstracted from them to create relations between two or more concepts, either superordinate or subordinate from the "source". The use of the terms, super- and subordinate brings us back to Barcelona's definition of domain from above. It was stated there that metaphorical domains must be two separate superordinate domains. Why is this so? Looking at the conceptual metaphor GOOD IS UP, e.g., *I'm so high, He climbed the ladder to success, She's on top of the world*, etc... the concept GOOD is comprised of the superordinate domain of WELLNESS and the UP domain of SPATIAL ORIENTATION. These domains do not ontologically share items in their groups. They are, for all intents and purposes, mutually exclusive. To create a metaphor, a member of the WELLNESS domain is mentally connected (i.e., *mapped*) onto a member of the SPATIAL ORIENTATION domain, producing a cross-domain mapping. If we were to use a concept from the same domain, i.e., inter-domain mapping of a subordinate concept, for example WONDERFUL, the construal GOOD IS WONDERFUL is produced, which is not metaphorical. We could do the same for UP, resulting in examples like, VERTICAL IS UP, which is also non-metaphorical. This is the reason Barcelona defines metaphor as concepts from separate superordinate domains accounting for metaphorical use.

Notice again example 131 from the second line of Dante's Inferno (Alighieri 2008), *I found myself in a dark wood...* Focusing on the SA event metaphor, the semantic subcomponents of *found*, i.e., the domain elements, must be delineated. Using the definition of *find* as 'discover or perceive by chance or after a deliberate search' (Oxford University 2015) and abridging *discover* or *perceive* as "to know", the concept FIND is mapped onto the concept KNOW, resulting in the conceptual metaphor FINDING IS KNOWING. This is combined with the schematic logic of the reflexive construction, such that 'reflexive knowledge is knowledge of oneself'. Thus, the combination of cross-domain mapping of [FIND → KNOW] in addition to the meaning of the reflexive construction produces the conceptual metaphor FINDING X-SELF IS KNOWING X-SELF. Consequently, the knowledge of oneself is the cognitive state of self-awareness.

But why would a speaker choose to construe and predicate the more complex SA event in lieu of a more simple, literal one such as *realize, ...is aware of, ...is conscious of*, etc.? Are there differences in construal that inspire its use? We saw in the previous paragraph that FIND contains or 'entails' subcomponents that mean 'discover or perceive something' (ibid.). Because the entailments of the TARGET are carried over to the SOURCE concept (i.e., FIND → SELF-AWARE), subtle meaning differences are also conveyed in the expression. In other words, *I was aware of my awkward silence* means something different from *I found myself in awkward silence*, and that subtle difference in meaning is due to the underlying semantics between the lexemes *aware* and *find*. Furthermore, this is precisely the reason why many languages have so many ways to say "basically" the same thing. Each component of an expression, from single phoneme to pragmatic element, adds to the whole and influences its meaning in both gross and subtle ways.

For the concept LOSE, conceptual entailments include 'previous possession of some thing$_x$ and current non-possession of thing$_x$'. Similar to the metaphorical process for FIND, when combined with meaning of the reflexive event, this comes to mean LOSING X-SELF IS TEMPORARY LACK OF SELF-AWARENESS. These conceptual subcomponents are compared to the situation in focus and help guide usage in context (Langacker 1987b).

133. *I found myself* blushing. (BNC:CEX 623)
134. *...she loses herself* in the cracks in the ceiling... (COCA:1998.MAG.PsychToday)

In 133 and 134, (repeated from above), domain subcomponents of FIND and LOSE are compared to domain subcomponents of the speaker's Self-Awareness in each situation.[25] The conceptual comparisons of Self-Awareness to FIND/LOSE connect the concepts. "A schematic relationship reflects a characterizing judgment based on comparison. The overall comparison between a schema and its instantiation summarizes over an indefinite number of local comparisons between corresponding substructures" (ibid.: 150).

One proposal by Grady that takes Awareness into specific account is the matrix in Figure 2, its explanation quoted in full:

> Here X represents the object of perception and X' represents knowledge associated with X as a perceptual stimulus. We experience scenes like the one schematized in Figure 2 many times each day - whenever we perceive something in our environment as it emerges from a containing space - and the association between the perceptual and inferential aspects of such scenes is likely to be very well-established in our cognitive structure (Grady & Johnson 2003: 539).

Figure 2. Primary Scene: Becoming aware by seeing (J. Grady & Johnson 2012: 541: Fig. 2)

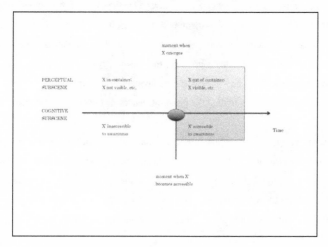

The matrix in Figure 2 reveals the tripartite interaction between the moment of Awareness, the internal/external perceptual stimulus and its conceptualization. This type of

---

[25] Note that 'awareness of a situation' and 'awareness of one's Self in a situation' are two different construals, SA events representing the latter.

'conscious attention to aspects of experience' is the foundation for the onset of Self-Awareness, shown in Figure 3. The upper dimension of the horizontal axis, called the Perceptual Subscene represents actual stimulus perception. The Cognitive Subscene below the horizontal axis represents the awareness of perception of that stimulus.

Figure 3. Primary Scene: The onset of Self-Awareness, based on Grady & Johnson (ibid.)

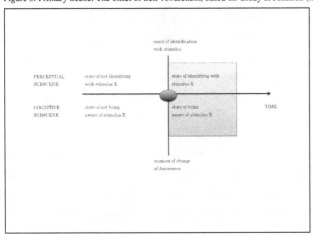

The vertical axis represents the Self-Aware onset point; left of the vertical axis represents stimulus that is pre-perceptual (upper) and pre-Aware (lower), right of the axis represents perceptually-registered stimulus (upper) and the awareness of the perception (lower).

> 135. ...*he found himself* squinting and raising his hand... (COCA:2007.FIC.Analog)
> 136. ...*she loses herself* in a conversation about the sixties... (COCA:1991.FIC.Atlantic)

Applying this matrix to example 135, in the upper-left quadrant the subject is *squinting and raising his hand*, but with no perception (his body may feel the direct stimuli, but his mind has not yet made sense of these neuronal signals). In the lower-left quadrant, the subject is not yet Aware of his/her situation. In the upper-right quadrant, the subject's mind perceives the physical acts of *squinting and raising his hand* (the mind interprets the nerve impulses). In the bottom-right quadrant, the subject is Aware of *squinting and raising his hand*. In other words, the focal point of Self-Awareness is the vertical Onset Point, i.e., the moment of perceptual and cognitive Awareness, which is then profiled in construal and the resulting predication.

For example 136, the same matrix efficiently explains the SA event *lose oneself* as well. The only revision is a reversal of the right and left quadrants on either side of the vertical Onset Point. When this is applied, direct stimulus perception and Self-Awareness in/of the situation is represented on the left side of the Onset Point (with upper and lower quadrants keeping their placement) i.e., she is aware of herself and the *conversation*, whereas the right side of the Onset Point represents the lack of perception and Awareness, i.e., she is only aware of the content of the *conversation*, not of herself engaged in that *conversation*. Here as well, the focal point of the construal and predication is the Onset Point of Awareness.

4.8 Chapter Conclusion

In conclusion to this section, the notions of image schema, domain and onset point strongly suggest positive conclusions for proposing Self-Awareness as a basic domain/image schema. The two reasons are that 1) the basis for Self-Awareness is a direct embodied stimulus/perception, not another conception, and 2) Self-Awareness is used as a base concept for which metaphoric (and non-metaphoric) construals and predications are based.

The discussion now turns to a more detailed survey of how Self-Awareness, as a basic domain, is mapped onto other domains to create metaphoric relationships.

Chapter 5: Cognitive Grammar

5.1. Introduction

This chapter begins with a review of the literal expression *The man found the cat* according to Cognitive Grammar (hereafter CG) (Langacker 2002: Chapter 6) and then proposes an original analysis for *The man lost the cat* based on that same model. Similarities and differences will be analyzed and discussed. Following this, a discussion of reflexive expressions in CG reveals that these are treated as special cases of Subjectification in which the viewpoint of the conceptualizer, commonly implicit, is included in the predication. Revision of previous models will be necessary to reflect the verbs *find/lose* as they occur metaphorically, especially with regard to the reflexive 'Subjective' elements contained in the overall construals. It will be shown that even an amalgamation of these elements cannot account for the full construal of SA events. This conclusion leads to the need for further analysis based on metaphorical mapping.

Because Cognitive Grammar differs drastically from more traditional semantic explanations, a brief summary of the basic tenets is provided hereafter. Langacker's Cognitive Grammar (1987b, 2002, 2008) was chosen specifically for this research due to its ability to provide an explanation for general cognitive abilities as well as psychological realities of the interlocutors as they relate to language use. This is crucial for the description of SA events where traditional syntactic and semantic methodology has difficulty accounting for the highly psychological nature of the Self-Awareness and its role in language.

5.2. Cognitive Grammar

Within CG, there is no ontological reality that language is required to assimilate. Each moment in time is processed through the mind of the speaker and hearer through sense stimuli and perception of these stimuli in the mind, as well as independent thought processes not directly connected to the physical world. The ideas we form (aka construal) and choose to convey linguistically (aka predication) have distinct semantic realities, although these may differ from any objective, ontological 'reality'. In order to be conveyed, this semantic reality needs some kind of form. In CG, the form is binary, having only phonological and semantic poles connected to each other by symbolic relations. The semantic pole (i.e., meaning) takes shape through the specific phonological pole (i.e., sound) by way of a symbolic relationship (i.e., phonology, morphology, syntax, etc.) previously decided on (however unconsciously) by the language users. Because there are only these two poles and the relationship between them that govern and control the creation and use of language, there is no need for an autonomous syntactic mechanism. There are no deep structures (i.e., underlying 'basic' grammar) from which the surface grammar emerges. The syntax represents schematic patterns of meaning that have been organized in a certain way and repeated often enough to become familiar and easily used without conscious effort. The patterns that emerge from language use form a general scale of abstractness, from fine-grained and concrete (such as phonemes) to abstract (such as syntax and discourse patterns). Each relates to and feeds off of the other, forming a type of meaning-form matrix driven by speaker and hearer intention. This meaning-form matrix has a fundamental experiential cognitive basis. It is supported by our natural ability to notice that some things are prominent in our consciousness (i.e. they are salient and 'stand out') and some things are not (i.e. they fade into the 'background'). Our minds are limited in capacity to access and analyze sensory input, and so we must pick and choose what to focus on and what to momentarily ignore (Langacker 1987b).

That this inborn, automatic cognitive process is the basis for linguistic structuring is no less than prodigious. From the patterning of sounds to the patterning of syntax, what each person, and ultimately culture, chooses to focus on for their language 'tools' depends very much on what they 'notice' in their physical and psychological environments. For example, all humans have the ability to produce a 'click' sound, but only a few cultures decide to use this in their phonetic inventory. In another example, all of us understand how some things in the world are naturally round and some things are naturally long and thin, but only some cultures 'decide' to overtly code these in their language system. These types of 'noticing' and 'ignoring' happen all the time at many levels of abstractness. This is the basis for CG's descriptions of the terms, 'figure/ground, base/scope, trajectory/landmark, and onstage/offstage'. Although these differ in their level of granularity, the fundamental principle of 'noticing' or 'ignoring' is the same and essential. For example, a foreground idea has more 'weight' than a background idea, and therefore takes prominence and is more likely to be explicitly coded and marked as topic or subject. On the other hand, a background assumption often takes a 'lower' status such as direct object or adjunct and may not even be explicitly predicated at all.

137. Well, he came home and he, he came running up the stairs…
(COCA:2011.SPOK.ABC_20/20)

For example, in example 137, *he* is the most 'noticeable' concept, and as such, it is explicitly predicated in topic/subject position. However, in the background lurks a mostly unnoticed speaker 'Point of View'.[26] If the listener were asked, "Where is the narrator's psyche now?", the answer would most likely be 'in the house, upstairs', because native speakers know that use of the verb *come* assumes 'a motion towards the self' (as opposed to *go* that assumes 'a motion away from self'). This knowledge stays in the background but provides psychological input for the 'shape' of the construal and predication.

5.2.1. Cognitive Grammar and find/lose

How is it that CG accounts for expressions using *find* and *lose* as they occur in language use?[27] In example 138, there are two nominals (i.e., 'things') and one verb (i.e., 'processual relation')[28].

138. The man found the cat.

"The base of FIND includes a search process of indefinite duration. Only the final stages of that process are actually designated by the predicate and hence profiled..." (Langacker 2002: 169). In other words, the action of FIND contains some kind of 'searching' but the 'noticed' construal that is predicated includes only the culmination of the process. This is true for many cases, shown in the (b) examples below. However, counter-examples in which *find* does not include a 'search' process are also construed.[29] For example, a base concept of 'search' is untenable in (139a) and (142a):

139 a. (John lost his wallet last night. John does not know Jenny.)

Jenny suddenly had a new wallet...Jenny found the wallet in the street.

b. (John asked his friend Jenny to look for his lost wallet.)

Jenny found the wallet in the street.

c. Jenny unintentionally/accidentally found the wallet in the street.

---

[26] 'Point of View' is used here in its specific definition according to CG.
[27] The original analysis (Langacker (1987)) discusses the Hopi language, but the methods and analyses supporting this are applicable to this proposal as well.
[28] 'Thing' and 'Relation' are CG specific terms. See Langacker (2002) for precise definitions. (In this example, the definite article will not be analyzed for ease of explanation.)
[29] This point was discussed previously.

140 a. (Harry went to the garden for some privacy, but to his surprise, his wife
   was already there.) Harry found his wife sitting in the garden.

   b. (Harry was searching for his wife.) Harry found his wife sitting in the garden.

   c. Harry inadvertently/coincidentally found his wife in the garden.

In (139a), *Jenny* does not know *John* and did not know he had lost his *wallet* and therefore there can be no 'search' conception involved for FIND. The *wallet* appears simply as a visual stimulus, at which point it is *found* (there need be no actual acquisition of the wallet for it to be found, although acquisition is probably the prototypical case).[30] In (140a), *Harry* does not go looking for *his wife*, but to his surprise, she is *in the garden* where he was heading. For these types of examples, lack of a 'search' construal can be further instantiated by the (c) examples, where *find* is modified with an adverb incompatible with 'search' and construes acceptable and even unmarked instances.

Figure 4. FIND-CAT-MAN, according to Langacker (2002: Fig. 7)

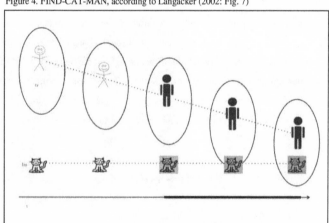

Langacker's analysis is accurate for 'search' instances of FIND as well as the observation that only the culminating event is profiled for FIND (for both 'search' and 'non-search' variations.) Furthermore, the mental scanning operation used for any relational process is valid here as well – the 'things' and their relationship to the scene are compared and

---

[30] The use of the definite article for the wallet presumes a narrative Point of View (POV), where the narrator knows that *John* lost his wallet, although *Jenny* does not. Taking a non-narrative POV would necessitate the indefinite article, i.e. a wallet. (For more on POV, refer to the discussion of Subjectification later in this chapter.)

contrasted through time (Langacker 1987b). For the 'search' FIND type, the scanning process is as explained above (also see Langaker 2002: 168: Fig. 3), but even the 'non-search' variation involves a scanning operation equivalent to 'perception of an object standing out from its surroundings', although there is minimal presence of linear time involved in the scanning process.

Because there are now two senses of FIND, the base construal of FIND is proposed as PERCEPTUAL AWARENESS OF A THING OR RELATION; furthermore, that 'search' and 'non-search' variations are 'immanent' (in the Langackerian sense) alternatives to this more schematic conception of FIND. Panther and Thornburg come to a similar conclusion for variants of FIND[31], stating, "…on conceptual grounds, it makes sense to derive the more complex second meaning 'come upon by searching' from the conceptually simpler meaning 'come upon' " (2009: 39-40). With full predications, FIND interacts schematically with its most prominent 'thing' or 'relational process' (i.e. 'trajector' (tr)) and the next most prominent (i.e., 'landmark' (lm)). The composite scene is created out of the relationship between the more abstract schema levels and more concrete levels, as needed by the speaker and hearer to decode the intended message.

Figure 5. Schematic representation of 'non-search' FIND in *The man found the cat*

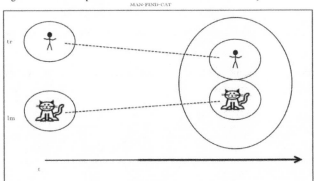

In Figure 4, a schematic is provided a for *The man found the cat* in which the 'search' type of FIND correlates with CAT and MAN. As proposed in this discussion, however, a new

---

[31] Their analysis is based on conceptual ACHIEVEMENT and ACCOMPLISHMENT metonymies of FIND. It proposes the metonymy RESULTANT ACHIEVEMENT FOR ACCOMPLISHMENT. See (2002: Chapter 6) for details of this hypothesis.

schematic for 'non-search' FIND is also necessary, provided in Figure 5. Only two sub-events are necessary for describing the trajector (tr) and landmark (lm) along the processual timeline (t). The first (left side) where *the man* (tr) is not 'aware' of *the cat* (lm), (i.e. the man is not searching for the cat), and the second (right side) where *the man* (tr) is aware of *the cat* (lm), (i.e. the man's awareness of the cat has emerged). The ellipse surrounding the man (corresponding to the tr perception of 'search'), is now representative of 'Awareness' (i.e., 'non-search' perception of stimulus). Thus, with only slight adaptations to account for the 'non-search, Aware' alternation of FIND, the CG model easily accommodates cognitive representations for both 'search' and 'non-search' variations.

A similar schema can be proposed for LOSE as in *The man lost the cat*, shown in Figure 6. Here, the 'search/Aware' ellipse in the final stage occurs only with *the man* (tr) due to the lack of perceptual contact with *the cat* (lm). The (tr) is, however, conscious of that fact, i.e., the man knows that he lost the cat. The dotted ellipse in the first time-frame (left side) represents this knowledge, i.e., the man previously had perceptual contact with the cat at an earlier point in time and recognizes this fact in the present, at which point *the cat* becomes *lost*. More schematically for LOSE, it can be stated that an (lm) cannot be LOST until the (tr) is aware that the (lm) is no longer in perceptual contact. Notice that this is a very different conception from that of the lm knowing that it itself is lost. In one scenario, the more likely conception/predication is that of the tr in an intransitive clause (i.e., *The cat is lost*, i.e., it cannot find its way home.) In another scenario, the tr has intentionally run away, and is therefore not *lost* (from its own perspective). However, in *The man lost the cat*, from the perspective of the tr, these scenarios may be identical iff the tr believes that *the cat* has not intentionally run away.

Figure 6. Schematic CG-type representation of *The man lost the cat*

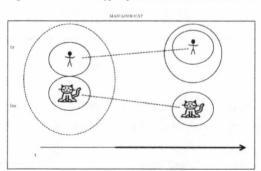

Having discussed the literal conceptions of FIND and LOSE as a starting point, we are now in position to discuss how reflexive, metaphorical events are construed using these same representative schemata.

5.2.2. CG and Reflexive FIND and LOSE

Complexity emerges when the (tr) and (lm) refer to the same entity, i.e., the reflexive construction:

141. Deliberately, *he pinched himself* on the thigh. (COCA:1996.FIC.FantasySciFi)

142. *She saw herself* once again in the cheval glass. (BNC:FPH.W_fict_prose)

143. ...and so *we found ourselves* in a brand new flat... (BNC:F82.S_interview_oral_history)

How can these reflexive events be represented schematically? In the simplest of schemata, a semi-circular line connects the coreferent (tr/lm), showing the relation between the referent and the referred. One other possibility is that a line starts from the (tr) and returns upon itself, forming a circle (Kemmer 1993; Langacker 2006). These are useful for schematically visualizing the situation in which the 'Point of View' (POV) is not a major consideration as in 141 and 142 above. However, when the POV needs to be specifically taken in account as well as for subtler metaphoric phenomenon, these schemata do not describe the semantic complexity of the event in enough detail to be useful.

One analysis that does take this 'viewing relation' (i.e., 'Point of View' or 'Subjectification' (Langacker 1985, 1990, 2002; 2006)) into account is that of Van Hoek (1997: 171-216), an analysis that goes a long way in delineating the construal for the reflexive schema. Examples such as 141 and 142 are claimed, supported by Faltz (1985), to be prototypical reflexive examples, where "the reflexive codes a landmark of the verb which corresponds with the trajector" (Van Hoek 1997: 173). The claim is that the difference between the reflexive and emphatic markers (both having the same morpho-syntactic form but differing in function) is based on the 'Subjectified' view of the referent. Noting that any first or second person account of an event constitutes some level of subjectification on the part of the referent and thus would not distinguish the pronoun and reflexive, Van Hoek's position on subjective reflexivity is provided in full:

The referent of the reflexive... is viewed semisubjectively within the onstage region. That is, some participant in the scene views him/herself semisubjectively. The semisubjective perception of the referent is part of the agent's experience, part of the conception being put onstage rather than just part of the speaker and addressee. This viewing relation is maintained throughout most of the extensions from the reflexive prototype (Van Hoek 1997: 175).

The extensions referred to in the last line indicate such things as metaphorical use, SA events included. She does not give further account nor examples of these, as her argument aims to distinguish between anaphoric and reflexive pronouns and their environments. Before describing the details of SA events, however, a more in-depth definition and description of 'Subjectivity' is necessary.

5.3. Subjectivity and SA events

Subjectivity is a subtle phenomenon that describes the relationship between the speaker, hearer, and the conception being conveyed. It concerns the conceptual 'stance' of a predication, the mostly implicit viewpoint from which the speaker codes meaning into a message and from which the hearer decodes that message. The conceptualizer creates meaning from a particular 'stance' that may totally exclude the conceptualizer such as *The boy walks the dog*, or greatly included in the conception, i.e., *I thought I would walk the dog*. There are various facets of these examples that could be described here, but the main concern for this discussion is 'Point of View' (POV) (Van Hoek 1997). All in all, is the speaker (i.e., conceptualizer) or his vantage point explicitly involved in the construal or does it remain implicit?

One example from the sport of golf might help to clarify this point. Golfers who have become fairly proficient will notice (or even learned) that when practicing, attention is paid to the mechanics of the swing; the stance, the weight distribution on the feet, the rotation of the pelvis in relation to the spine and shoulder girdle, the body position in relation to the lie of the ball, etc. However, once the player is involved in a tournament, the mechanical aspects (hopefully) fade into the background. The focus of attention is on the target (the fairway, green, pin and cup) and the object (the ball) that needs to reach that target. Players 'in the zone' experience a total lack of self-reference and a complete goal-oriented mindset. This 'goal-oriented' mindset can be equated with the 'objective scene' described in the example *The boy walks the dog* from above. There is no explicit mention of the conceptualizer in the construal/predication. It is an objective viewpoint -- an 'optimal viewing arrangement' -- where the conceptualizer remains 'offstage', as it were (Langacker 1985, 1990; 2006). On the other hand, *I thought I would walk the dog* represents a much more subjective viewpoint, an 'egocentric viewing arrangement' (ibid.) in which the conceptualizer (and possibly the conception itself) is explicit and even focused on, i.e. put 'onstage'. In sum, and quoting in full:

> The optimal viewing arrangement...can be equated with the conceptualization focused primarily on OTHERS—the role of the conceptualizer S is then subjective to the extent that S loses conscious awareness of this role. The egocentric viewing arrangement ...corresponds to instances where S is specifically concerned with SELF and consequently functions as both the conceptualizer and an object of conceptualization (Langacker 1985: 123).

Various stages or degrees are present between these extremes, Langacker claiming at least five (2008). Due to space constraints however, only those which are directly relevant to SA event construal and predication will be discussed. Specifically, the SA event construal represents an 'egocentric viewing relation' in which the 'S' (conceptualizer) is at maximum 'Subjectification'. "The observer S is thus situated within the boundaries of this more extensive objective scene, reflecting the fact that S is no longer simply an observer, but also to some degree an object of observation. SELF-consciousness therefore attenuates the subjective/objective distinction" (Langacker 1985: 122).

144. I was in the hospital.
145. *I found myself* in the hospital.

Examples 144 and 145 above elucidate the difference between a simple Subjective schema and an SA event schema, represented schematically in Figure 7, below. In the left-side schematic (example 144), the square box labeled 'H' represents the conceptualizer placed inside a structure, *Hospital*. Since there is no processual element involved, no timeline appears below the schema. Example 144 represents a viewing arrangement where the Ground (G) element (viewpoint of the conceptualizer S) is semi-subjective -- SELF is part of the conception. It is also included within the 'scope of predication' (dotted square), i.e., it is 'onstage'. In general, this is the conceptual basis for construal and predication in the first person. "Rather than fading from awareness (as subjectivity demands), the SELF is placed on stage and viewed in basically objective terms. The observer/observed asymmetry is essentially neutralized, and the subjectivity of G is minimal" (ibid.: 126).

Figure 7. CG models comparing simple Subjective event and SA event with FIND

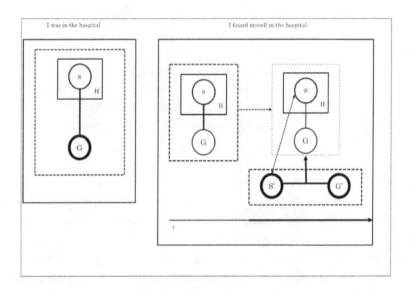

The SA event (right-side schematic) for sentence 145 represents a construal in which Awareness (S') of the event is 'profiled' by the conceptualizer (S). Because Awareness (S') is profiled, (although both (S') and the conceptualizer (S) are put 'onstage'), (S) loses its main profiled status (but keeps some hint of profile, i.e., SELF is still some part of Awareness). It remains linked to profiled (S'), predicated by way of the reflexive pronoun. In essence, the conceptualizer's Awareness is put onstage as the profiled object of conceptualization, while the sub-event, *I was in the hospital*, no longer receives main profiling, (but remains within the scope of predication). A profiled bold connecting line between S' and G' represents the 1st person conceptualizer as the one that *finds* the Ground (Self-Awareness). This relationship, in turn, relates to the sub-event being construed (i.e., self *in a hospital*), a solid arrow depicting this connection. The dotted arrow connecting the overall left and right components indicate that this is a processual relation, however momentary that process may be. FIND, as a (search or non-search) process, includes a time (t) element (outside the 'scope of predication' – i.e., an implicit reference point). Only the end result of the process is profiled, as discussed above for the literal use of FIND within the CG framework.

There is another construal for the predication FIND X-SELF that appears in English and must be addressed. In these cases, it is not the 'Awareness of perception' that is profiled, but the 'Awareness of a transcendental or deep Self'. The differences between the two can be illustrated by sentences 146 and 147:

146. I'd be terrified if *I found myself* alone in London...

(BNC:CBC/W_newsp_other_social)

147. You know, I didn't do so well. But *I found myself*...These are the values I have.

(COCA:2011.SPOK.Fox_Oreilly)

The first difference lies in the viewing scene. In 147, the conceptualizer construes the SELF as a completely separate entity, as a 2nd person within the physical confines of the first. This is representative of the 'divided self' or 'true Self' metaphors, discussed in detail in Chapter 5.

The second difference is seen in the 'degree of adjunctiveness' of the post-SELF elements. In 146, the prepositional phrase is (mostly) obligatory in order to convey the meaning of the SA event construal; however, in 147, post-SA event elements are optional; in fact, they are often lacking in the corpus data (see Part III).

How can the difference in construal be depicted using CG-type schematics? 146 is represented similarly to the construal of the right side of Figure 6 above. 147 is shown below in Figure 8 and represents "...a detached outlook in which the speaker treats his own participation as being on par with anybody else's..." (Langacker 2002: 328). This is a matter of degree. Example 147 displays this criterium to a high degree. However, the claim being made here is that the SA event in 146 represents a maximum degree of 'egocentric viewing arrangement', i.e. there is only a very ambiguous 'object' to ground the subject referent. The 'objects' in SA events are limited to the cognitive function of Awareness emerging within the Conceptualizer. Thus, as visualized in Figure 8, SELF assumes all roles of Subjectivity and Objectivity, and for SA events, construes those roles as maximally egocentric. The Subject of Perception (S) and Object of Perception (P) are maximally connected and onstage (OS); in other words, the conceptualizer [SELF] and the conceptualizer's [AWARENESS OF PERCEPTIONS] are inextricably bound entities. In the schema, the semi-subjective stance from which the construal is conceived (S') is connected to the onstage construal by a dotted arrow, representing the scene as construed semi-subjectively from the offstage Ground (G), yielding a [[SELF] VIEWING [SELF-AWARENESS]] construal.

Figure 8. Maximally egocentric construal of the SA event I found myself

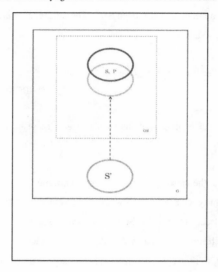

Schematizing the LOSE X-SELF sentence 148 below presents an interesting challenge:

148. I lost myself in the world of imagination.   (COCA:2001.FIC.VirginiaQRev)

Figure 9. CG model for I lost myself in the world of imagination

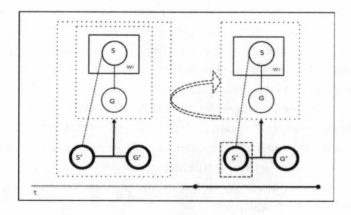

As discussed above, LOSE metaphorically extends to mean LOSS OF SELF-AWARENESS when contained within the reflexive event. However, this construal includes the presupposition that at some previous time SELF-AWARENESS was present. In figure 9, this concept is represented by the central, dotted, arching arrow. Precursory Self-Awareness (the left portion of the diagram), although falling within the scope of predication, remains offstage (surrounding dotted boxes for the conceptions of SELF-AWARENESS and *world of imagination*). Only the relationship between the Conceptualizer (S'), the Ground (G') and the event (vertical arrow) remain profiled (bold lines). The final event (right portion of the diagram) of the timescale (bold line due to its final-stage profiling) represents the LOSS OF SELF-AWARENESS, as the conceptualizer's (S') Awareness was totally absorbed in *the world of imagination* (WI) (but is not anymore[32]). The Ground (G') is profiled (i.e. SELF-AWARENESS is explicit) but is removed from the 'scope of predication' (small square dotted box), SELF-AWARENESS now being totally Subjective in viewpoint (offstage) and "serving only as a point of reference for situating those entities that attract the focus of viewing attention" (Langacker 1985: 124). Because of the 1st person vantage point, however, the coreferential conceptualizer (S-S') still maintains the profiling and onstage status. This is possible due to the past tense of the processual relation. The event has already passed - it is complete, and the conceptualizer is relating the event that is no longer in progress. This is represented by the blunt-end profiled timeline, the left dot in the timeline representing the onset of the *loss of Self-Awareness* and the right dot representing the time of predication of the event, which is no longer in progress. Similar to Figure 7, a profiled bold connecting line between S' and G' represents the 1st person conceptualizer as the one who has here lost the Ground. This relationship, in turn, refers to the sub-event being construed (i.e., world of imaginings), a solid arrow depicting this.

In conclusion to this section, CG schematic representations can delineate the subtleties of SA events, however, implementation can be intricate and the resulting description quite opaque. This is due to the extremely abstract quality of the construal of both the metaphorically extended predicates as well as the pseudo-reflexive coreferent nominals.

---

[32] The metaphorical extension of [[LOSE] + x-self] is heavily biased towards the past tense (see Part III). This is likely due to the cognitive idiosyncrasy of the function of awareness. We are not able to be in the midst of [LOST AWARENESS] and simultaneously vocalize that experience. In other words, to say *I have now lost awareness* is technically an oxymoronic statement, because consciously vocalizing that state of being is to not be in the state of being [LOST].

A different type of Cognitive Linguistic analysis proposes a distinct, semi-independent psyche, a phenomenon often called the 'divided self', where one part of the mind is 'at odds' with or 'exerts force upon' another part of the mind/body and even interactively among individuals and social groups (Gilquin 2010b; A. Lakoff & Becker 1992; G. Lakoff 1996b; Langacker 1985; 1987b; Lederer 2013; Talmy 2000a, 2000b). Research conducted on the causative forces influencing linguistic construal and predication (Gilquin 2010b; Talmy 2000a) has proposed that: 1) objects (Agonists) can apply, block or remove physical and/or psychological force to/from other objects 2) objects (Antagonists) can have physical and/or psychological force applied or freed (blockage removed), 3) exertion of these forces is not binary but exist on a cline, and 4) the way we view the effects of force in a particular situation is the way it is construed and predicated. Applications of force dynamic principles to various types of construal and predication are ubiquitous; "...force-dynamics thus emerges as a fundamental notional system that structures conceptual material pertaining to force interaction in common ways across a linguistic range: the physical, psychological, social, inferential, discourse, and mental-model domains of reference and conception" (Talmy 2000a: 409).

Force dynamics is proposed as the base or image schema for various levels of force in construals of causative constructions:

149. Tommy spilled the milk.
150. The milk spilled all over the table.
151. Tommy tried not to spill the milk.
152. Tommy wanted to spill the milk.
153. Tommy prevented the milk from spilling.

Due to space constraints, an in-depth analysis of causation will have to be put aside here. However, one specific point directly related to SA events will be discussed. This is a subcategory of force dynamics called 'Psychodynamics' (Talmy 2001a) where a psychological force is exerted upon one or both of the participants in a construal. Within psychodynamics can be found the specific case of reflexive constructions, termed 'coreferential causative constructions' (Gilquin 2010b; Talmy 2001a).

154. He held himself back from responding.

155. He exerted himself in pressing against the jammed door.   (Gilquin 2010b)

The psychodynamic situations in these examples are intriguing. If force is applied from one object to another, what and how is the force being manipulated during a reflexive event? It has been proposed that one part of the Self (a peripheral part) acts upon another part of the Self (a central part)[33]. The fundamental concept behind this 'divided self' phenomenon is a two-tier system comprised of the following (depending on one's terminology): Ego, Id, Subject, Super-ego and Self (Talmy 2001a: 32), one of these being the 'core' or 'center' of consciousness and the other the 'mundane' or 'peripheral' action-based part. In some cases, one part of the Self exerts force upon the physical body, in other cases, the Self exerts control over another part of the psyche. Different levels and types of force can be exerted which guide the choice of construal and predication. Gilquin's (2010b) discussion of the 'divided self' is based on Talmy (2010b) and includes much detail as well as corpus evidence supporting her arguments. Being specifically a study of causation limits its applicability to SA event construal and predication, however. The type of energy construed for SA events is very different from that of causative physical or psychological forces. There are similarities that cannot be ignored, however.

156. After 30 days of chanting "OM", *Mary found herself.*

In 156, a 'peripheral' part of Mary's SELF searches[34] for some 'central' part, and subsequently *finds* (i.e., becomes aware of) this part of her psyche which was perhaps psychologically hidden or underdeveloped. This construal adequately corroborates the 'divided self' phenomenon (without explicit causation[35]). The construal can be represented as maximally egocentric, i.e., the Subject views the Self in the same way as an independent Object. However, 157 exemplifies a different construal.

157. After 30 days of dieting, *Mary found herself* in the kitchen at midnight.

---

[33] Talmy uses the terms 'peripheral' and 'central' to refer to general patterns of Agonistic/Antagonistic forces, respectively. He claims that the basic state of the 'central' part is 'repose' or inaction, while the 'peripheral' part 'exerts' the force. Many construals lend themselves to this kind of analysis, but it is proposed here that SA events are not one of them.

[34] I assume here that the reason for her chanting was to 'search' for her deeper Self.

[35] There may be a secondary causation, however, as the force of chanting provoked the 'central', deeper Self to become known to 'peripheral' consciousness.

In 157, although two SELVES seem to be predicated, the construal is actually a singular [SELF-AWARE] cognition of certain perceptions, in this case, spatial location (*in the kitchen*). There may be a minor, fleeting recognition of the 'divided self' as the literal construal is quickly compared but then subsequently denied. The claim here is that this predication construes and refers to the cognition of Self-Awareness as a singular entity. It is along this parameter that the differences in meaning between 156 and 157 may be understood and delineated.[36]

Lakoff and Johnson (2000a, 2001a) examine the 'divided self' by way of the folk theory of 'Essence', whereby "...each person is seen as having an Essence that is part of the Subject ('center'). The person may have more than one Self, but only one of those Selves is compatible with that Essence. This is called the "real" or "true" Self" (1999). Due to the importance of this explanation with regard to SA events, the following quote is provided in full:

> In the general Subject-Self metaphor, a person is divided into Subject and one or more Selves. The Subject is in the target domain of that metaphor. The Subject is that aspect of a person that is the experiencing consciousness and the locus of reason, will, and the judgment, which, by its nature, exists only in the present. This is what the Subject is in most of the cases; however, there is a subsystem that is different in an important way. In this subsystem, the Subject is also the locus of a person's Essence-that enduring thing that makes us who we are. Metaphorically, the Subject is always conceptualized as a person. The Self is that part of a person that is not picked out by the Subject. This includes the body, social rules, past states, and actions in the world. There can be more than one Self. And each Self is conceptualized metaphorically as either a person, an object, or location.
>
> (G. Lakoff & Johnson 1999: 242)

In 158 and 159 below, the central part of the SELF metaphorically *gives* (= assigns) and *asks* (= questions) the peripheral part of the physical/mental SELF, respectively. These cases are clear and unequivocal examples of the divided-self phenomenon, where not only are there two aspects to the SELF, but the deeper construal of the metaphor is also congruent with these two aspects. In other words, TO ASK/GIVE SOMETHING OF/TO SOMEONE IS SUBJECT ASKING/GIVING SOMETHING OF/TO ONESELF. This is the reason for including the 'true-Self' metaphor into this category, being two 'divided', interacting aspects of the SELF.

---

[36] One interesting aspect of (157) is that both meanings may be construed, the 'divided self' and the SA event. It seems that intonation and/or sentential stress divide the two phenomena; heavy phonological stress placed on *found* construes the 'divided self' whereas the post-SA adjunct is stressed for SA predications (native speaker inquiry). In usage, collocational idiosyncrasies divide the two. See Part 3 for further details concerning corpus analysis.

158. *I gave myself* a task...　　　　　　　　　　　(COCA:2005.SPOK.CBS_Morning)

159. And then *I asked myself* the question... (COCA:SPOK.THE CHARLIE ROSE SHOW)

160. *I kicked myself* for being so stupid.　　　　(COCA:2002.MAG.BoysLife)

161. ...*James Brown found himself* back at home, alone in his old room...

　　　　　　　　　　　　　　　　　　　　　　　(COCA:1998.MAG.Ebony)

162. No one could imagine *Lucy losing herself* in sensuality...

　　　　　　　　　　　　　　　　　　　　　　　(COCA:1999.FIC.NewEnglandRev)

Example 160 represents an interesting case, however. Here, even though two aspects of SELF (Subject-Self) are predicated, the construal of the expression is non-dualistic in nature. To *kick oneself* means to regret doing something (McGraw-Hill 2002). The event as a whole metaphorically refers to an emotional feeling of regret. It is not inherently based on the dualism of Subject-Self. It is only at a shallower stage of construal, closer to the level of predication, that the divided-self construal emerges from the metaphorical form of the predication.

It is along these lines that SA events are construed as well. For examples 161 and 162, even though the dualism of the predication may momentarily form a divided-self image in shallow construal, it is quickly replaced with the meaning of the deeper construal, i.e., the emergent FIND or temporary LOSS of Self-Awareness. The complexity of this cannot be overstated. Self-Awareness is in itself a type of dualistic phenomenon in that a Subject's Awareness of Self (i.e., perceptions of stimuli) defines the cognitive function of Self-Awareness. In other words, it is an additional perspective (i.e., viewpoint, vantage point) from which the mind notices other aspects of mental and bodily experiences. However, as a metaphorical expression, reference to that specific mental function is a singular, non-dualistic event (i.e., *I find myself* = I am aware.) Whether or not the cognitive function is dualistic in nature is irrelevant (for the purpose of the metaphoric meaning). Sentence 161 means that *James Brown's* Self-Awareness of his surroundings suddenly and acutely emerged at that moment in time. And in 162, *Lucy*, not being prone to emotionalism nor romanticism, would probably not get so intensely absorbed in sensuality that her Self-Aware cognitive function is temporarily disengaged by it. Both of these SA events construe the emergence or lack of a single cognitive function, Self-Awareness. The 'divided-self' metaphor, certainly present at some level of construal, must give way to the more schematic, inclusive construal that is reference to the single cognitive function of Self-Awareness.

Thus, although Psychodynamics and the 'divided self' phenomena help clarify many metaphorical reflexive instances, the precise construal of SA events still remains outside these parameters. Therefore, this discussion continues on to the specifics of how SA events come to have the metaphorical meanings they have with the predications they are given.

5.5. Mapping of Metonymy and SA events

In cognitive linguistics, the term 'mapping' is used to describe a relationship between two or more concepts. Regarding metaphoric expressions, it describes a concept from one domain related to a concept of another domain (Barcelona 2002; Croft & Cruse 2004; Fauconnier 1985; G. Lakoff 1993b; Langacker 2009; Panther et al. 2009). These domains may be basic or abstract but the mapping usually proceeds in only one direction for metaphor, from the concrete to the abstract category, as opposed to metonymy, which are in general reversible (Kuno 1987; Panther et al. 2009). The term 'source' (a.k.a. 'topic') is used for a concept's foundational domain, the domain from which the concept is taken. The term 'target' (a.k.a. 'vehicle') is used for a concept whose domain is used in the expression.

For example, *Sally is an absolute angel* means that *Sally* is profusely imbued with angel-like qualities. The speaker intends to convey that the positive qualities displayed by *Sally* such as compassion, joy, generosity, tenderness, etc., (i.e., the source domain concept) are mapped onto those conceived qualities usually (deemed by a particular culture) displayed by *angels* (the target domain concept). The mapping is only partial because there are many qualities that *angels* have besides those mentioned above; for example, they have wings, halos, they are able to fly, come down from heaven and convey messages from God, etc. In our understanding of the metaphor above, we do not map wings, halos, flying from heaven, onto *Sally*. *Sally* has a specific and limited number of traits of the source domain concept,[37] but not all of them, because if the mapping were total, the concepts would be identical and indistinguishable. In this way, metaphorical concepts 'connect' to their conceptual origins.

Another type of mapping that is a major factor in the delineation of SA events is the mapping of concepts within the same domain, called 'metonymy'. This has often been cited as being referential in nature and many definitions of metonymy include this referential aspect (Croft 1993; Goossens 2002; G. Lakoff & Johnson 2008; Langacker 1987b; Littlemore 2015).

---

[37] See Lakoff for further details of metaphorical mapping especially with regard to conceptual constraints, i.e., the 'Invariance Hypothesis' (Barcelona, 2000; G. Lakoff, 1990a)

However, as pointed out (Langacker 2009; Ruiz de Mendoza & Díez 2002), there are metonymies that are not directly referential; for example, *Mary is just another pretty face*, where *pretty face* does not directly refer to any one person's pretty face but *beauty* in general. Due to this type of non-referential construal, referentiality may be excluded from a general definition of metonymy. An alternate definition based on domain inclusion/exclusion, metonymy being the former and metaphor the latter, is proposed. This is similar to Goossens' definition, " ...the crucial difference between metonymy (as well as synecdoche) and metaphor is that in a metaphoric mapping two discrete domains are involved whereas in the metonymy, the mapping occurs within a single domain" (2002: 351). This definition is concurrent with others as well (Barcelona 2000; Kovecses 2006; Littlemore 2015).

Mendoza and Velasco (2002) further characterize metonymy based on whether a specific characteristic of the concept is being highlighted within the domain, called 'source-in-target', or whether the domain as a whole is being used to stand for a particular member of that domain, called 'target-in-source'. These have traditionally been labeled WHOLE FOR PART and PART FOR WHOLE relationships (Feyaerts 2000; Kovecses 2002; G. Lakoff 1990a, 1993b; Littlemore 2015).

163. The ham sandwich is waiting for his check. (G. Lakoff & Johnson 2003, p. 35)
164. A lefty can't just sit anywhere they want. (Hunt 2016)

The underlined parts of 163 and 164 show metonymic construal of the PART FOR WHOLE (i.e., 'synecdoche') and WHOLE FOR PART types, respectively. In 163, the predication, *ham sandwich* corresponds to a PART of the person, specifically the part that ordered the *ham sandwich* which corresponds to the entire person. In 164, *A lefty* corresponds to a WHOLE group of people that display left-hand orientation and corresponds to a specific person (PART) who becomes an archetype.

WHOLE FOR PART metonymy is applicable to SA events. It is the WHOLE person (predicated as a reflexive pronoun) that stands for a PART of the person, i.e., Self-Awareness of a particular perception and/or experience.

165. The plane began to fall. *Barry found himself* stepping on the gas.

(COCA:1998, FIC.Bk:WasItSomething)

166. After 14 months of unemployment, *he found himself* lying drunk
on the floor of a room... (COCA:1999.NEWS.Atlanta)

167. She goes from Rome to Greece, where *she* basks in the sun and
loses herself in reading about the mythic lives of the gods and goddesses.

(COCA:1997.FIC.BK.PassionDreamBook)

168. ...setting aside their identity in the outside world and (*visitors* to the Gallery) *losing themselves* in the art on the walls... (COCA:2003.ACAD.ArtBulletin (my parenthesis))

The reflexive pronouns in 165-168 do not refer to dualistic entities which are seen in 169 and 170 below:

169. Bernard Goldberg published a book titled 100 People Who Are Screwing Up America and *I found myself* listed as culprit number 80. (COCA:2011.ACAD.AmerScholar)

170. Father, I fear *I* have badly *lost myself* in the woods. (COCA:2005.FIC.FantasySciFi)

Example 169 represents what is described as Picture Noun Phrases (Kuno 1987) or 'displacement' (Langacker 1987a). Here, some 'alternate world' is conceived where the Self is an actual entity, whether in a picture or other form. In 170, the literal meaning is construed, and the physical Self is literally *lost* in some spatial location. In contrast, for the SA events in 165-168, the construal of the whole event must be considered, i.e., an emergent or absent Self-Awareness, and as such, the reflexive pronoun cannot refer to the antecedent in a simple one-to-one relationship. If this were the case, the meanings of 165-168, and all SA events, as well as a select number of other metaphorical reflexive events, could not be construed accurately. Their metaphorical construal would be inaccessible. For SA events, the construal of the predicate as a whole (i.e., emergence/lack of Self-Awareness) dictates to what the reflexive pronoun refers. The pronoun is metonymic in the sense that the concept of Self-Awareness is contained within the superordinate domain of Self. There is no cross-domain mapping. In 165-168, what is *found* or *lost* is not the physical person, not the gestalt psychological person, not the 'true-Self'. What is *found* and *lost* is the cognitive function of Self-Awareness of a particular perception or experience, the reflexive pronoun metonymically 'standing for' that Self-Aware construal, i.e., a WHOLE FOR PART relationship.

5.6. Conceptual Metaphor and SA Events

How do we get from the literal, *I am suddenly aware that I am in the kitchen* to the metaphorical *I found myself in the kitchen*? Looking at the specific logic of conceptual metaphor for SA events, KNOWING IS SEEING (G. Lakoff 1993b; G. Lakoff & Johnson 1999) represents a well-known conceptual metaphor that plays a role in SA event construal. This is instantiated by examples such as:

> 171. I see what you mean. (COCA: 2011.SPOK.CNN.Behar)

For this metaphor, one cannot KNOW what one does not SEE, and as such, KNOWING IS SEEING represents the conceptual logic underlying the linguistic metaphor. FINDING IS KNOWING is another common conceptual metaphor, instantiated by examples such as:

> 172. So many people find it very very difficult... (BNC:G3V.S_classroom)
> 173. ...Students found this exercise helpful... (COCA:2009.ACAD.CommCollegeR)

Furthermore, if FINDING IS KNOWING then it is logically possible to construe LOSING IS HAVING KNOWN[38], exemplified by 174 and 175:

> 174. Your generation has lost touch with solitude... (COCA:2012.FIC.MassachRev)
> 175. ...the Government has lost sight of their stated aims...
>
> (BNC:K5D.W_news_other_report)

The metaphors FIND to mean KNOW and LOSE to mean HAVING KNOWN are proposed here to be the base conceptual metaphors for SA events. However, due to the intent to construe KNOWLEDGE OF SELF, i.e., SELF-AWARENESS, the reflexive construction is employed for the linguistic metaphor:

> 176. One night, *I found myself* at a party with Naomi Campbell...
>
> (COCA:2012.SPOK.ABC_20/20)
> 177. *I lost myself* in thoughts of meeting kind people... (COCA:2008.FIC.Triquarterly)

---

[38] As discussed above, the inherent meaning of LOSE contains previous perceptual contact that is no longer available.

In 176, a particular kind of SELF-KNOWLEDGE, i.e. Self-Awareness of unexpectedly being at the same *party* as *Naomi Campbell* is conveyed by *I found myself*, while in 177, gestalt, perceptual SELF-KNOWLEDGE that was present but is no longer is conveyed by *I lost myself*.

Two further conceptual metaphors are needed to complete the logic of SA events in their entirety. One is THE MIND IS A CONTAINER FOR OBJECTS (G. Lakoff & Johnson 1999) and the other is MENTAL STATES ARE OBJECTS (Yu 2008). When we think of the mind, we imagine it as a container that holds things like ideas, dreams, hallucinations, theories, etc. We imagine putting things in the mind as well as taking things out of the mind. For example, in 178 and 179:

> 178. I had other people in mind as well actually. (BNC:FM2.S_meeting)
> 179. That's one of those things I think I blanked out of my mind.
>
> (COCA:2012:SPOK.ABC_20/20)
> 180. His mental state has been very stable... (BNC:CBF.W_newsp_other_report)
> 181. ...there are no fresh ideas on how to do it. (COCA:2012:SPOK.CBS_NewsEve)

The mind can also be in different states, and each of these can be thought of as some kind of object. For example, emotions can be light or heavy, ideas can be stale or fresh, logic can be strong or weak, etc. Examples 180 and 181 are instances of the conceptual metaphor MENTAL STATES ARE OBJECTS.

In order for SA events to be able to convey SELF-AWARENESS, three conceptual metaphors above need to work in collaboration: FINDING IS KNOWING, THE MIND IS A CONTAINER FOR OBJECTS, and MENTAL STATES ARE OBJECTS. Now, two SA event-specific metaphors can be proposed: FINDING ONESELF IS AWARENESS OF SELF and LOSING ONESELF IS UNAWARENESS OF SELF. The following conceptual logic for SA events is as follows:

1. FINDING IS KNOWING and LOSING IS HAVING KNOWN
2. THE MIND IS A CONTAINER FOR OBJECTS
3. MENTAL STATES ARE OBJECTS
    a. SELF-AWARENESS IS A MENTAL STATE
    b. OBJECTS CAN BE FOUND OR LOST

Therefore,

4. SELF-AWARENESS IS AN OBJECT THAT CAN BE FOUND OR LOST

This is not to say that every time an SA event is predicated the interlocutors consciously go through all steps in order. What is proposed here is that entailed within the SA event construal are the conceptual metaphors of (1-3) collaborating with the ontological facts of (3a) and (3b), culminating in (4). These are immanent to the understanding of SA event metaphors. This information is crucial for the proper construal and delineation of SA events. By carefully taking heed of the specific conceptual environments of SA events, it can be gleaned that both WHOLE FOR PART metonymy as well as Conceptual Metaphor are present within SA events.

5.7 Categorizing SA events: metonymy and metaphor

Goossens (2002) proposes cases where metaphor and metonymy are both at work within the same expression. He describes four main types but only one type, 'metonymy within metaphor', will be discussed here, SA events being instances of this type.

> The typical case… is that a metonymically used entity is embedded in a (complex) metaphorical expression. The metonymy functions within the target domain. As we found out in the instances we analyzed, this often, but not necessarily, goes together with a metaphorical reinterpretation of the relevant entity in the donor domain (Goossens, Pauwels, Rudzka-Ostyn, Simon-Vandenbergen, & Vanparys 1995: 172).

> 182. Surprised, *Colby found himself* recalling a distant, early memory…
> (COCA:2011.FIC.AntiocRev)
> 183. *I* ignored her and *lost myself* in the joyous simplicity of munching on a perfectly vine-ripened tomato.   (COCA:2000.FIC.Bk:SullivansIsland)

A crucial element in the description and delineation of SA events is the metonymic characterization of the reflexive pronoun. The main argument here is that Self-Awareness is a unique cognitive function able to be identified and referred to independently of its Conceptualizer/Agent. The next step is to reveal the mapping from the reflexive pronoun onto that cognitive function, showing an intra-domain mapping that leads to the metonymic construal. According to Ruiz de Mendoza and Velasco (2002), the metonymic aspect of SA events would likely be categorized as a 'target-in-source' metonymy, a situation in where a whole domain stands for a part of the domain, in other words, WHOLE FOR PART. They call this a domain reduction due to the highlighted feature (thus, a type of conceptual narrowing) of the domain matrix being central to the conception. For SA events, the conceptually gestalt reflexive pronoun stands for the specific cognitive function of Self-Awareness (a part of oneself), shown in Figure 10.

In the source domain, *a person finding an object* is mapped on to *a person aware of his/her perceptions/experience*. In the TARGET domain there is a metonymic interpretation of Self-Awareness in which the reflexive pronoun is in a WHOLE FOR PART relationship with the specific cognitive function of Self-Awareness. The construal of this, however, is dependent on the metaphoric construal of the predicate. In other words, depending on the construal of the predicate, the metonymic mapping of the pronoun changes, and both of these mappings are sensitive to pre- and post- event contexts.

Figure 10: 'Metonymy within metaphor' mapping of SA events, based on Ruiz de Mendoza and Velasco (2002)

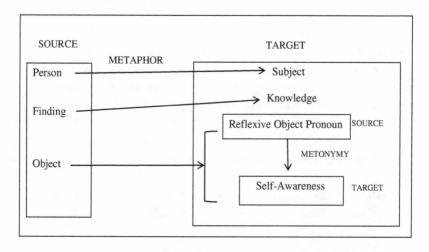

184. (158) *I gave myself* a task...   (COCA:2005.SPOK.CBS_Morning)
185. (159) And then *I asked myself* the question...
                                                (COCA:SPOK.THE CHARLIE ROSE SHOW)
186. (160) *I kicked myself* for being so stupid.   (COCA:2002.MAG.BoysLife)
187. (161) ...*James Brown found himself* back at home, alone in his old room...
                                                (COCA:1998.MAG.Ebony)

188. (162) No one could imagine *Lucy losing herself* in sensuality...

(COCA:1999.FIC.NewEnglandRev)

In 184-188 (reproduced from (158-162)), conceptual entailments of each of the verbs (metaphorical or not) conceptually point the interlocutors towards plausible reflexive pronoun-antecedent referent construal. In 184, the verb *give* entails the transfer of something from one entity to another, and thus, the reflexive pronoun refers to the receiving part of Self (whatever that may be which is appropriate for the situation). In 185, the verb *ask* designates an interrogative verbal act, thus the reflexive pronoun is assigned to a part of the mind that can 'hear' the question being posed. In 186, it is not only because *kicking oneself* is literally quite difficult that the metaphoric interpretation is construed, but also because the post-event adjunct, *for being so stupid*, "urges" the interlocutors towards the metaphoric interpretation of *kick*. That being established, the reflexive pronoun is easily assigned metonymic construal, i.e., *myself* STANDING FOR the part of the mind that receives the scolding, an intra-domain mapping. 187 and 188 are SA events and have already been described in detail, but again, FIND / LOSE entail KNOWLEDGE of perception/experience (or loss thereof) along with the inherent meaning of the reflexive pronoun entailing that the action occurs back on the Self, thus KNOWLEDGE must be of the Self, i.e., Self-Awareness.

5.8 Chapter Conclusion

Concluding this section, SA events cannot be precisely delineated without reference to their total pre- and post- event conceptual contexts that contribute vital information to the interlocutors for conceptual decision-making. SA events contain 'target in source' or WHOLE FOR PART metonymic construals wrapped inside a larger metaphoric event which is hinged upon the conceptual entailments of the predicate, a phenomenon Goossens calls 'metonymy within metaphor'.

PART III Corpus Analyses[39]

CHAPTER 6

6.1 Introduction

> The old grey donkey, Eeyore stood by himself in a thistly corner of the Forest, his front feet well apart, his head on one side, and thought about things. Sometimes he thought sadly to himself, "Why?" and sometimes he thought, "Wherefore?" and sometimes he thought, "Inasmuch as which?" and sometimes he didn't quite know what he was thinking about (Milne 1926: 11).

Linguistic research sometimes seems to totter on the precipice of Eeyore-hood, meaning that in the search for more and more explicit explanations and explications, we sometimes lose ourselves in the lingua-stratum and need to catch ourselves, take a few long, deep breaths, and find ourselves again. Part III attempts to do just that, i.e., to clarify and exemplify, by way of corpus analyses, the theories and ideas presented in the previous chapters. In particular, this investigation presents corpus data and analyses of Self-Aware (SA) Events, defined as reflexive events which metaphorically construe Perceptual and Situational Self-Awareness. It will demonstrate conceptual subtlety and ambiguity but also uncover structure and order within that 'fuzziness'. Numerous examples and contexts will be analyzed in order to specify the precise metaphorical construal of that ephemeral mental state called Self-Awareness when predicated within the reflexive construction.

The incentive for the present research originates from the need to concretely delineate the construal of Self-Awareness in expressions such as [NP + find/catch/lose + x-self]. Many aspects of the reflexive construction and its various meanings have been explored in detail in the literature from various perspectives, but Self-Awareness is rarely mentioned, and when it is, details are lacking, are purely intuitive, or fail to account for a wide breadth and depth of data. This research differs greatly from those descriptions, methodologically speaking, in that it explores the reflexive construction from a corpus-based side of the fence, so to speak. Instead of outlining the structure and meanings of the reflexive construction in an effort to explain how and why Self-Awareness is construed and predicated (as in the previous chapters), Part III examines first how to, fundamentally, identify metaphorical construal and predications within

---

[39] Corpus data is accurate as of September, 2012.

the reflexive construction. It then proceeds to delineate relevant predications from collocational and broader contextual perspectives. In this way, it is a much more pragmatic endeavor. It explores general and specific methodological issues for identification, retrieval and analyses of metaphor in a linguistic corpus. It also examines collocational environments surrounding metaphors in an effort to understand the role that they play in the metaphor's construal and predication. This part of the research, then, is basically a bottom-up endeavor; it begins with corpus data retrieval and analysis and concludes with hypotheses based on those analyses.

Specifically, evidence for the theoretical claims made previously in Parts I and II is essential. Without this, justification for these claims seem shallow, even if intuitively warranted. Considering the vast amount of corpus data now readily available and the functionality of modern user interfaces, validation (or not) for the previously proposed hypotheses can be readily obtained. Overall, three questions guide the present corpus-based inquiry; 1) Is there collocational evidence for posing the mental state of Self-Awareness as an image schema, 2) Is there collocational evidence for posing find/catch/lose (and other verbs) as metaphorically mapping onto Self-Awareness when reflexively predicated? and 3) Can corpus evidence be found for SA Events as described in previous chapters?

In order to investigate these questions as objectively as possible, a new method of inquiry is required. Previous chapters assumed that there was a metaphorical phenomenon called 'SA Event', having theoretically described it. This approach is inadequate for the present inquiry, as theoretical assumptions may taint objectivity. This research hopes to rectify this, and aspires to answer a common methodological issue, 'Can metaphor be objectively identified, observed and evidenced in a corpus?'

Data from both the British National Corpus (The British National Corpus (BNC XML Edition) 2007) and the Corpus of Contemporary American English (Davies 2008) are examined. This research proposes a unique, quasi-corpus-driven approach and demonstrates a method of corpus research methodology for metaphor retrieval and analysis that is proved useful both in quantitative and qualitative terms. The results uncover a wealth of information and allow for coarse- and fine-grained analyses. This method begins with the query, "what verbs are instantiated within the reflexive construction?" In this respect, it is methodologically similar to collostructional analysis in that the search "always starts with a particular construction and investigates which lexemes are strongly attracted or repelled by a particular slot in the construction…" (Stefanowitsch & Gries 2003: 214). This is followed by the question, "which of the verbs that appear in the reflexive construction are used metaphorically and how can these be evidenced?" Once metaphorically-construed verbs are objectively identified, they are grouped into categories based on the semantics of the verbs. It is only at this point in the process that possible verbs that metaphorically express Self-Awareness are identified. These are analyzed, token by token, with an effort to 'allow the data to speak to the researcher', as it were. In other words, an effort was made to keep theoretical assumptions to a minimum. It is at this stage that Self-Aware Events are positively identified. As shown below, many unpredictable results also emerge, confirming the method as a productive tool for uncovering under-specified and undetermined conceptions and construal.

It has been noticed that corpus retrieval of metaphors is "almost impossible for the simple reason that conceptual mappings are not linked to particular linguistic forms" (Stefanowitsch & Gries 2007: 2). This refers to corpus-based metaphor studies that mine data using metaphoric SOURCE conceptions as their input search parameters. However, the present research methodology overcomes this disadvantage by limiting itself to the reflexive construction, an easily-searchable syntactic parameter. Second, the method searches for metaphoric cross-mappings by objectively identifying TARGET domain samples and only then are SOURCE domain mappings proposed, analyzed and categorized according to semantic content, context and collocational patterning. In this way, the method provides a way to uncover previously undetermined and underspecified metaphoric SOURCE data. This method has proven to be advantageous, resulting in a number of important findings, the details of which are presented in the next chapters.

6.2. Metaphor Identification Method

The process of distinguishing between literal and metaphorical expressions is clearly the most basic and crucial stage in any study of the nature and patterning of metaphors in language, and is therefore fundamental to any attempt to extrapolate conceptual metaphors from linguistic data (Heywood, Semino, & Short 2002: 35).

The procedure adopted (and adapted) for this investigation for determining and analyzing possible metaphors mined from corpora are the basic operations from the Metaphor Identification Procedure (MIP). "...the purpose of MIP is to provide a procedure that starts from the actual discourse, and inductively builds the case for why a particular word was used metaphorically in context" (Group 2007: 34). However, I have not adopted this process in its entirety. Only its basic methodology is used here, providing a simplified decision-making tool for distinguishing between the metaphoric and literal use of a word and phrase. It differs from the MIP in that a strict adherence to analyzing the data with respect to linguistic propositions has been forgone, in other words, an expression's truth value is not taken into account. This is due to this research not being directly concerned with the non-human, computational processing of the literal vs metaphor nor linguistic vs conceptual metaphor distinction. Interpretation and analyzation of metaphor by the reader/hearer is considered a necessary function of metaphor comprehension. In agreement with Goatly (2002) and Gibbs (2002), human conceptual processing is always necessary when deciding between linguistic and process metaphors. For the purposes of metaphor identification, proposing an artificially created dichotomy between these such as some propositional level of metaphor is therefore unnecessary. Furthermore, and in line with Kövecses (2002), the level at which semantic propositions are proposed for text analysis (in the MIP) is different from that of the standard analyses of conceptual metaphor, whether the data is taken from corpus sources or not.

This research is specifically concerned with efficient methods for mining and analyzing collocational patterns that instantiate metaphoric use. More specifically, a procedure was needed for deciding relevant cross-domain mappings of TARGET domain samples taken from large corpora. Thus, I have omitted some details of the MIP version of text analysis (and its reliance on propositions (Crisp 2002; Heywood et al. 2002; Steen 2002)) and incorporated only the essential procedures that make data retrieval and analysis more systematic and reliable. For this research, the most recent version of the MIP, called the Metaphor Identification Procedure Vrije Universiteit (aka MIPVU) was used as a framework. It is a more encompassing and intuitive version (Steen et al. 2010) in which the following 6-step guideline is recommended for the identification of metaphors within a text:

1. Find metaphor-related words (MRWs) by examining the text on a word by word basis.
2. When a word is used indirectly and that use may potentially be explained by some form of cross-domain mapping from a more basic meaning of that word, mark the word as metaphorically used (MRW).
3. When a word is used directly and its use may potentially be explained by some form of cross-domain mapping to a more basic referent or topic in the text, mark the word as direct metaphor (MRW, direct).
4. When words are used for the purpose of lexico-grammatical substitution, such as third person personal pronouns, or when ellipsis occurs where words may be seen as missing, as in some forms of co-ordination, and when a direct or indirect meaning is conveyed by those substitutions or ellipses that may potentially be explained by some form of cross-domain mapping from a more basic meaning, referent, or topic, insert a code for implicit metaphor (MRW, implicit).

5. When a word functions as a signal that a cross-domain mapping may be at play, mark it as a metaphor flag (MFlag).

6. When a word is a new-formation coined, examine the distinct words that are its independent parts according to steps 2 through 5.   (Steen et al. 2010: 25-26)

Because not all of the above steps are necessary for the present objectives, the following steps were employed in this investigation for delineating metaphorical use within reflexive events:

1. Reflexive construction parameters are input into the corpus search field, with the verb slot 'open' or 'filled' by the researcher.

2. Check the retrieved data for 1) antecedent-pronoun consistency (noun$_1$ + verb + refl. pro$_1$), 2) reflexive meaning (i.e., compared to emphatic, benefactive or logographic, etc.), and 3) missing antecedents or pronouns (ellipses).

3. Check data for metaphor-related words (MRWs) by examining the text on a word by word basis by referencing 'base' meanings in a corpus-based dictionary (as per MIPVU).

4. If a word's use is considered metaphorical, analyze TARGET → SOURCE mappings.

5. Find contextual and/or collocational evidence corroborating the mapping in #4.

6. Analyze data statistically and confirm results.

From the above six procedures, only number three is the same as the MIPVU. Original MIPVU procedures one and two were combined and cross-domain plausibility checks were limited to the reflexive verb, anaphoric NP, and the reflexive's immediate adjuncts. Procedure number two was added to distinguish reflexive from non-reflexive anaphors as well as to confirm antecedent-pronoun agreement. The decision to perform this procedure at this time was more practical than theoretical. Simply, it was more efficient to weed out the non-reflexive, non-anaphoric tokens before proceeding with the more time-consuming metaphoric identification and analyses. For procedure number four, various metaphorical interpretations were possible for many tokens in the data, and it was critical to remain open to all possible interpretations. This was sometimes difficult, and the expanded context of tokens were consulted frequently. Procedure number five was added in order to confirm collocational and broader contextual evidence when encountering ambiguous metaphorical interpretations. Although this was time consuming, it allowed for more objective judgements to be made for metaphorical interpretation. Finally, in step six, the data is analyzed statistically and the results are categorized according to parameters set by the researcher.

6.3.Research Method

This research makes use of two corpora, the British National Corpus (BNC), (The British National Corpus (BNC XML Edition) 2007) comprised of 100 million words, and the Corpus of Contemporary American English (COCA) (Davies 2008), currently comprised of over 500 million words. The web interface used for both was the corpus query interface at Brigham Young University. By using data from both corpora, a more encompassing and balanced data set was available for analysis. Although this could not eliminate all the idiosyncrasies of the collected works inherent in each and any corpus, by including two regions whose native language is English as well as different registers contained within the corpora themselves, the culminative data set added inferential value to the research.

Although there are many statistical tests used for corpus analysis, the Fisher Exact test of independence was used here as a variable relations significance test, with corpus frequency ratios[40] used as input values, rounded to the nearest whole number. Although the related Chi Square test is also common, the Fisher test "neither makes any distributional assumptions nor does it require any particular sample size" (Stefanowitsch & Gries 2003: 218). Further, although t- and Z-scores can show relative significance along a single parameter (such as relative frequency) within a corpus, Fisher Exact tests show relations between two or more sets of data and whether there is attraction or repulsion of one lexeme with regard to the collostruction to which it is compared (Stefanowitsch & Gries 2003). Because the current research attempts to find the relational significances of different semantic construals within the reflexive construction, the Fisher Exact test was considered the most appropriate tool for this endeavor.

In this way, corpus research supports theoretical and intuitive research by adding a level of *significance in use*, a parameter that assigns weight value to an expression as used in society. But it still stands that this data must be analyzed by human eyes, with a human mind knowledgeable in the language and the patterns being analyzed. Patterns can be found by a computer program, but these patterns need meaning. Statistics can help to uncover hard-to-find patterns and trends, but exceptions to these often also reveal fascinating insights. It is to this general end, then, that this investigation attempts to combine this more straightforward, transparent method of corpus analysis with the human factor necessary (in the present era, at least) for the analysis of metaphor.

---

[40] In general, frequency ratios (i.e., percentages) were used as the input values of the significance tests due to the different total items among the corpora (for cross-corpora analyses) and among the pronoun data sets (for intra-corpora analyses). When raw frequencies are used, it is duly noted.

6.4. Preliminary Corpus Analysis and Methodological Considerations

For this first step, the COCA and BNC corpora were mined with the search parameter syntax, [v*] [ppx*], i.e., any verb lemma followed by any reflexive pronoun. The 500 most frequent verb lemmas analyzed. The 500th-ranked verb had a frequency of 16 in the COCA and 18 in the BNC. For the next step, reciprocals (i.e., [v*] [each], [v*][one]) were deleted, leaving 462 total hits in the COCA and 468 in the BNC. A cross-corpora comparison was then conducted and a list of common verbs was created (see Appendix 1). The motivation for this cross-corpora comparison is that it lessens the influence of region-specific varieties of English.[41] Each of the verb lemmas from this data was then entered into each of the respective corpus search engines in order to retrieve tokens of that particular verb within the reflexive construction, e.g., [find][ppx*]. If more than 100 hits were retrieved for any pronoun group, a random sample[42] (n=100) was chosen for the analysis. The results were then checked for metaphoric instantiation using a corpus-based dictionary, as per the methodology discussed in section 6.2. At this stage, the *potential* for metaphoricity, not the specific cognitive mappings nor motivations for those mappings, was determined. If a token was suspected of being used metaphorically, a corpus-based online dictionary was consulted (LDOCE 2014) to determine the verb's 'base' or 'literal' meaning. Because metaphors are syntax-sensitive[43], the syntax of the data was preserved for the dictionary consultation. All conceptually ambiguous tokens were compared with dictionary definitions to ensure data accuracy and objectivity. In some cases, these were not easy decisions. For example, when the physical, concrete meaning of a verb was archaic and currently not well entrenched in contemporary meaning, that meaning was not considered a 'base' for the metaphor, because metaphoricity involves some sort of comparison to 'normal use' (Ronald W Langacker 1987b). If that 'normal' use is not part of a person's working cognitive lexicon, there can be no cross-domain mapping comparison from which to draw. If, however, a 'base' meaning and 'figurative' meaning comprised a fairly obvious cross-domain mapping, the instance was marked metaphoric. Admittedly, this is not as cut and dry as it seems, but the

---

[41] Although a fully international data set of all native (and non-native) varieties of English is ideal, it is beyond the scope of this research.

[42] The data sample is truly random, according to Davies, "…a routine in SQL Server randomly assigns a number to each one, and then I just take the top 100 or so, based on those random numbers" (2016).

[43] A simple example of this is the word *dog*. When used metaphorically as a noun, it means a man with low moral values, as in *He's a dog*, but when used as a verb, it means to pursue with intensity, for example, *The police dogged the criminal.*

utmost effort was made to ensure reliability and consistency throughout the data by adhering to published (i.e., dictionary) sources.

One issue that arose during this stage was whether or not post-predicate (adjunct) verbal constructions were phrasal verbs or verb + preposition, and whether to count these as metaphoric or not. The dictionary was consulted here as well, and verb + preposition was considered a single phrasal verb (and metaphoric if it displayed cross-domain mapping.) This choice was motivated by the way these phrasal verbs were subcategorized under the main verb listing, i.e., one complete meaning sense within a subset of the main meaning.

Lastly, tokens were categorized according to metaphoric sense. Shown below, the surrounding linguistic contexts proved invaluable as a decision-making resource. When context was directly related to the construction's meaning under analysis and was deemed a necessary semantic component of the construction, it was labelled Focus of Awareness (hereafter FoA), a label that conveys the conception under immediate consideration for the construction. For Self-Aware Events, the FoA is the Conceptual Object of Self-Awareness. In other cases, it is the object referred to by the metaphor. Shown in the examples below, the main metaphoric components are in *italics*, and the FoAs are <u>underlined</u>.

189. *Wade finds himself* <u>feeling like the papa bear</u> to a bunch of frisky cubs.

(COCA:2009.MAG.SportsIll)

190. How ironic that *her eulogy found itself* <u>in an issue</u> whose lead articles treat

the evils of tobacco...   (COCA:1998.MAG.America)

In the first SA Event example, what is *Wade* aware of (i.e., what does he *find*?) He is distinctly aware of his paternal feelings. This is the Focus of the Awareness (FoA). In the second example, categorized as a Picture Noun Schema (Kuno 1987), what is being noticed or realized (i.e., *found*)? It is that the *eulogy* was written in a certain *issue* of a magazine or newspaper.

One complication at this stage arose because decisions needed to be made from only one line of text (i.e., the token). In many cases, there were no obvious or predicated antecedent referents for the metaphor and/or the FoA. In these cases, the token's expanded context was consulted, consisting of approximately 180 words of text, and in most cases, this resolved the uncertainty. "Any instance of language depends on its surrounding context. The details of choice shown in any segment of a text depend – some of them—on choices made elsewhere in the text, and so no example is ever complete unless it is a whole text" (Sinclair 1991: 5). Reference to longer and more complete contexts led to more accurate and confident decisions about the FoA, the metaphoricity of the construction, and thus, the reliability of the analysis and its results.

6.5. Results

A total of 67 metaphorically-construed verb lemmas concurred with the procedural criteria described above that were instantiated in both the COCA and BNC. 42 verbs were considered non-metaphorical. There were 12 metaphorically-construed verbs whose 'base' meanings were difficult to assign due to the high number and variety of metaphorical and non-metaphorical senses, some of them functioning as auxiliary verbs. These verbs were: *do, get, give, have, hold, keep, make, put, set, take,* and *turn*. These verbs were eliminated from the analysis. The remaining data were grouped into four metaphorical and six non-metaphorical semantic categories. These categories were not predetermined, although they occasionally overlap with established verb categorizations (see: Levin 1993). The present data-based categorization procedure was determined necessary to ensure consistency for the current research methodology. Shown below are the four metaphorically conceived categories (verbs listed alphabetically, category marker in parenthesis).

1. Self-Perception (P): be, catch, check, feel, find, identify, immerse, lose, perceive, regard, see, watch
2. Self-Causation (F)*: assert, bring, catch, check, drag, draw, drive, fling, force, hang, haul, help, kill, launch, lock, pull, push, resign, set, shake, steel, throw, work
   * (F) stands for 'Force-dynamic' conception.
3. Societal Interaction (SI): align, attach, behave, call, commit, distance, distinguish, establish, excuse, expose, express, identify, involve, lend, lower, present, prove, raise, sell, show, suit
4. Self-Maintenance (M): brace, compose, feed, help, resolve, save, settle, shoot, support, treat, watch, wrap

Listed below are the six non-metaphorical categories.

1. Sense-Perception & Physicality (P'): hear, know, manifest, seat, sit
2. Self-Causation (F'): allow, busy, calm, let, steady, stop, will
3. Social Interaction (SI'): avail, extricate, identify, introduce, reveal, concern
4. Self-Communication (C): ask, blame, remind, repeat, teach, tell

5. Self-Judgement (J): believe, fancy, feel, hate, imagine, pride, think, trust

6. Self-Maintenance (M'): calm, ease, enjoy, prepare, rid, organize, protect, steady, surround, transform

Two verbs construed more than one category, *catch* and *check*. In these cases, the verbs were counted once for each category due to unique conceptions being construed for each of the predications.

6.6. *Verbs of Self-Perception*

Metaphoric and non-metaphoric categories having been determined, the question of construal type may now be addressed. Specifically, is Self-Awareness metaphorically construed and predicated within the reflexive construction? The categorization procedures above were necessary to identify verbs that *might* convey this meaning, with as little subjective interference as possible. Likely candidates for construed Self-Awareness are found among the first metaphorical category, Self-Perception (P). This category comprises TARGET-SOURCE, cross-domain mappings referring to one's physical, psychological or spiritual perceptions. All of the verbs in this category use sense perceptions as well as cognition and ontology as their SOURCE domains. Admittedly, ontology is not traditionally used in a perceptual sense, but here it is warranted due to the *true nature of one's being* coming under consideration, as in the 'True-Self' or 'Loss-of-Self' metaphors (A. Lakoff & Becker 1992; G. Lakoff 1996a) discussed previously and below (see Chapters 7 and 8). From this category (P), the verbs that have their SOURCE domains in sense perceptions are *be, catch, check, feel, find, identify, immerse, lose, perceive, regard, see,* and *watch.* The task now is to determine if any of these metaphorically construe Self-Awareness. It was previously claimed and is repeated here that Self-Awareness is defined as an image schema or basic domain because Self-Awareness is a direct experience and is not based nor built upon any other conception. Self-Awareness can be regarded as a meta-sense perception because the mind becomes aware of a specific or total sum of sense perceptions at a particular moment in time. The antecedent-pronoun pairs in this category reflect metonymic mappings of the reflexive pronoun onto some self-perception and this synchronizes with the semantics of the reflexive construction to reverse the expected action of the predicate object from an 'other' onto the antecedent itself. Thus, the metaphorical construal of a reflexive construction for which a Self-Perception verb is predicated may[44] describe the Awareness of a particular or gestalt perception, i.e., an SA Event.

Examples from the metaphoric perceptual verb category (P) above which convey reflexive self-perception are the following:

BE: The metaphoric sense of *be oneself* means 'to be aware of one's deep, basic, or 'real' Self, and then taking some action to establish that Self'.

> 191. ...what *you* really need to do is let people get to know you, *be yourself*.
> (COCA:2015.SPOK.CBS)

CHECK: This may take the meaning of 'self-awareness of one's action, thought, or situation'.

> 192. But the whole notion of society and manners forces *you* to *check yourself* if you have those tendencies.　　　　　　　　　　　　　(BNC:ED7.W_pop_lore)

This may also express the meaning of self-causation (Gilquin 2010a; Talmy 2001b), meaning 'to stop or prevent oneself from doing something', and as such, it is also listed under the (F) category.

> 193. It was as much as *Millie* could do to *check herself* from saying,' Oh, I don't think I should do that.　　　　　　　　　　　　　(BNC:CK9.W_fict_prose)

FEEL: When used metaphorically, *feel* is used to convey the meaning of 'think or believe'.

> 194. And when I'm with the other *I* just *feel myself* to be a better person.
> (BNC:A08.W_fict_prose)

IDENTIFY: When metaphorically expressed, this means 'to align or understand oneself to be similar in some way with a group, person or thing'.

> 195. Sixty-two percent of *respondents identified themselves* as either not religious or atheist, placing the country behind only China...　　(COCA:2015:NEWS.CSMonitor)

---

[44] 'May' is used here to convey the polysemy that often occurs within the reflexive construction.

IMMERSE: When metaphorically construed, this means t'o completely engage one's efforts in some activity'. At first glance, this seems to convey the same concept as *lose x-self*, and the activities performed are, in many cases, similar. However, even though one is totally involved with an activity here, there is no loss of other perceptions nor loss of a deeper Self, as seen by the examples below. Even when *immersed* in the various situations, one can still engage normally with other people. This is not possible with SA Event *lose x-self* nor the 'loss-of-self' metaphor.

196. *They* visited pubs all over the country, *immersing themselves* in pub culture -- playing darts and drinking with the lads. (BNC:K1V.W_news_script)

197. I was thinking of ethnography, which means *you* have to *immerse yourself* in the situation and talk to the people involved like an anthropologist would.
(BNC:EC7.W_ac_medicine)

PERCEIVE: This means 'to think of oneself as... or understand oneself to be some 'type' of person'.

198. *Many women* who served in the military *don't perceive themselves* as veterans...
(COCA:2007.NEWS.CSMonitor)

REGARD: This means 'to think of oneself as... or understand oneself to be some type of person'.

199. ...*I* do not *regard myself* as disabled, I have a disability... (BNC:J9D.S_meeting)

SEE: This means 'to think of oneself as... or understand oneself to be some type of person'.

200. ...*he* began to *see himself* not as cursed but blessed, ... (COCA:2013.FIC.ParisRev)

Another meaning is 'imagining oneself being or doing something'.

201. So what sort of targets do *you see yourself* setting? (BNC:KLX.S_meeting)

WATCH: This means 'be careful' and is the only usage besides the literal. This could also be put into the Self-Maintenance (M) category due to its meaning of physical or mental caution.

> 202. Richard jump down. Oh dear. *Watch yourself* there now.   (BNC:KB8.S_conv)

> 203. And Lightening (horse's name) is a stubborn as they come. If *he* doesn't *watch himself*, he won't be pulling a carriage for much longer. (my parenthesis)
>   (COCA:2013.FIC.Bk:FlirtingWithTexas)

Besides these verbs, three other verbs are discussed in detail below. These verbs metaphorically express meta-self-perception, i.e., Self-Awareness, when contained within the reflexive construction. These verbs are *find*, *lose* and *catch*.

CHAPTER 7: SELF-AWARE EVENTS

7.1 FIND X-SELF

Theoretical issues for SA Events were presented in the Parts I and II. In these discussions, two points in particular helped clarify the meanings of *find x-self* and possible motivations for its use. The first is the semantics of the reflexive construction. It was seen that the reflexive pronoun marks an unexpected event, i.e., the self as object for a transitive verb, where the prototypical unmarked form takes an object that is 'other-than-self' (Faltz 1985). This lexical mirativity (i.e., unexpectedness or surprise) affects the subject's perceived participation in the event (Calude 2007; Faltz 1985; Fukaya 2002; Kemmer 1993). Reflexivity weakens the transitivity of the event, drawing it closer to the transitivity found in middle events. Barlow (1996), from the standpoint of corpus research, also notes this:

> Other verbs that occur frequently with the reflexive in the corpus have what we call middle semantics...Many of the middle-like uses of the reflexive are highly idiomatized expressions with their own special semantics, such as find myself, consider myself, control myself, expose myself, and feel myself. These phrases are non-compositional (in the sense that the meaning of the phrase is not completely predictable from the meaning of the constituent parts) and should be distinguished from the ordinary productive reflexive device in English (Barlow 1996: 7-8).

Barlow's mention of *idiomaticity* in line 2 was shown to be comprised of the metaphoricity of the overall expression (anchored to the verb), as well as the metonymy of the pronoun, i.e., metonym within metaphor (Goossens 2002). The second point regarding the delineation of SA Events is the denotation of the verb *find*. It was shown previously that *find x-self* does not necessarily include a semantic entailment of 'search', and that a meaning of 'non-search', unexpected or sudden 'coming upon an object' is also viable and productive. The object of this 'sudden coming upon' was shown through Conceptual Metaphor and Cognitive Grammatical models to be the experiencer's Self-Awareness, metonymically mapped onto the reflexive pronoun. And so, the semantics of *find* together with the semantics of the reflexive event both contribute to the construction *find x-self* meaning 'to be aware of oneself' physically, psychologically, spiritually and/or situationally. These points are briefly mentioned in research by Barlow (1996), as he introduces his schema-based approach to grammar (Barlow & Kemmer 1994). He mentions and provides corpus data on a variety of verbs, one of them being the construction vp[find + REFL Participle Phrase]. The research presents frequency and t-score results to evidence the ubiquity of this construction in use.

> This preliminary corpus study shows that the verb occurring most frequently with the reflexive form is find. The very high frequency of occurrences of the lemma find compared with the other verbs in this corpus suggests that the association between find and reflexives will be found in the language in general - an association, which has, as far as I know, never been mentioned in any discussion of reflexives (Barlow 1996: 8).

The focus of Barlow's research is the common associations of various components within the reflexive construction and what these might mean, providing valuable data and methodology upon which more detailed and encompassing analyses can be undertaken. Although the present research is independent of Barlow's, it is congruent with many of those results, specifically, his brief mention of *find + x-self* containing the meaning of 'self-observation' (i.e., self-awareness) as well as the semantic entailment of surprise, mentioned above.

> The meanings associated with the find plus reflexive construction involve self-observation, in particular with some degree of distancing of the protagonist from the action. It is as if someone is observing his/her own actions from a distance and is even surprised by what is taking place (Barlow 1996: 6).

The lack of detail and elaboration on these points is unfortunate; however, his research was not specifically focused on the *find x-self* construction but on the many types of verbs that appear within the reflexive construction and their associative frequencies. The detection of self-observation, aka self-awareness, is further exploited at length in the present research.

Barlow's analysis of *find* plus reflexive construction constitutes an example of what is coined here 'Self-Aware Unexpected-Event' (hereafter SA-UE). However, the Self-Aware (aka SA) event is completely absent from this analysis, leaving about 40 percent of the data unaccounted for, as seen in Figure 11. The following corpus analysis examines both of these events in depth.

Figure 11: Frequency ratios for all semantic categories in the COCA & BNC

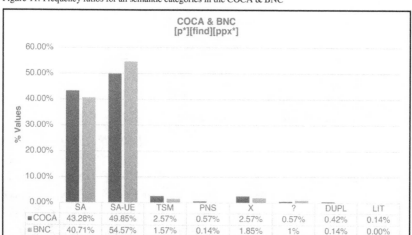

COCA & BNC
[p*][find][ppx*]

	SA	SA-UE	TSM	PNS	X	?	DUPL	LIT
■ COCA	43.28%	49.85%	2.57%	0.57%	2.57%	0.57%	0.42%	0.14%
■ BNC	40.71%	54.57%	1.57%	0.14%	1.85%	1%	0.14%	0.00%

SA=Self-Aware Event, SA-UE=Self-Aware Unexpected Event, TSM=True-Self Metaphor, PNS=Picture Noun Schema, X=non-reflexive, ?=indeterminate, DUPL=Duplicate, LIT=Literal use

Other research that examines *find x-self* is by Fukaya (2002), who labels the construction FINDSELF. This investigation begins by introducing Barlow's research above and then discusses the discourse functions of FINDSELF by way of corpus analysis using the Bank of English corpus. Mirativity is a continuing theme here, dictionary and corpus examples are provided as evidential support, and the high frequency of FINDSELF is established. It is here that common ground with this research ends, however. In that brief article, FINDSELF is discussed in relation to: main and subordinate clauses, background vs foreground, collocations including prepositions, adjectives and adverbs, data on different corpus registers, verb tenses and pronouns that are tentatively related to the function of FINDSELF as a localization device. The topics discussed are numerous and due to the very select and limited nature of the data, evidential support for the claims made there are sparse and tenuous. For example, he offers evidence and supports conclusions from Taoka (1999, 2009), who investigated FINDSELF from a corpus of two fiction writers' novels. In that discussion, two subcategories are proposed for the FINDSELF construction, the first being: a. emotions, b. reactions to emotions, and c. passives, and the second: a. identifying one's position, and b. un-intentionalization. She lists examples for the first subcategory as:

a. …found himself getting angry

101

b. He found himself sputtering.

c. Adam found himself pushed down...

And examples for the second subcategory as:

a. ...find herself in the elevator with him.

b. ...find herself staring into Brenda's face.

(1999: 131-134. In Fukaya 2002)

Questions immediately arise as to the overall validity of these subcategorizations. In subcategory one, (a) and (b) refer to emotional states whereas (c) refers to a syntactic construction. This incongruence is left unexplained. Furthermore, in (1b), the example *sputtering* is cited as a reaction to emotions, and if this example is cited because it is the ideal, then the subcategory is suspect. In a corpus collocate search (+/- 4) conducted here with the lemma [sputter], the most frequent collocate is *engine*, referring literally to the sound an engine produces when not in good condition. The next most frequent is *economy*, referring metaphorically to the lack of power or health of an 'economic engine'. Of the most frequent 100 collocates with the lemma [sputter], the following nine had some connection to emotional states: *rage, laughter, red-faced, cursing, muttering, outrage, helplessly, indignation* and *swore*. However, the total token frequency ratio of these is only 6.7% (*n*=52). Although there is usage related to emotional qualities or reactions to those emotions, more detailed and comprehensive data supporting the claim of reactions to emotions would have further clarified and supported the arguments. Since there are none, we must presume that *sputter* is their ideal case, which is accurate only perhaps for the very small corpus used therein, and not congruent with a variety of registers and a larger data set.

Other questions arise about Takao's categories and Fukaya's support of them. For example, if subcategory (1c) refers to passives and (2a) refers to identifying one's position, assuming that these categories are mutually exclusive, we are forced to choose between one or the other. But *finding oneself pushed down* can be construed either as passive and/or as identifying one's position. (literally and/or metaphorically). Similarly, and more importantly, un-intentionality in (2b) seems to cover all examples above. As stated in previous sections above, un-intentionality is a part of the basic entailment of both one meaning of *find* and of the reflexive construction. Fukaya's acceptance of these categorizations along with his own corpus analysis lead him to the conclusion that 'localization' (from categorization (2a) of Takao and from Barlow's comment about a 'distancing relation' (1996: 6-7)) is the determining factor and reason FINDSELF is used so ubiquitously. Granted, Fukaya's is a discourse-based study, not strictly linguistic, but his data collection and reporting methodology is imprecise and his conclusions are incongruent. The corpus data used there show differences in the frequencies of the use of FINDSELF between main and subordinate clauses, when-clauses, and their associated conjunctions and coordinators, concluding that:

> ...the FINDSELF construction has a general tendency to occur more often in the subordinate clause than in the main clause because of its function of backgrounding. But it is also possible to highlight the background by placing the subordinate clause after the main clause...it tends to make its appearance in the background position in a complex sentence; however, in coordinate sentences, it occurs more often in the foreground second clause position...the common function of FINDSELF is to localize the subject of the second conjunct depending on the semantics of the verb find and the reflexive pronoun, and consequently to put the location in the foreground information (ibid.: 82-83).

Needless to say, these conclusions warrant a more accurate delineation of the FINDSELF construction that can account for more data in a more systematic and efficient way. This is not an easy task, especially for such a common and flexible metaphorical conception as *find x-self*. This complexity in the corpus data is the subject of discussion of the next section.

7.2. Subtleties in the Corpus Data

Eight categories are proposed for the data retrieved for the search parameter [find][ppx*] (i.e., the lemma find followed by any reflexive pronoun). These categories were not predetermined from some model but are based on the data, and thus can be seen as moderately corpus-driven, in line with Sinclair, who states, "Without relinquishing our intuitions, of course, we try to find explanations that fit the evidence, rather than adjusting the evidence to fit a pre-set explanation..." (1991: 36). The categories are as follows:

1) Self-Aware Event (hereafter SA) is an event in which the specific object of Awareness, aka the Focus of Awareness (FoA), is the experiencer's embodied self-perception.
2) Self-Aware Unexpected Event (hereafter SA-UE) is an event in which the specific object of Awareness (aka FoA), is an externally initiated and unexpected situation.
3) True Self Metaphor (G. Lakoff, 1996a)(hereafter TSM) is the Awareness of an internally deep or central part of the psyche.

4) Picture Noun Schema (Kuno, 1987)(hereafter PNS) is an event in which the experiencer's physical or psychological self-representation (picture, film, statue, hallucination, etc.) is present in the scene.

5) LIT is the literal use of the construction.

6) X is the non-reflexive use (e.g., emphatic, benefactive, etc.) of the construction.

7) ? is the marking for cases that were categorically inconclusive or unintelligible.

8) DUPL is the marking for duplicates in the data.

Within the four types of metaphoric construal found in the data (i.e., SA, SA-UE, TSM and PNS), the most frequent are the two types of Self-Aware Events, SA and SA-UE. The distinctions between these are construed and predicated by speakers and writers, evidenced by collocational data (see section 7.3.1). Although clear-cut cases are the norm, there is a cline of metaphoricity within these events. In the present research, data suggests a metaphorical continuum that extends from a personal, direct perceptual Self-Aware Event, where *Maggie* is aware of her own physical, visual perceptions, in the example below,

> 204. In the light, *Maggie found herself* staring directly at Bryce...
> (BNC:AN7.W_fict_prose)

to an event that is much more situationally external from the experiencer's point of view, as in the following example.

> 205. The place in which *he found himself* was a tall grimy building with a long
> passageway...   (BNC:CKD.W_fict_prose)

Intermediate cases, although harder to categorize, are also interesting in terms of the subtleties of construal and predication. For example, in cases when the experiencers are a collection of people, a situation can be construed as perceptual, but not directly perceptual for the individual experiencers. For example,

> 206. Upon hospitalization, even for brief and simple interventions, *people find*
> *themselves* in an extremely awkward public space: sharing rooms with strangers...
> (COCA:2009.ACAD.AnthropolQ)

In this and similar cases, the situation of being *in an extremely awkward public space: sharing rooms with strangers* is construed as a perceptual experience, evidenced by the exactness of the time frame *upon hospitalization*. In addition, the adjective *awkward* suggests immediate emotional reactions on the part of the experiencers. However, the event is describing the experiences of a collection of people and of some external location and is therefore perceptually distant and/or removed from the direct perceptual stimulus of a single individual. Because of this contextual evidence, this example is labeled SA-UE. Subtleties like these as well as more straightforward cases will be examined at length in the following sections.

7.3. Results for [find x-self]

In a search of the most frequent 500 tokens for the lemma find + reflexive pronoun (i.e., [find][ppx*]) in the COCA corpus (see Table 4), the total frequency was 47,498 (excluding reciprocals (v+each; v+one), compared to a total 101,403 tokens with any verb (lemma) + reflexive pronoun (i.e., [v*][ppx*], (excluding reciprocals). This yielded a *find x-self* frequency ratio of 46.8%. For the most frequent 500 tokens in the BNC corpus, from a [v*][ppx*] total of 35,661, [find][ppx*] yielded 5,426 tokens, resulting in a *find x-self* frequency ratio of 15.2%.

It may be argued that *find x-self*, as a unique construction consisting of the verb *find* used within the reflexive construction, is not statistically salient. In other words, that the instantiation ratios are comparable to the patterning ratios of the verb *find* when placed within any construction. This was tested for both corpora using the Fisher Exact test and the results are significant (p=0; p<.05) [45] (Stangroom 2017). This suggests that the verb *find* and the reflexive construction display dependence and differ in collocational profiling from *find* + *non-reflexive constructions*. Thus, both the raw frequency ratios together with the Fisher Exact results reveal the great extent that the *find* is used with the reflexive construction, corroborating Barlow's (1996) findings. This was strong motivation to continue with a more in-depth and fine-grained investigation.

In an expanded investigation (see Table 5), the total frequency of [find][ppx*] in the COCA was 27,188 (*n*-lemma=3000, (n≥10)), excluding reciprocals. The total frequency for [v*][ppx*] was 276,810, yielding a [find][ppx*] frequency ratio of 10.18%. In the BNC, the same

---

[45] The contingency table values are as follows: COCA corpus: Categories= [find], [v*]: Groups=[any Construction], [ppx*]. [find]+[not ppx*]=525,022; [v*]+[not ppx*]=89,318,707; [find]+[ppx*]=27,643; [v*]+[ppx*](minus [find])=278,801. 5000 hits max., lemma sorting, n ≥10. In the BNC corpus: [find]+[not ppx*]=88,686; [v*]+[not ppx*]=16,483,316; [find]+[ppx*]=5102; [v*]+[ppx*](minus [find])=51,326. 5000 hits max., lemma sorting, n ≥5.

[find][ppx*] search yielded 5,064 tokens ((n≥5), excluding reciprocals)), while the total [v*][ppx*] frequency was 51,626 (n-lemmas=1997(n≥5))[46], yielding a [find][ppx*] frequency ratio of 10.19%.[47] Although the results are statistically not significant, the cross-corpora frequency ratios of over 10% are consequential in that *find x-self* use can be considered common and consistent across both regions. Although frequency in and of itself does not prove linguistic entrenchment, it does suggest it. This is corroborated by the query sorted by register (see Appendix 2 & 3, and section 7.5) where, although the fiction register yields the highest number of tokens, other registers are also commonly instantiated.

The frequency of metaphorical Self-Awareness for the *find x-self* construction as an overall semantic category (i.e., SA + SA-UE) yielded a frequency ratio of 93.1% in the COCA and 95.3% in the BNC (mean= 94.2%), far outranking all other metaphorical categories. Uncovering the ubiquity of the Self-Aware event for *find x-self* is an important observation at this point because it evidences Self-Awareness as an authentic and unique conception and provides motivation for further, more in-depth analyses.

Table 4. Results of most frequent 500 token search for [v*][ppx*] and [find][ppx*]

Corpus	[v*][ppx*]	[find][ppx*]	ratio of *find x-self*	Fisher Exact results
COCA	101,403	47,498	46.8%	
BNC	35,661	5,426	15.2%	
Total	137,064	52,924	38.6%	p=0; p<.05 = significant

Table 5. Results of expanded search (lemma n=3000) for [v*][ppx*] and [find][ppx*]

Corpus	[v][ppx*]	[find][ppx*]	ratio of *find x-self*	Fisher Exact results
COCA	276,810	27,188	10.2%	
BNC	51,626	5,064	10.2%	
Total	328,436	32,252	10%	p=0.942485; p<.05 = not significant

Differentiating between SA and SA-UE (the two sub-categories of Self-Aware events) also proved informative. In a cross-corpora analysis, SA-UE instantiated an mean of 65.2% while

---

[46] A minimum token frequency was set at ten for the COCA (n≥10) and five (n≥5) for the BNC. Although the COCA has five times more data than the BNC, and therefore minimum frequency may be adjusted for this (i.e., minimum frequency (n= 2) for the BNC), due to idiosyncratic and/or one-off linguistic use concerns, I decided to set the minimum frequency at five for the BNC. This decision, however formally un-statistical, seemed a reasonable compromise between theory and practice.

[47] Due to the large data set, this particular analysis does not delete emphatic and other non-reflexive anaphor tokens. These are, however, filtered out in all other analyses below.

SA yielded a 28.7% mean across seven pronouns. In other words, there is a preference for using *find x-self* to describe the 'awareness of oneself in an unexpected situation' in both American and British English compared to the more visceral and internal SA construal. This is again congruent with Barlow's explanation for *find x-self* in that a majority of examples construe the 'self-observation… with some degree of distancing" (1996: 6).

The frequent instantiation of the Self-Aware Event as a metaphorical category in both corpora lends strong support to the previous theoretical proposals. Compared to the Self-Aware event, the True-Self Metaphor (TSM) and the Picture Noun Schema (PNS) categories yielded much lower frequencies, 2.1% and 3.5%, respectively. These results illustrate the advantages of using corpus data to support (and perhaps ignite) theoretical and intuitive research, providing social context and statistical weight to theoretical claims.

One of the benefits of corpus research is being able to test assumptions and 'hunches' against empirical data. For example, TSM construal seemed, at precursory glance, to occur clause-finally. This was tested here and the results show a 92% likelihood for the TSM construal to be in clause final position (clause-final position (*n=26*); other (*n=2*)). These results thus support this 'hunch' and is objectively confirmed.

One component of the *find x-self* construction that seemed important for distinguishability of construal was the type of antecedent in the event, i.e., whether the antecedent was predicated as a pronoun or full noun. The motivation for this seemed to be the metonymic construal of the full noun antecedents, as in the following example.

> 471. **America** *found* **itself** deeply and violently divided about its national purpose.
> (COCA:1991.MAG.AmHeritage)

Although I am not familiar with any research that overtly analyzes subject pronoun vs. full noun distinctions for the overall metaphoricity of the construction within a corpus framework, due to the presence of these types of examples in the data, this was specifically examined in the present investigation for all three constructions, *find x-self*, *lose x-self*, and *catch x-self*.

7.4   Results for PRONOUN + FIND X-SELF

The parameter [p*][find][ppx*] (i.e., any pronoun followed by the verb lemma *find* followed by any reflexive pronoun) was input into the two corpus search engines. Each pronoun category consisted of a random sample (*n=100*; pronoun categories *n=7*), totaling 700 tokens. A minimum frequency of ≥10 was set for the COCA data, and ≥5 for the BNC. The cross-corpora total frequency ratios (i.e., *n*=200, per pronoun) for [p*][find][ppx*], according to semantic category and corpus, are provided in Figure 12 (duplicated from Figure 1). These data are shown in more detail and charted according to pronoun and semantic category in Table 6. At the outset, a few of the values and relationships are readily discernible. The first is from Figure 12 and concerns the relationship between the COCA and BNC data for the SA and SA-UE categories. The graph visibly shows a difference and this may entice one to conclude that there is inherent meaning in these differences, but the results of the significance test do not support such an assumption. By inputting the values of the two corpus groups (COCA, BNC) and the two categories (SA, SA-UE) into the Fisher Exact contingency table, the resulting value is 0.662 (at p < 0.05), which is not significant. In other words, SA and SA-UE are, for all intents and purposes, equally construed for *find + x-self* in the COCA and BNC when the antecedents are pronouns. The discrepancy between this and the more general [find][ppx*] results are interesting and point to the possible importance of making this type of antecedent distinction for other kinds of metaphoric analyses.

Figure 12: Frequency ratios of [pro+find+x-self] according to semantic category

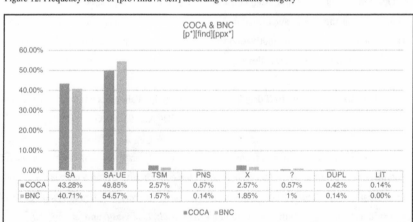

	SA	SA-UE	TSM	PNS	X	?	DUPL	LIT
■COCA	43.28%	49.85%	2.57%	0.57%	2.57%	0.57%	0.42%	0.14%
▣BNC	40.71%	54.57%	1.57%	0.14%	1.85%	1%	0.14%	0.00%

■COCA ▣BNC

With the exception of Barlow mentioned previously, cognitive linguistic and semantic research has mentioned Divided Self metaphors (e.g., True-Self Metaphor (TSM)) and Picture Noun Schemas (PNS), but the corpus results here point to a much greater frequency of Self-Aware events for *find x-self*. What is the frequency distribution for TSM, PNS, SA and SA-UE events? The data from Table 6 below reveals that, compared to the SA event category, TSM has a much lower frequency for all instantiated pronouns except the impersonal *it*, where TSM is more frequent (+ 2.5%), although much less frequent than the SA-UE construal category (-84.5%). For all pronouns, SA instantiates 28.7% and SA-UE 65.2% on average, whereas TSM instantiates only 2%. PNS has even lower frequency rates across the board, instantiating at most 0.5% for only four pronouns (*we, she, you, it*) and zero for the others. Needless to say, PNS is a minor event within the reflexive construction with the verb *find*. This does not in any way discount the conceptual experiences of *seeing/viewing/finding oneself in a newspaper, movie, picture, etc...*, but it can be stated with confidence that for *find x-self*, PNS instantiates rarely. Self-Aware Events dominate the metaphorical construal of [pro + find x-self].

Table 6. Cross-corpora frequency ratios of [p*+find$_v$+ ppx*], by pronoun and category

	he	they	she	I	you	it	we
SA	26.5	11.5	59	55	30.5	1	17.5
SA-UE	70.5	86.5	33.5	41.5	61	85.5	78
TSM	2	1	2.5	1	2	3.5	2
PNS	0	0	0.5	0	0.5	0.5	0.5
X	1	1.5	3.5	1	4.5	0.5	1
?	0	0	0	0.5	0.5	0	0
literal	0	0	0	0	0.5	0	0
DUPL	0	0	0	0	0.5	0	1

Another observation from Table 6 concerns the SA to SA-UE frequency ratios for the plural pronouns *they* and *we* and the impersonal pronoun *it*. By far the most frequently instantiated subcategory is the SA-UE construal, with a difference of 75, 84.5 and 60.5 points, respectively, compared to the SA construal. Upon reflection, however, the results for the plural pronouns are logical. An embodied, internal perceptual awareness is difficult to describe for a group of people, each person usually having their own individual perceptions and awareness. Thus, describing this generally or holistically for number of people is counterintuitive. However, this does not account for the 84.5-point value differentiation for the pronoun *it*. A likely motivation for *it* to show similar frequency patterning is that *it* refers to a singular, non-human, non-sentient antecedent. As such, describing an embodied, perceptual awareness is also counterintuitive. This can be seen in the following SA-UE examples. The first one is reference to Iran's nuclear program's computer system, called *Stuxnet*:

207. And then, depending on where *it found itself*, Stuxnet was supposed to self-
destruct.   (COCA:2010.MAG.Newsweek)

Another example construes the human *body* as non-sentient (i.e., THE BODY IS A MACHINE conceptual metaphor).

> 208. But the body is very efficient, " says Maxwell. " It adapts quickly to <u>whatever</u> <u>position or movement pattern</u> *it finds itself* <u>in</u> most often.
>
> (COCA:2014.MAG.MensHealth)

The next example construes a metonymic antecedent in which *Atlanta* stands for the Atlantic Olympic Committee organizers, referred to by the impersonal pronoun.

> 209. When Atlanta started bidding for the 1996 summer games, *it found itself* <u>in</u> <u>a pair of expensive, no holds barred competitions.</u>   (COCA:1999.SPOK.ABC_Nightline)

Thus, there is really nothing unusual about the high rate of association of *it* with the SA-UE category, once the antecedent and its semantics are delineated according to their 'function in use' across a spectrum of genres and in sufficient number within context.

Another observation concerns the difference in frequency between the singular and plural first-person pronouns, *I* and *we*. There is a much more balanced differential for SA and SA-UE for the singular than the plural, *I* instantiating 55% and 41.5% for SA and SA-UE, respectively. In contrast, for *we*, SA instantiated 17.5% compared to 78% for SA-UE, a 60.5% difference. The results of this are significant ($p=0$, $p<.05$)[48]. The motivation for this can be proposed again here as the awkwardness of construing SA with anything other than a singular, first person experiencer. However, when the experiencer is the first person singular, the likelihood of instantiating SA vs. SA-UE is almost equal.

As with much data-based research, there are anomalous results in the present data here as well. Specifically, the third person masculine pronoun shows a higher association with SA-UE construal while the feminine associates more frequently with the SA construal, the difference being significant (p-value$=.0000001$, at $p<.05$)[49]. This is perhaps, at first glance, a counter-intuitive result. Why would masculine and feminine pronouns display significant differences for the two types of Self-Aware events? A few examples may help to clarify this:

---

[48] Contingency table: Categories=SA, SA-UE; Groups=I, we.
[49] Contingency table: Categories=SA, SA-UE; Groups=he; she.

210. For decades, *he found himself* at the center of the nation's biggest crises
    and most perilous challenges…   (COCA:2015:NEWS.USAToday)

211. Morrissey is a product of the political climate *he finds himself* in, a period of
    the reformist Left…   (BNC:CAE.W_pop_lore)

212. …that mystical source of everything Claire held true. In weaker moments,
    she found herself thinking, "What if it wasn't real?"

                                                (COCA:2015.FIC.Bk.FirstFrost)

213. Her patience in equally short supply, *she found herself* exasperated, not for
    the first time, by Peony's snide tongue.   (BNC:A0D.W_fict.prose)

A possible motivation for the feminine vs. masculine SA-UE results, shown in the examples above, derives from social, gender-biased stereotypes, where male-dominant models control business, politics and financially-oriented situations. As such, they often describe external situations (i.e., the SA-UE construal). On the other stereotypical side of the fence, so to speak, is the feminine model, one of introspection and emotion, often describing thoughts and feelings, and thus, the high frequency of the more internal and perception-based SA-type construal. This proposal is based on the data, not on sociolinguistic theory. But linguistic and/or social gender bias is not a novel concept. It is plausible, and indeed likely, that this kind of social gender bias is reflected in language and the mass media that disseminates the language. Sociolinguistic analysis, however, not being the focus of the present research, will not be discussed at length. The issue is raised here only as one likely explanation for the discrepancies in the third person masculine and feminine pronoun data. Although the data cannot cover all possible language registers and scenarios, it would be an interesting (albeit monumental) undertaking to discover to what extent these results change (if at all) when a wider variety of registers and regional varieties of English are included.

7.4.1. Fuzzy construals for [p*][find][ppx*]

It was sometimes difficult to determine whether an event construed self-awareness of an embodied perception (SA) or the experiencer's awareness of being unexpectedly involved in an external situation (SA-UE), especially for plural and impersonal pronouns. This was due to the various types of metonymic antecedents that were predicated, e.g., animal(s), groups of people, company(s), government(s), etc. However, even though many of these pronouns were metonymic in their mapping, the main criteria for determining SA and SA-UE categories remained unchanged. For SA Events, the direct perceptual involvement in the action centers the action within the perceiver/experiencer, in contrast to SA-UE events in which the focus of the construal is an external event in which the experiencer's internal, embodied perceptions only play a relatively minor part in the event action. The FoA, i.e., the immediately relevant object of the construed awareness, is a critical factor for resolving the ambiguity between SA and SA-UE. For example, in the sentence below, even though two people are involved in the event, (which often takes the SA-UE construal due to the difficulty of simultaneously expressing two people's embodied perceptions), the following example was determined to be SA due the direct perceptual content of the action (*back in bed*, i.e., having intercourse)[50] as well as the emphasis on each subjects' perceptual awareness of those actions.

214. ...*they* almost always *found themselves* either screaming at each other or
back in bed where words were rendered meaningless...   (COCA:2004.FIC.Iris)

An SA-UE event, on the other hand, construes a situation that is external to the experiencer. In these cases, the experiencers are construed as having little control over their situations; they are circumstantial participants in an unfolding event that is, often suddenly, brought to their attention.

215. What adolescents say they will do may be very different from what occurs
when *they find themselves* in the middle of an emotionally charged situation.
                                        (COCA:2007.ACAD.SocialWork)

The word *situation* is used in example 215 and therefore seems at first glance to be an SA-UE construal. However, the supporting context *adolescents say they will do* (construing an internally-initiated action) as well as the adolescents being *in the middle* of an *emotionally charged situation* (construing and focusing on the feelings of the experiencers in the present moment) overrides the SA-UE conception categorization. The example was marked SA due this contextual evidence.

---

[50] The first FoA, *screaming at each other*, was not considered here due to its reciprocal (i.e., non-reflexive) function.

Another issue concerns the first-person plural pronoun *we* which is used both for two or more individuals as well as for a group of people. The same criteria were used here as with impersonal pronouns discussed above. If the experiencer displayed metonymic and/or metaphoric properties and the FoA referred to an awareness of some embodied self-perception, it was marked SA Event, as in sentence 216 below. Both experiencers (plural and therefore typically SA-UE) are sharing the action of *ringing the bell*. The physical action is originated and completed by both experiencers, construed as shared performers of the action, and they are both perceptually aware of themselves performing that action.

216. But surely hotels are open to guests? It seems not. <u>On arrival</u> *we find ourselves*
<u>ringing the second bell</u>.   (BNC:AHC.W_newsp.brdsht_nat_misc)

If the FoA were an externally-conceived event, as in psychodynamic force (Gilquin 2010a; Talmy 2001b) shown in example 217 below, then it was marked SA-UE. In this example, being *unable* to do something is a preventative force, and that force is initiated outside the Self:

217. ...the South of England in particular, whose support we need.' If *we find ourselves*, as we
did, <u>unable to campaign, to argue, to debate</u>...   (BNC: W_newsp_brdsht_nat_misc)

One example of how complicated an event construal can be is the following:

218. *We found ourselves* <u>in the kitchen</u> where a well-groomed girl was washing up...
                    (BNC:A2C.W_newsp_brdsht_nat_social)

When the token alone is considered, this seems to be an SA event relating to the internal, perceptual awareness of the Self in some physical space. However, upon examination of the expanded context (below), this example is revealed to be a film review. The pronoun *we* is used as a general reference, referring to all of the film's viewers being shown a spatial location in the film, an externally-placed event. This is not in reference to any particular individuals' perception, except for the visual experience happening on screen, (the visual scene being external to all involved in the action). Because of this evidence, this example was marked SA-UE.

Expanded context for example number 483:

> SOME months ago I saw a television documentary on hostels for young homeless people in London. The voice-over described the need for accommodation for the thousands of unemployed youngsters who pour hopefully into London every year, while the camera panned around the sparse but well-kept lodgings. *We found ourselves* <u>in the kitchen</u> where a well-groomed girl was washing up -one of the tasks for which residents were responsible in this co-operative household. As the narrator explained that' Jane would soon have to move on', because she was reaching the limit of her maximum stay in the council-owned hostel, we watched her rinse the sink, wipe the draining board and hang up the dishcloth.

Thus, proper construal of an event is dependent on the context in which it is construed and predicated. To better understand the immediate context of *find x-self* (and other constructions discussed below), further delineation of the FoA is discussed in the next section.

7.4.2. More about the FoA

Descriptions of the FoA for SA Events show it to be a obligatory part of *find x-self*, not optional nor adjunctive in its construal. The FoA can be considered the semantic linchpin for the proper delineation of *find x-self* constructions. In previous descriptions, relatively simple FoA examples were provided for ease of explanation. As might be expected, though, conceptual transparency is not always the case. For example, there were instances where the FoA was itself metaphoric, leading to ambiguity of the conceptual status of the overall event. In these cases, concise mapping of the FoA construal as well as broader contexts were necessary. Again, at the risk of repetitiveness, what this means is that taken together, the specific *find x-self* construction, the FoA and the support context are often all necessary conceptual components for appropriate meaning retrieval.

> 219. ...time and again, *artists have found themselves* <u>in a barren field wondering how to revivify art</u>. (COCA:2010.ACAD.AmerScholar)

In order to illustrate this, consider example 219 above. The FoA *in a barren field* is metaphoric, the SOURCE being understood along the lines of 'insubstantial artistic production'. Without knowing this, the literal meaning of the FoA may be mistakenly construed (i.e., the artists are literally *in a barren field*). Upon review of the expanded context below, the appropriate metaphoric construal can be resolved, i.e., that *barren field* refers to, or is mapped onto, 'a slump in artistic fervor or production', and the artists, experiencing this slump, are 'wondering how to renew their endeavors' (i.e., *revivify art*).

Expanded context (abridged):

If their solution called for an immersion in culture, Caravaggio turned once again to the very careful study of nature. Such bursts of wonder seem inevitably bracketed by slumps: time and again, *artists have found themselves* in a barren field wondering how to revivify art. Moments of great fertility alternate with drought. Bursts of energy are followed by exhaustion. As our tour continues, the Baroque itself becomes conventionalized, and we wander disconsolate through acres of 18th- and 19th-century Italian art. Yes, little seeds can be found in the chaff, and " occasionally even full-blown glories like Tiepolo. (COCA: 2010.ACAD.AmerScholar)

The FoA alone invites a choice of readings. One is the choice between literal vs. metaphorical (i.e., literally or metaphorically *in a barren field*). Another involves the overall predication and the choice between a construed embodied perception (SA) vs. some externally initiated situation (SA-UE). In the above example, this reflects the difference, respectively, between the focus on each individual artists' *wondering* vs. the focus on 'the creative sterility of the artistic community'. There can be, of course, no 'absolute' determination. Even if consultation with each speaker/author were feasible, the reasons for a particular use of an expression might be subconscious, and reflection on the expression in afterthought might not be completely accurate. In the above example, an SA event determination was deemed appropriate due to the awareness of the active, embodied, perceptual thought-emotion of the FoA, i.e., *wondering* (about an artistic slump, metaphorically in a barren field).[51] This kind of decision-making, based on contextual clues, is vital for the proper evaluation and calculation of data and their analyses. It also demonstrates how various subtleties and choices are available for the construal of a given expression and the importance of consulting expanded contexts for any detailed analysis, especially metaphoric expressions.

As just mentioned, the function and construal of the FoA in relation to the main event is critical for proper analysis. If one assumes that the FoA is only a typical adjunct (i.e., optional) to its clause, what are the consequences of this with regard to Self-Aware events? The result is that a different conception is construed, this being the True-Self Metaphor. Using the previous example, according to the meaning of the TSM construal, *artists* have become aware of their

---

[51] The phrase *in a barren field* was analyzed as metaphorical due to the plural marking of the antecedent *artists*. It would be highly unusual (although admittedly, not impossible) to construe many artists literally walking into a barren field just to *wonder* about their situation, especially since they would all be entering the same barren field due to the singular marking of the noun *field*.

deep psychological or spiritual Selves and this happens metaphorically or non-metaphorically *in a barren field* (perhaps a special field conducive to self-realization?) where they *wonder* about their art:

> 220. ...time and again, *artists have found themselves* (in a barren field wondering how to revivify art). (COCA:2010.ACAD.AmerScholar)

Parentheses are used here so that the adjunct can be easily differentiated from the main clause, but the TSM event is easier to construe if the location is changed, as in example 221 below:

> 221. ...time and again, *artists have found themselves* (in a yoga ashram wondering how to revivify art.)

This conception becomes even more clear once the FoA is deleted altogether:

> 222. ...time and again, *artists have found themselves*.

In the original SA-event example 219, the FoA *in a barren field* is not conceptually adjunct. It is a crucial component that cannot be deleted or changed without changing the main event's core meaning. This shows how complete and relevant contexts must be considered when analyzing metaphoric examples. An interpretation within the boundaries of the token alone often cannot resolve the intended construal. Broader contextual clues guide the choice of construal and predication and these must be incorporated into the analysis for proper denotation and delineation.

Concerning the types of construal expressed in the FoA for *find x-self*, there often appear variations of the following: *in a situation, in a position or location, involved in/with something, etc.* Although perhaps counter-intuitive, the presence or absence of these terms alone was not complete verification of the SA vs SA-UE distinction. These needed to be analyzed carefully in order to distinguish between the two. For example, 'location' in and of itself was not a definite determiner of SA-UE for the following:

> 223. As the crowd gathered around the elevators, *a man* in a blue maintenance coverall *found himself* next to a little black girl. (COCA:1991.FIC.Bk:FromDuskTill)

Even though this may be construed situationally as SA-UE, i.e., '*the man* realized his close proximity to *a little black girl*', this case was determined to be the SA-event type because the *man* is suddenly and unexpectedly aware of his physical, spatial perception, an internally-based experience. This is supported by the double-underlined context appearing in the clause before the metaphoric main clause, its temporal aspect (i.e., simultaneous actions, instantiated by the preposition *as*) perhaps priming the conception of 'sudden perceptual awareness'.

> 224. In the early '70s *I found myself* in Columbus, Ohio, at a church.
> (COCA:1992.FIC.Analog)

On the other hand, example 224 above was marked SA-UE because the temporal event is spread out over a decade, making it difficult to construe a direct, embodied perception of a single experience. Here, there are two competing viewpoints within the conception; one at the time of the event and the other at the time of reporting of the event. Only supporting context can help verify the dominant construal of the token.

> 225. SA: Last month, *I found myself* in an unknown place. No idea how I got there.
> (BNC:HA0.W_fict_prose)

> 226. SA-UE: Next morning *Lucy found herself* seated alone at the corner table,
> and when Jean brought her breakfast... (BNC:HHB.W_fict_prose)

Related to this, for FoAs that construe spatial locations, a distinction needed to be made between being 'proprioceptively aware of oneself in a location' compared to being 'situationally aware of oneself in a location'. Basically, this amounts to the same distinctions made thus far regarding the differences between SA and SA-UE, although more specific to spatial location. In examples such as those above, when deciding whether [[find x-self] + FoA^{location}] was SA or SA-UE, conceptual premeditation, i.e., intention, was also used as a guiding factor. If the experiencer arrived at a location that was planned, foreseen or habitual, it was labeled SA-UE. If, however, the experiencer arrived at a location suddenly with no previous intentions, then it was labeled SA. The rationale for this decision is that the non-intentional event is comparable to a 'sudden awareness of proprioceptive stimuli in relation to one's surroundings'. To be in a planned, foreseen, or habitual location does not demand this kind of attention to spatial perception unless some other new or noteworthy action occurs within that space. This difference adds credence to the previous Langackerian analysis where it was postulated that two meanings of *find* be proposed, a 'search' construal (in which one searches for and finds an object), and a 'non-search' construal (in which one happens upon an object unintentionally). Lending support for this proposal are SA Events in which (un)intentionality (aka 'mirativity') are overtly construed in the event, as in the example below:

Expanded context:

> Mr-RUSH: It's true. Life had been kind of upside down for a little bit, and *I'd* just gone through a divorce and <u>suddenly</u> *found myself* living in Wyoming, <u>to my astonishment</u>, and I was in this little log house right next to the Snake River by the foot of the Tetons.
> SIMON: I mean, I have to ask. Did you just, like, stop the car 'cause you were cold and decided to live there? *Or what do you mean, you found yourself* in Wyoming <u>to your surprise</u>?
> Mr-RUSH: Well, there was this woman...
> SIMON: Oh, right. OK.
> Mr-RUSH: ... who is now my wife. And she was involved, actually, with bringing the gray wolf back to Yellowstone.
> SIMON: Mm-hmm.
> Mr-RUSH: So <u>I ended up in Wyoming</u> and basically that's what the song is about.
>
> (COCA:2000.SPOK.NPR_Saturday)

In the dialogue above, the meaning of the Self-Aware event expressed by the interviewee, *Simon*, is confirmed by the interviewer, *Mr. Rush*. The interviewer specifically asks about the meaning of *suddenly found myself living in Wyoming*. Why would this need confirmation? Because under 'normal' circumstances, one usually plans a change of residence; it is an important decision that involves some intention and is rarely a surprise to oneself. To *suddenly* do this without intention needed further elaboration for clarity of proper meaning. This example evidences the complexity and subtlety of the Self-Aware event construal but also shows that consulting the full context can resolve many issues concerning ambiguous construal.

These conceptual ambiguities do not only stem from different conceptions of the verb and its metaphoricity and/or from nuances of the FoA. Conceptual 'fuzziness' also occurs due to the type of antecedent that is predicated, the topic of the next section.

7.5. Nouns as Antecedents: [n*][find][ppx*]

The aim of this section is to explore in more depth the components that make up the antecedent-experiencer, specifically, the differences in the conceptual coding of full nouns when occurring as Antecedent/Experiencers of the *find x-self* construction.

A search was conducted (see Appendix 4) in which the antecedent-experiencers were full nouns, not pronouns. The input search parameter was [n*][find][ppx*]. In the BNC, the search, sorted by lemma, yielded 111 tokens ($n \geq 5$), instantiating 16 nouns, 75% of which were feminine names. Proper names hit at a rate of 29.7% and overwhelmingly construed the SA event type at a rate of 98.6%. The opposite result was yielded for all other types of nouns, where SA-UE dominated the data at a rate of 85.7%. This is statistically significant (p=0). In other words, there is a positive correlation between proper names and SA construal and 'non-names' and SA-UE construal, the two types being strongly predictable in these contexts. Thus, it can be confidently stated that for British English, when the experiencer-antecedent is a proper name, the SA type will more likely be construed and when all other types of nouns are predicated as the antecedent, it is highly likely that SA-UE will be construed. Although there is no way to test this prediction for all cases (spoken and written) in the language at large, the strength of the data here provides good reason to believe that this will be so.

One noteworthy result was the lack of masculine names. One possible reason for this may be, again, a reflection of social gender bias. Many of the above scenarios reflect a lack of social control of female gender roles (there are many cases in the FoA in which women are *following a man, moved by a man, staring at a man, in a man's arms or embrace*, etc.) Taken from the opposite (and perhaps more feminist) viewpoint, another explanation may be that this result indicates society's perception of women as being endowed with enhanced or keenly developed mental and/or emotional self-awareness. In other words, women may be viewed and perhaps more socially encouraged to introspect thoughts and emotions. Although intuitively plausible, due to space constraints, in-depth sociolinguistic analysis will have to be left for those specialized in such areas, but this is likely a productive area of future research.

Having proposed possible motivations for the results of the data related to proper names, a note of caution is now timely. The retrieved data, coming entirely from the FICTION register, is limited in its applicability across the spectrum of language use throughout the whole of society and may not represent the actual social environment nor attitudes of the general populace. More specifically, of the 12 female names ($n= 70$), 17 different sources were represented, many of them romance-type popular novels. This is hardly representative of the British fiction register in general, or of the overall corpus. What can be stated here, without reservation, is the significance of noun types to SA events in the respective data sets retrieved here for the search parameter [n*][find][ppx*].

In the BNC data, there were no examples of TSM, PNS nor LIT, but there was one antecedent token that was not congruent with the predication's 'true' antecedent, and this was categorically corrected. This example is presented below:

227. Too many *teachers* of deaf people *find themselves* learning communication skills on the job -- a slow process...   (BNC:FPJ.W_ac_soc_science)

In this case, the antecedent-experiencer is not *deaf people*, but *teachers*. This issue of antecedent-pronoun accuracy was an overall point of concern, for obvious reasons, and was specifically discussed previously in the methodological procedures (procedural step two) used for this research. There were samples where a token's antecedent was actually part of larger, complex antecedent-experiencer and the tagged 'noun' was actually an adjective. For example, in the COCA example below, the preverbal noun was *countries*, e.g., *...countries found themselves...*, but the actual Experiencer was *junior diplomats*.

228. *...junior diplomats* from both countries *found themselves* ...
                                            (COCA:2012.MAG.HistoryToday)

For all of these types of cases, the noun-experiencer was amended and categorized appropriately for analysis.

In the BNC, all cases of Experiencer proper names construed the SA-type, with one exception, example 229, and all are of the [W_fict_prose] register, except one from the [W_biography] register (see 230, below).

229. SA-UE: Guido and Agnese had so much to talk about, and *Ronni found herself* included with perfect ease.   (BNC:JXT.W_fict_prose)

230. But it was a haste they paid for dearly in emotional terms. *Laura found herself* repeatedly hurt by accusations in the press that they had become tax exiles...
                                            (BNC:GU9. W_biography)

Table 7. Contingency table (integer values) for SA vs. SA-UE and fiction vs. non-fiction in the BNC

	SA	SA-UE
[W_fict_prose]	70	1
all other registers	3	33

It is timely to comment briefly on what was and will be shown throughout the discussion to be the high frequency of tokens in the fiction register in the data (labelled FIC and fict in the COCA and BNC corpora, respectively) for the SA-type construal, and vice versa for the non-fiction register and SA-UE event data. The data can be analyzed along these four parameters, namely, SA vs. SA-UE and fiction vs all other registers, shown in Table 7. The BNC values are significant (p=0), meaning that the relationships between fiction and SA and between all other registers and SA-UE are dependent. One reason for this relates to discourse point of view, specifically that of the narrator/author in relation to the main character within the text. For the fiction register, because the author *is* the character (in reality), it is quite easy for the author to place him/herself mentally inside the psyche of the character. The author can then express that character's perceptual self-awareness using the literary voice of the narrator while predicating the third person noun antecedent. This is rare in discourse. To assume knowledge of another person's perceptual awareness is perhaps an intimate step too far. Although it is presumptuous to assume to intimately know the internal mental state of another person with which one is linguistically engaged, this is easily attained in the fiction genre due to the intimacy of the author with the character(s) in the text. Again, this proposal is borne solely out of the results of the data and therefore is likely accurate, but also possibly double-edged. In other words, this data-driven hypothesis is objective but it lacks the expert knowledge of literary theory. For the purposes of here, the former must take precedence.

The same search parameter in the COCA corpus, i.e., [n*][find][ppx*] (sorted by lemma, $n \geq 10$), yielded 678 tokens and 43 noun lemmas. In this data set, however, only one token was a feminine name, *Mary*, (n=12, 1.8%), and two were masculine names (n=31, 4.6%), these being the former U.S. Presidents *Bush* and *Clinton*. In total, proper names hit a mean of 6.3%, differing from the BNC by 23.4%. In the COCA, *Mary* instantiated an SA-type rate of 83.3%, somewhat similar to that of the BNC (98.6%). There is no BNC data to compare masculine names, but within the COCA data, the tokens had different construal profiles from each other. *President Bush* instantiated an SA-type rate of 31.6% while the SA-type rate for *President Clinton* was 45.5%. This result is likely due to register difference. When analyzed by individual register, the correlations are weak; however, it was determined that all registers (i.e., SPOK, MAG, NEWS) be tallied as a set, as everything presidents say and do, due to their wide-ranging clout and influence, is fodder for all forms of mass media. Supporting this decision is the fact that there are zero hits for the FICTION register. Thus, calculating the amalgamated register group (i.e., SPOK + MAG + NEWS), the frequency ratios comparing SA to SA-UE are 36.7% and 60%, respectively, revealing a roughly twofold preference for the SA-UE-type construal when the antecedent-experiencers are American presidents. This now seems logical and even obvious. High-profile politicians are often thrust into various externally-initiated situations that they might not have foreseen. This result was unexpected and again reveals how, by engaging in corpus research, one is able to uncover various types of distinctions and test claims with some degree of reliability.

Another pattern revealed from the analysis of the COCA data is the number and type of metonymically-construed Experiencers. Although the literally-construed plural noun *people* was the most frequent (*n*=81; 11.9%), and other plural or general nouns were the majority (e.g., *woman, man, child, family etc.*), metonymically-construed Experiencers were a prominent factor in the data, the frequency ratio of metonymically-construed nouns being about 25%. Total frequencies and ratios as well as SA and SA-UE ratios of metonymic Experiencers are shown in Table 8.

Table 8. COCA data for [n*][find$_v$][ppx*]: Frequencies and ratios for SA and SA-UE-types for metonymically construed experiencers

Metonymically-construed Experiencer + (pro^{refl})	FREQ, ratio	SA	SA-UE
State (itself)	n=40, 5.6%	15%	85%
Government (itself)	n=25, 3.5%	24%	76%
Administration (itself)	n=21, 2.9%	27.3%	71.4%
Church (itself)	n=18, 2.5%	44.4%	66.7%
Company (itself)	n=15, 2.1%	13.3%	86.7%
Industry (itself)	n=15, 2.1%	33.3%	66.7%
U.S. (itself)	n=12, 1.7%	16.7%	83.3%
Country (themselves)	n=11, 1.5%	9.1%	91%
Country (itself)	n=11, 1.5%	27.3%	72.7%
Total mean ratio		23.4%	77.7%

Within the metonymically-construed Experiencer data, the SA-UE to SA ratio is roughly 3:1, dominated by the conceptual metonym ORGANIZATION STANDS FOR THE PEOPLE

IN THE ORGANIZATION, similar to the conceptual metaphor ORGANIZATIONS ARE PEOPLE (G. Lakoff & Johnson 1980). Due to the reflexive construction, supposed sentience of the antecedent-experiencer is necessary in order for the *find x-self* metaphor to be appropriately construed (how can a non-sentient object be aware of itself?), and so the antecedent-experiencers are construed in sentient terms. References to 'individual people in an organization' are replaced by 'the name of the organization'. As such, for these types of examples, due to the specific metonymic mapping of the antecedent-reflexive pronoun pair and not the overall metaphor, and its reliance on the metaphorically-construed verb, this is coined "conceptual metonym".

For cases in which the antecedent-experiencer is metonymically construed, the SA-UE type is 54.3% more frequent. The likely reason for this is the nature of the metonyms' mappings. Because the metonyms in this data are politically and/or financially related, they are more likely to be mapped onto situations in society, not on an individual's mental state per se, but on the experiencers' realization of some surprising or unexpected external situation. We can calculate these registers using the same parameters used previously for the BNC data, i.e., the aggregate set [SPOK + MAG + NEWS + ACAD] and compare it with the FIC register. As seen in Table 9, there is almost triple the frequency ratio (72.3%) for the aggregate set than the FIC category (27.7%). When specifically looking at the SA-type construal for each of these metonyms (see Table 8), none of the 47 SA-type tokens are from the FIC register, further supporting this 'situational' hypothesis for metonymic experiencer-antecedents.

Table 9. COCA search [n*][find][ppx*] : Frequencies and per million totals by register

	FREQ	PER MIL	ratio (%)
SPOKEN	575	5.3	10.3
FICTION	1479	14.1	27.7
MAGAZINE	1225	11.1	21.9
NEWSPAPER	1166	11	21.6
ACADEMIC	976	9.4	18.5
Total	5421	50.9	100%

Lastly, all of the metonymically construed nouns pairs with the singular impersonal pronoun *itself*, except for *Country*, which is construed as both plural (*countries find/found themselves*) and singular (*country finds/found itself*). The frequencies and ratios here are noteworthy. Whereas the plural form expresses the SA-UE type construal 91% of the time, the singular form construes SA-UE at a ratio of 72.7%. Conversely, the SA-type construal is more frequent (27.3%) when the antecedent-experiencer is singular than when plural (9.1%). This is significant (p= 0.00149) and adds support to the claim here that it is more common and natural to construe the SA type for a single experiencer than it is for multiple people or a group. This has to do with the nature of perceptual self-awareness being a highly intimate mental state and is therefore easier to express a single entity's perceptual awareness than it is to generalize about a number of individuals or group.

7.5.1. Nouns as Antecedents: sorted by 'word'

Due to limitations of mining certain aspects of the data in the above lemma-based search such as tense, aspect and number, another search was conducted in which tokens were sorted 'by word' in order to test whether other collocational patterns (Hunston & Francis 2000; Sinclair 1991; Stefanowitsch & Gries 2003) would emerge. The input search parameter [n*][find][ppx*] was entered (*n* = most frequent 100). The total number of tokens was 837 in the COCA and 305 in the BNC (see Appendix 5).

The most frequent construction in both corpora was [*people find themselves*] (COCA: *n*=63 (7.5%); BNC: *n*=21 (6.9%)). Again here, as seen in the lemma sorting query, the BNC had many more proper name tokens (77%) than the COCA (25%).

Analyzing the COCA data with respect to past and present verb tense (N + find$_{past/present}$ Pro$_{refl}$), there was only a marginal difference (4.9%) between the past and present tense, (present= 439 (52.4%); past= 398 (47.6%); discrepancy ratio= 4.8%)). However, there was a large discrepancy in the BNC (present= 71(23.3%); past= 234 (76.7%); discrepancy ratio= 53.5%)). The values for the BNC are significant (p= 2.3E-05). Motivations for this are tentatively attributed to regional variation. Thus, when the antecedent is a noun, in British English (or at least within the texts represented in this corpus) the past tense is likely to occur whereas in American English there is no direct relationship found.

Perhaps more telling is the relationship between verb tense and antecedent number. In both corpora, there are significant dependencies between these categories (p=0) (see Table 10). For [n*][find][ppx*], there is a greater likelihood that a singular antecedent and past tense verb occur together, and conversely, that a plural antecedent and present tense verb occur together. When these results are added to the previous results suggesting that singular-person nouns more often construe SA-type events (and vice-versa), the overall findings add empirical support to the claim that meaning and form cluster together into collocational patterns and that those patterns have meaning (Deignan 2007; Hunston & Francis 2000; Stefanowitsch & Gries 2007).

Table 10. Frequencies of [n*][find][ppx*] according to tense and subject number

COCA	present	past	TOTAL
singular	134	233	367
plural	315	148	463
BNC			
singular	14	240	254
plural	59	4	63
TOTAL	522	625	singular total = 621 plural total= 526

Turning attention to the type of metonymy of the antecedent, in the COCA there were many more metonymically-construed antecedents (n=219, 26.2%) than in the BNC (n=25, 8.2%). The metonymic antecedents (in alphabetical order), their singular/plural frequencies, and present/past tense frequencies in the COCA and BNC are shown in Tables 11 and 12, respectively.

Table 11. COCA search [n*][find][ppx*]; metonymically construed antecedents, sorted by word

	singular	plural	present tense	past tense
administration	21	-	13	8
allies	-	5	-	5
America	6	-	6	-
church	17	-	10	7
city	5	-	5	-
company	15	-	6	9
countries	-	14	7	7
country	9	-	9	-
families	10	-	5	5
family	8	-	-	8
government	25	-	11	14
groups	-	5	5	-
industry	11	-	-	11
Iraq	5	-	5	-
police	-	5	-	5
president	17	-	10	7
states	-	30	15	15
U.S.	7	-	7	-

universities	-	7	7	-
world	7	-	7	-
TOTAL	163	63	128	101

Table 12. BNC search [n*][find][ppx*]; metonymically construed antecedents, sorted by word

	singular	plural	present tense	past tense
BBC	2	-	-	2
Britain	2	-	-	2
council	6	-	6	-
family	2	-	2	-
Germany	2	-	-	2
house	2	-	2	-
institutions	-	2	2	-
Korea	2	-	-	2
police	-	2	2	-
schools	-	3	3	-
TOTAL	18	7	17	8
[COCA+BNC] TOTAL	181	70	145	109

In the COCA, metonymic singular antecedents are twice as frequent than the plural forms ($n=14$ and $n=7$, respectively). When this is combined with the data on tense, however, no significant relationship[52] is found (p=0.2541). Similarly for the BNC, metonymic singular antecedents are slightly more than twice as frequent ($n=7$ vs. $n=3$, respectively), and here as well, this is not significant when a relationship to tense is tested (p=0.0573). Thus, even though use of the past and present related to antecedent number is significant for the whole data set [n*][find][ppx*], when the antecedent is construed metonymically, no significant relationship is found, except on a single axis, i.e., the antecedent is about twice as likely to be singular, regardless of tense. Further, the present tense is more than twice as likely than the past tense, regardless of antecedent number. These findings occur in both corpora and differ from the more generic [n*][find][ppx*] (i.e., metonyms not taken into consideration), where [singular + past tense] cases are 20% more likely.

These results reveal just how complex and subtle metaphoric data can be. Why do the results of the data differ when antecedents are metonymic? The singular antecedent is the easier of the two to explain, namely, that many of the antecedents are construed as collective nouns,

---

[52] For this and the next calculation, integer frequency values were used in the Fisher Exact contingency tables.

i.e., singular entities that contain within them the individual people, e.g., administration, America, family, police, etc. Although this is fairly straightforward, the difference in verb tense remains unresolved. Why should the present tense be more frequent when the noun is metonymic? The analysis here has not revealed any identifiable pattern, and so, at least for the moment, this point remains for future research. This uncertainty leads into the next section concerning the analysis of ambiguous metaphoric construal for full-noun antecedents.

7.5.2. 'Fuzzy' construals for [n*][find][ppx*]

In the present era and with the technology we now possess, description of language conception, construal, and predication is still an imprecise business and so the utmost effort must be made for transparency and reliability (and repeatability) of the data and its analysis. Thus, along with uncovering systematic consistencies that explain much of the data, the importance of revealing and delineating ambiguous cases cannot be overstated. SA Events are verifiable with few exceptions, proving to be a reliable conceptual paradigm for metaphoric *find x-self*. However, there are vague examples whose categorizations are not easily made. The discussion in this section describes this decision-making process and challenges related to such cases.

When antecedent-pronoun pairs are metonymically construed, there were some instances where the difference between SA and SA-UE were difficult to distinguish.

> 231. SA: *The Alberta government found itself* trying to battle a tax it had vigorously objected to during the summer...   (COCA:2004.ACAD.CanadianStud)

> 232. SA-UE: ...that *the federal government found itself* wasting taxpayer dollars that were supposed to be helping young people go to college...   (COCA:1995.MAG.WashMonth)

As explained thus far, the criterion used to distinguish between SA and SA-UE-types of construal was being able to construe (or not) an internal perceptual awareness as opposed to a situational unexpected awareness, respectively, for the metonymic antecedent. In the SA example 231 above, *the Alberta government* is construed as a sentient being (i.e., conceptual metonymy = GOVERMENT STANDS FOR GOVERMENT EMPLOYEES), which is trying *to battle a tax* (i.e., conceptual metaphor = ARGUMENT IS WAR). *Trying to battle* is construed as an internally based action and its perception, the force of the struggle, is being viscerally felt by the metonymic experiencer. This is supported by the double-underlined, emotionally-charged context, *vigorously objected to*. These pieces of contextual evidence reinforce an SA-type analysis. In the next SA-UE example 232, on the other hand, even though the *federal government* is construed metonymically as a PERSON, *wasting taxpayer dollars* does not correspond to any internal perception on the part of that metonymically construed entity. The construed action of *wasting* here is involuntary and as such, this action is considered based outside the realm of direct and embodied perception and thus an SA-UE-type construal.

As explained earlier, one other criterion for supporting the decision of SA or SA-UE was whether the experiencer was specific or general. When the experiencer referred to a specific person or people and their internal perceptions were described in an immediate and direct context, the event was labelled SA. In the example below, it was noticed, after reviewing the expanded text, that the antecedent refers to a particular family having ten individually-construed *children* and that the event takes into account each of their personal experiences in the social welfare system. Thus, the direct perceptual experiences of these *children* as individuals (as well as a group) added weight to an SA determination for this context.

> 233. SA: *The children found themselves in a foster care system* the state itself acknowledges is overwhelmed... (COCA:2003.SPOK.NBC_Dateline)

This is contrasted with the following SA-UE example in which *children* in general are aware of some external situation:

> 234. SA-UE: ...something must be done to improve the settings in which *the vast majority of children find themselves for at least part of the day.* (COCA:2004.ACAD.CanadianStud)

It was mentioned previously that phrases such as *situation, position*, etc. may influence the type of construal, but that it was not the sole determiner. In cases as those above and for most experiencers, when nouns in general are referred to, immediate, direct awareness of perceptions is difficult to justify and therefore they are more likely to be construed as SA-UE, as example 234 above with its situational cue *settings*. But again, each of these needs to be examined on a case-by-case basis, carefully considering the FoAs along with their expanded contexts.

Examples 235-236 below show the difference between SA and SA-UE events and the conceptual subtleties involved therein.

235. SA: ...the invasions of Afghanistan in 2001 and Iraq in 2003, *the*
United States found itself engaging in reactive transformation...
(COCA:2009.ACAD.ForeignAffairs)

236. SA-UE: By the end of the 1960s, *the United States found itself* engaged in
what political scientist Robert Justin Goldstein called " a cultural war...
(COCA:2007.MAG.MilitaryHist)

In 235, an SA-type example, *the United States* is a metonym for the members of the United States government, and the metonym construes those members as though they are a single, sentient being. As such, they may undergo the same kinds of direct experiences as any singular sentient being. The internally-initiated activity, *engaging in reactive transformation*, along with the support context of self-initiated *invasions*, encourage the SA categorization. Although the SA-UE example of 236 is similar to the first, it is categorized differently due to the metonymic experiencer's awareness of being involved in an external, unexpected situation, one that the experiencer is much more passively involved. The double-underlined, supporting contexts for both examples reinforce these differences. In 235, the experiencer takes the action initiation of *invading*, whereas in 236, there is only an indefinite time-frame, *by the end of the 1960's*, to set the conception. Here, the FoA verb tenses (*engaging* vs. *engaged*) are related to this conceptual difference. Although tense of the main verb sometimes plays a functional role in conception, as discussed earlier, this difference is not statistically significant and therefore cannot be said to play any major role in the overall analysis and results. However, because FoAs have such a strong influence on their metaphor's construal, each FoA must be analyzed critically. In examples 235 and 236, both main verbs are in the past tense but the tenses of the FoAs guide the reader/listener into conceptions in which the experiencer is more actively participating and initiating action in the first event (235) but is a more distanced and more passive participant in the second (236).

Another example showing how the FoA guides the conceptual differences between SA and SA-UE is the following:

237. *The Bush administration found itself* attacking Iraq militarily after years of supporting it
financially.   (COCA:1992.SPOK.ABC_Nightline)

An SA-type analysis considers the FoA verb *attacking* as an internal, directly perceived activity of the experiencer. On the other hand, for an SA-UE-type analysis, a group-oriented decision would strongly be taken into account in which the action is not solely based within a single metonymic experiencer *Bush administration*. Here, the metonym is more loosely interpreted, and members of *the administration* share in the decision-making process, thus, not strictly an internally initiated action and awareness. But along with these issues, other points need consideration for appropriate analysis such as the nature of the corpus register, in this case [Spoken: TV news program], as well as other contextual clues (double-underlined) found throughout the expanded context (see below). Taken together, the data suggests an internally-construed event, i.e., SA event, for example 237 above. Interestingly, the fourth line of the expanded context includes another case of *find x-self*, but in this case, SA-UE is the determination due to the externally-initiated action of accusations of *criminal actions* by the Democratic party to which *the President and his advisors* are suspected. Thus, a variety of contextual clues given by way of the FoAs and other related context assist to appropriately interpret the experiencer's activity/passivity in the event, and thus the quality of the Awareness of that event.

Expanded context (abridged):
When the United States and its Arab allies drove Iraqi troops out of Kuwait less than 18 months ago, it ended a bizarre turnaround in American foreign policy. *The Bush administration found itself* attacking Iraq militarily after years of supporting it financially. Now *the President and his advisers*, *find themselves* suspected, not only of bad judgment, but of possible criminal actions. For months, Democrats in Congress, have been exploring what they see as the policy mistakes, and George Bush's role in them. (COCA:1992.SPOK.ABC_Nightline)

Further complicating decisions about 'fuzzy' examples are tokens in which the FoA is itself metaphorical:

238. SA-UE: *Bush finds himself* swimming in similar historical tides, forging his own alliances... (COCA:2002:NEWS.Atlanta)

In this example, the FoA is metaphorical (e.g., *swimming in similar historical tides*) and denotes Bush's awareness of himself being in situations which are comparable to historic events. Even though the FoA verb *swimming* is a self-initiated action, it is metaphoric and thus here, the SOURCE loses its literal sense of 'aquatic physical self-propulsion' but keeps its sense of being 'surrounded by liquid'. This is supported by the metaphoric *tides* that construes an image of strong currents over which floating objects have little control. Thus, the metaphor means '*Bush* had little personal control over his external situation', a typical SA-UE construal.

One example where SA is warranted for a metaphoric (and/or metonymic) FoA is the following:

239. SA: As the week went on, *Bush found himself* saying in one breath that he wants to change the tone in Washington and work across the aisle, and in the next, laying into Gore for seven and a half years of failure. (COCA:2000.SPOK.NPR_Saturday)

Saying in one breath...and in the next is a fairly idiomatic (i.e., non-compositional) FoA, but the construal is considered an SA-type due the actual physical verbalizations of the experiencer and his awareness of those physical sensations. Granted, this is a borderline case and an SA-UE interpretation is also possible, e.g., one where *Bush* had uttered contradictory statements, but his awareness of those contradictions occurred at a later date and so they were unexpected and surprising even to him. However, in this case, due to the likely and very real possibility of the experiencer's direct perceptual awareness of his first utterance immediately followed by his second verbal assault on *Gore*, the SA-type categorization was deemed appropriate.

Another fuzzy example is the following:

240. SA: *Bush finds himself* under attack from both sides on abortion.
(COCA:1999.NEWS.Atlanta)

This example, perhaps contrary to expectation, has been categorized as SA because even though *under attack* implies the experiencer's unexpected involvement in the *attack*, it is proposed here that being *under attack* is the awareness of the direct physical and/or psychological sensations of being *attacked*. Again, in this and all fuzzy cases, event construals need to be analyzed on individual bases. Here, *under attack* is a conceptual metaphor (i.e., ARGUMENT IS WAR) that construes a situation in which the experiencer is surrounded by arguments from two sides. The FoA is the experiencer's awareness of the direct stimulus of that *attack*, a condition deemed within the experiencer's realm of immediate, internal perception, and as such, an SA-type construal. The expanded context corroborates this analysis. Here, *Bush*'s many controversial decisions are described, decisions that he directly instigated and initiated, and he therefore had direct knowledge and awareness of them and of their consequences, incongruent with an *unexpected event* analysis.

For similar examples in which total context is indispensable for appropriate construal, the words *situation* and *caught up in*, as part of the FoA are typically labeled SA-UE due to the construal of an external stimulus. However, in the following case, the experiencer is construed as more active in the embodied perceptions, evidenced both by the adverbials preceding the experiencer (i.e., *shocked*, *scared*) and by the psychological addendum (*overwhelmed*) in the sentence following the event. Therefore, in this case, the example is considered an SA event construal.

241. SA: ...no one has made a plan for this situation, and *shocked and scared family members find themselves* caught up in a maze of choices. They're overwhelmed.

(COCA:2013.MAG.SatEvenPost)

In another example of this type, the immediacy of the perceptions along with the focus on the experiencers' physical struggles support an SA event decision.

242. SA: Luckily, within moments the boat rolled upright again. But *crew members found themselves* caught in a maze of twisted rigging and ropes, struggling to get free...

(COCA:1999.SPOK.NBC_Dateline)

Examples containing *to face something* or *face to face with something* as part of the FoA were categorized as SA due to the metonym/metaphor *face*, suggesting a more intimate physical construal.

243. SA: *Scrooge finds himself* <u>face to face with a strange-looking being</u>.

(COCA:2006.FIC.Read)

244. ...*districts* <u>already facing the difficulty</u> of supporting teachers in high-poverty schools *find themselves* <u>with the extra burden of providing extensive In-service training</u>...

(COCA:2013.ACAD.RuralSpecEd)

245. But *a company finding itself* <u>in a crisis today faces pressures</u> far different in a landscape much more treacherous...

(COCA:2007.MAG.Fortune)

Cases in which an externally-based 'force-dynamic' construal was part of the FoA were marked SA-UE. This is due to the origin of the force being extrinsic to the Self, as discussed previously. This can be demonstrated by the following example:

246. SA-UE: When *I found myself* <u>having to learn French</u>, to memorize maps of Montreal, I had to quit the club.

(COCA:2010.Bk:GhostsDoingOrange)

Having to learn expresses an unwanted situation that one was perhaps not in control of, as far as the self-initiated action of *learning* is concerned. The extended context below supports this by evidencing the lack of control the experiencer felt.

Expanded context (abridged):

Once, when New York City was still New York City, I'd belonged to a squash club on Fifth Avenue. Someone I played with got it into his head that I was Canadian, introduced me to someone else - I let it go. It seemed impolite to insist. Within weeks I was tangled up in explanations, recriminations, and invented histories. When *I found myself* <u>having to learn French, to memorize maps of Montreal</u>, I had to quit the club.

In most cases, modal auxiliary verbs[53] (see Appendix 6), which express various states and levels of necessity and/or possibility, contribute a more indirect, externally-construed awareness of an event, and as such, typically, an SA-UE marking was determined appropriate, as in the examples below.

> 247. SA-UE: *She'd find herself* alone on the savannah, a fine treat for a bunch of lions.
> (COCA:2013.MAG.NewRepublic)

> 248. SA-UE: Could *she*, Colene, *find herself* trapped in this towerlike edifice?
> (COCA:1992.FIC.BkSF:FractalMode)

In examples 247 and 248, the events are not yet actualized (i.e., real) and this lends a conceptual quality that is not-yet-perceptually-embodied, i.e., more distanced, from the experiencer's point of view. On the other hand, sometimes even with a modal auxiliary, the actions have been actualized (at some point) or are a very real possibility and therefore the experiencer can be immediately and perceptually aware, as in the SA examples below.

> 249. SA: And every once in a great while, *I might find myself* peeling away a worthless canvas to find a Ver-meer beneath.   (COCA:2013.FIC.Bk:AppleOrcahrd)

> 250. SA:...*you may actually find yourself* getting weaker because your muscle will constantly be in the broken-down phase...   (COCA:1993.Mag.MensHealth)

Due to the possibility of either the SA-UE or SA event being construed, each token in this investigation was analyzed individually and given a designation based on the general guidelines discussed in previous sections.

One last example concludes this section.

> 251. ...some staffs over-schedule, one reason *patients* often *find themselves* waiting.
> (COCA:1990.NEWS.WashPost)

---

[53] In a search with parameters [_vm* [find][ppx*]] (i.e., [modal + find + any reflexive pronoun]) sorted by lemma, there were 1942 tokens in the COCA (n ≥10) and 535 in the BNC (n≥5).

In example 251, is the FoA *waiting* used from a personal, direct perceptual point of view (i.e., the experiencer *waiting*) or from a more external and situational point of view (i.e., the situation of *waiting*)? After examining the expanded context below, the overall topic of that news article was, *"The question your doctor doesn't ask: Are you satisfied?"* This article refers to an overall situation of health care and to a group of people who, according to the writer, probably share similar unpleasant situations to whom the writer then gives advice. The writer is not describing the awareness of a single individual's direct perception of *waiting*. Furthermore, as discussed in the previous section, plural and group antecedent-experiencers often take the SA-UE construal due to the difficulty of assigning the awareness of a direct perception onto more than one individual. For all of the above reasons, the example was marked SA-UE.

Expanded context (abridged):
We ask a lot of doctors. Patients must equally ask themselves: If I want to be satisfied with my care, what can I do? # I would say: # Show up on time for appointments. If you can't, phone as early as possible. " No shows " -- too frequent -- make some staffs over-schedule, one reason patients often find themselves <u>waiting</u>. # Know what you want to ask or learn well before you enter the doctor's examining room.   (COCA:1990.NEWS.WashPost)

7.6. Discussion: find x-self

What are the implications of the results discussed in Chapter 7? First and foremost, corpus and collocational evidence strongly points to the cognitive state of Self-Awareness as the fundamental conception for the majority of metaphoric *find x-self* data. That being the case, Self-Awareness is thus most likely functioning as an image schema (aka basic domain), as defined earlier. This is no trivial point considering the limited amount of corpus data used as evidence for many theoretically-based discussions on the matter. It is claimed here that Self-Awareness is the embodied, functional foundation for Self-Aware events which contain two sub-types of construal; the Self-Aware type in which awareness of an experiencer's internally-based, direct perception(s) is described, and the Self-Aware Unexpected Event type which describes the experiencer's awareness of an externally-initiated, unexpected situation. The discussion above provided numerous and varied accounts of these phenomena and discussed fuzzy cases and their possible resolutions.

Second, the method implemented for delineating metaphor and metonymy of these predications was created out of pragmatic necessity. The combinatory use of the fundamental tenets of MIPVU (i.e., objectively identifying metaphors) followed by in-depth corpus analyses of selected metaphors within the reflexive construction, proved to be a productive and transparent methodology. Each of these steps were deemed essential for objectivity of the data-based core upon which successive steps of the inquiry could proceed. Although no research can be one-hundred percent objective, by eliminating as many intuitive assumptions and statements in the first stages, in-depth analysis was able to proceed with as little 'noise' in the data as possible.

Finally, the corpus-based inquiry for *find x-self* revealed four metaphorical senses; 1) Self-Aware Events, 2) Self-Aware Unexpected Events, 3) True-Self Metaphors, and 4) Picture Noun Schemas, as well as literal meanings. This is impressive on two counts; first, it takes into consideration only one verb contained within a narrowly defined construction, i.e., *find* within the reflexive construction, and from this, five different senses are construed and predicated. Second, it presents strong evidence that collocation plays an important role in semantics. That such a limited construction can have so many conceptions is both daunting and freeing. It is daunting because it forces one to reevaluate previously held notions about the relations between grammar, context and meaning. It is freeing because once the data are viewed from relatively unbiased perspectives, one needs only to employ appropriate methodology to uncover various patterns within that data and to describe them with efficiency and clarity.

One study that illustrates these points comes from comparative research on a parallel corpus. Analyzing English and Norwegian text translations from the English Norwegian Parallel Corpus (ENPC+), Ebeling and Ebeling (2013) compared the use of *found REFL* (i.e., *found x-self*) in original English text sources and their Norwegian translations. It was shown that where the English glosses used *found x-self*, there were various Norwegian verbs that were used as translations. The sample size was limited and they retrieved significant frequencies only for the past tense *found* along with three pronouns, *himself*, *herself*, and *myself* (although they included *themselves* to increase the sample size). However, they conclude that a colligational approach to these translations is beneficial. Analyzing the colligations that occur after the reflexive pronoun (i.e., the FoA), three patterns are focused on based on the entry for *find* in the Collins Cobuild Advanced Learner's Dictionary. By separating and analyzing each of the post-REFL colligations as individual meaningful units, the researchers were able to roughly correlate the translation glosses.

Their first analyzed pattern, [found REFL (NP)dO (direct object)], which was noticed to be indicative of the non-reflexive use of the anaphoric pronoun, has mainly benefactive meaning;

252. *He* himself crawled into his lair, *found himself* a back to lie against, doubled up and fell asleep.   (KAL1T)

This pattern yielded the highest ratio of congruent (word-for-word) translations (Norwegian, BEFINNE REFL) but will not be commented upon further here due to the non-reflexive meaning of the construction.

The other two main post-REFL patterns that were instantiated were [found PP/Adv] and [found V-ing]. These glosses are mostly non-congruent. It was shown that by separating the two colligational types, the translations were more semantically consistent. "... we concluded that the same pattern (i.e., *found REFL*) is used in two different extended units of meaning. When followed by [V-ing] the semantic prosody is neutral, suggesting that the subject found out that he/she was doing something by accident; similarly, when followed by a PP, the semantic prosody is also fairly neutral, suggesting that the subject found out that he/she was situated somewhere by accident" (ibid.: 150, my parenthesis).

253. found V-ing: "Yes," she found herself saying.   (AnCl1E)

254. found PP: A quarter of an hour later they found themselves in a darkened bomb crater of a street.   (JoNe2TE)   (ibid., p. 136)

As for the meaning of these post-REFL patterns, the results of the study only really differentiate between the function of predicates and prepositions in general, viz. to describe actions and to describe the relationship between two things, respectively. The only difference they note is in the added conception of 'discovery' or 'unintentionality'. Furthermore, and more importantly, their English source examples included a variety of construal types; SA, SA-UE, and PNS construal types[54] were exemplified, complicating the analysis. In other words, the research did not distinguish between the different metaphorical meanings of *found x-self* as discussed in the present research. By examining and categorizing the English source texts in this way, many of the inconsistencies of verb-to-verb glosses may be resolved. For example, sentences 10.27 through 10.29 from that research all instantiate *found REFL* as the construction, glossed by three different Norwegian verbs. Upon examination from the viewpoint suggested here,

---

[54] The authors state that they could find no examples of the 'deeper-self' (i.e., TSM) in the ENPC+ nor in the BNC, although it has been shown here that there are, in fact, a few examples of this in the BNC.

however, the English source texts construe three different meanings of *found x-self*, PNS in 255 (10.27), SA in 256 (10.28), and SA-UE in 257 (10.29):

255. (10.27) …and found himself reduced to a detail in oil paint in a garish illustration… (JH1)

256. (10.28) The carriage was hot, and several of the people he found himself crushed up against clearly hadn't bathed that morning. (PeRo2E)

257. (10.29) So Perez found himself sat at a table with Willy…(AnCl1E)

(ibid., p. 143)

Thus, although in general agreement with regard to the importance of the post-REFL elements (i.e., the FoA) for appropriate construal of an event, questions arise about their analysis due to the lack of semantic categorization of the events' most distinguishing elements, i.e., the different metaphoric senses of *found x-self*. Focusing only on the syntax of the FoA may account for specific and limited translation glosses but it does not address the fundamental conceptions of *find x-self*, now known to be essential for proper construal, and thus, translation. That being said, the authors do acknowledge the importance of this polysemy, as they state, "The contrastive analysis has revealed that the pattern found REFL is highly versatile and is used in a number of different contexts…it could be argued that found REFL is polysemous, and as such gives rise to two different extended units" (ibid.: 150). The present research proposes that the construction gives rise not only to two extended units, but four metaphorical senses and one literal sense that are involved intricately with their respective FoAs, ipso facto complicating the accuracy and efficiency of translations. Although the present research does not directly deal with comparisons across languages, it does discuss comparisons between British and American English as well as different corpus registers, and thus, can relate to translation studies in a methodologically important way.

Having shown that the methodology implemented here for *find x-self* is productive for uncovering various semantic and collocational patterns as well as idiosyncrasies, it is now timely to investigate whether this method is useful with other verbs that appear in the reflexive construction. Corpus analysis, results, and discussion of the *lose x-self* construction will follow in Chapter 8.

CHAPTER 8: LOSE X-SELF

8.1. Introduction

In the previous chapter, metaphorically construed *find x-self* was discussed in detail and was found to construe different meanings depending on context. Four of these meanings are metaphorical, two of which contain perceptual Self-Awareness as an image schema used for the metaphoric construal. It will be shown in this section that *lose x-self* is also metaphorically construed, includes Self-Awareness as a conceptual image schema, and that the results of the data are verifiable through corpus analysis.

To begin this chapter, the following quotation is offered:

> From our tour of the metaphor system for the Self, we will find that, first, we do conceptualize a single person as divided. Second, the divisions are not consistent with each other. That is, we have a system of divisions that don't fit together into a simple general scheme. Third, we reason and talk about these internal divisions in terms of relations between external individuals (G. Lakoff 1996a: 101).

The phenomenon described above is called the Divided-Person Metaphor. This is proposed to be the basis for different metaphors that concern the Self. Among those outlined by Lakoff are the following: Object-Subject, Loss-of-Self, Split-Self, True-Self, Real-Me, General Inner-Self, True-to-Yourself, Absent-Subject, Scattered-Self, Self-as-Companion, Self-Sacrifice Complex and Self-Control-Is-Up (ibid.) Although instances of these are found throughout English, two of these are of immediate concern for the topic at hand. These are 'Loss-of-Self' and 'True-Self'. The discussion that follows proposes that the underlying conception of 'Divided Person' may not be the most efficient conceptual categorization for the verb *lose* when used within the reflexive construction. The results of the analysis suggest that the notion of Self-Aware event accounts for more data, more efficiently and with fewer exceptions.

A brief account of what Lakoff (1992, 1996a) calls the 'Loss-of-Self' metaphor is as follows:

> What does it mean to lose yourself in some activity? It means to cease to be in conscious control and to cease to be aware of each thing one is doing…In the Loss-of-Self metaphor, conscious control is conceptualized as position of the Self by the Subject, and ceasing to be in control is loss…The Loss-

of-Self metaphor is thus a way of conceptualizing a wide range of very real experiences, both positive and negative (1996a: 103).

According to this definition, *to lose yourself in some activity* means (1) to cease to be in conscious control. This is conceptualized as position of the Self by the Subject, and ceasing to be in control is *loss*, and (2) to cease to be aware of each thing one is doing. Lakoff merges these two definitions, but what will be shown in the following analysis is that the most common type of construal for *lose x-self* is that in which one ceases to be aware of anything, with one caveat, that awareness is lost for *all but that which is focused upon*. Lakoff's definition deals primarily with *lack of control* (of Self), and his use of *aware* in line 2 occurs only with respect to this control. In contrast to this, the definition presented here deals primarily with awareness as a perceptual congnitive state, where the conception of LOSE X-SELF is *the lack of awareness of general perceptions except for the Focus of Awareness (FoA)*.

Lakoff's use of the concept of *control* is a natural one in the overall Divided Self paradigm and the metaphorical use of the word *lose* in the metaphor seems to instantiate that. After all, to lose a thing once possessed is to lose control of that thing. To demonstrate this, Lakoff maps the 'Loss-of-Self' metaphor, shown below:

> (i)   The Self is possession of the Subject
> (ii)   Control of the Self by Subject is possession
> (iii)   Loss of control is loss of possession

Knowledge Mapping:
Source Domain Knowledge: if a possession of yours is taken, then you no longer have it.
Target Domain Knowledge: if something takes control of you, you no longer have control.

Subcase 1: Positive loss of Self: freedom from normal concerns
>   Examples: I lost myself in dancing. Only in meditation was she able to let go of herself. She let herself go on the dance floor.

Subcase 2: Negative loss of Self: emotional and demonic possession
>   Examples: I don't know what possessed me to do that. I was seized by a longing for her. I got carried away. He's in the grip of an intense hatred. He was possessed by the devil. He's in the grip of his past.

(ibid: 104)

We see here the focus on *control of the Subject over Self* in the mapping based on the Target Domain Knowledge required to understand this metaphor. Lakoff's interests here are to show that Loss-of-Self metaphors exist as Conceptual Metaphors. This goal differs from the main purpose here which is to show how and to what extent the *lose x-self* construction is metaphorically construed and predicated by employing an empirically-based methodology as a way to define collocational patterns and semantic categorizations that may arise from the data. When this methodology is adhered to, the results are surprising. The Loss-of-Self metaphor does not express itself in the data. This does not mean it does not exist in other constructions, or in other corpora. However, Lakoff's use of the first example in Subcase 1 from above, i.e., *I lost myself in dancing* and similar such examples are shown not to be based on *loss of control* but on *the intensity of concentration on a single object to the detriment of general perceptual self-awareness*. The evidence for this is twofold as discussed in previous chapters: 1) the metonymic referent of the reflexive pronoun is the cognitive state of Self-Awareness, and 2) the contextual FoA is essential for proper construal. When these points are taken into consideration, the Self-Aware Event emerges as a simple and efficient explanation for most of the data.

The other conceptual metaphor proposed by Lakoff is the True-Self Metaphor. However, it takes on a slightly different meaning when instantiated in the *lose x-self* construction. For *find x-self*, it referred to the realization of a deeper, more core Self which is realized. For *lose x-self*, it refers to the (temporary) absence of this innermost Self usually due to some psychological trauma or experience. It will be seen that, contrary to opinion (G. Lakoff 1996a), *lose x-self* and *find x-self* can thus construe opposite meanings. Considering the frequency of the True-Self Metaphor in the data, however, the typical categorization for the *lose x-self* construction is proposed as the Self-Aware event. Again, although frequency itself does not directly instantiate entrenchment within a language community, it does provide a litmus test for commonness in use. What is of immediate concern here, methodologically, is the direction in which the data points. In order to explore this, an effective method for data retrieval and analysis needs to be elucidated.

8.2. Method

The initial steps of metaphor identification and categorization for *lose x-self* are the same as those described in the previous chapter. However, based on the data for *lose x-self*, analyses revealed idiosyncrasies that did not appear in the *find x-self* data. Compared to *find x-self*, it was much more difficult to delineate many of the tokens for *lose x-self* and expanded contexts needed to be consulted numerous times for accuracy. There were a few examples where categorization was impossible to determine absolutely and/or in which two or more construals were ultimately plausible. These cases were marked accordingly as '?'.

According to the data retrieved from the COCA and BNC corpora, one semantic categorical change from *find x-self* concerns the literal (LIT) category. There were three meanings that were grouped together under this label[55], although admittedly, the third one is not literal in the strict sense. The decision to include this idiomatic use in the LIT category was based on extending the meaning of LIT 2, *to be unanimous amongst a group of people or objects*. With this in mind, the LIT 3 sense construes *the main topic of conversation getting lost amongst other topics and trains of thought*. The three LITERAL subcategories are:

LIT 1: to be lost in a location:

258 ...*he* had accepted the same invitation, stepped through the entrance and within three minutes *lost himself* helplessly in a second-floor cul-de-sac. Kaldren had taken half an hour to find him. (COCA:2014.FIC.WestHumRev)

LIT 2: to be unidentifiable amongst a group of people or objects:

259. It had the cunning of the vole. Like the owl, *it could lose itself* in the forest. (BNC:HTM.W_fict_prose)

LIT 3: to get off topic in one's narrative:

260. ...were packing up wholesale (pause) so (pause) erm (pause) *I've lost myself* a little bit now. (SP:PS08Y) No, you were talking about er (pause)... (BNC:KC0.S_conv)

Besides these literal senses, there were three metaphoric senses that were either very narrow in their conception, were non-compositional (i.e., their meanings were fixed and components were mostly non-interchangeable) and/or had extremely low frequency. I have thus considered these idiomatic cases and marked IDIOM (IDI). These three idioms are:

---

[55] When analyzing the data, each type of LITERAL and IDIOMATIC case was individually marked, i.e., LIT 1, 2, 3 and IDI 1, 2, 3, respectively.

<u>IDI 1</u>: to have sexual intercourse:

261. ...and let her see how human he was as *he* merged with her and *lost himself* inside her.

(BNC:JYD.W_fict_prose)

<u>IDI 2</u>: to die:

262. ...*she* realized we were kindred spirits, or knew in her final moments that in *losing herself*, she saved me. (COCA:2006.FIC.Analog)

<u>IDI 3</u>: to abruptly leave or go away:

263. Candace gave her little brother a cutting worldly look. " *Go lose yourself.*" # Stefan began to retreat, gladly. (COCA:1996.FIC.FantasySciFi)

In the *lose x-self* data, there were no examples of the SA-UE category. The reason for this is proposed as inherent in the meaning of the metaphoric sense, i.e., although the circumstances causing one's loss of self-awareness are varied (i.e., internally or externally initiated), only the resultant, internally-perceived mental state (i.e., the loss of awareness) is reported. Unexpected external events may have triggered the loss of self-awareness and are sometimes the locus of the attention, they are never construed from the viewpoint of that external locus. The event is always construed from the resultant internal loss of perceptual awareness and as such, it is construed and marked as the SA-type construal.

264. When he could, *he* enjoyed *losing himself* in research.

(COCA:1995.FIC.Bk:HarmonyFleshBlack)

265...he will get relaxed, perhaps playing a little PlayStation Vita. Then *he will lose himself* in rap songs by Waka Flocka Flame or Machine Gun Kelly... (COCA:2012.NEWS.Denver)

One last point concerning the methodology specific to categorizations of *lose x-self* is that there were more than an average number of non-reflexive, (i.e., 'X') category tokens for the second person pronoun yourself (*n*=6). This was due to the instantiations of the song title by the rap artist Eminem named, 'Lose Yourself'. These were excluded from the data set.

8.2.1. Complexities and Subtleties

It was sometimes difficult to decide whether a token was a LIT or SA category, for example:

266. <u>To brush up on your Southern authors</u>, head north to Blue Bicycle Books, owned by local scribe Jonathan Sanchez, *to lose yourself* <u>in the narrow aisles</u>.

(COCA: 2012.MAG.NationalGeographic)

At first glance, *lose oneself in the aisles* suggests a LIT (1) categorization. However, the first part of the sentence contains the support context (double-underlined) for the FoA in the construal, in which the 'reading of books' is the action performed in those *narrow aisles*, and thus <u>losing oneself in the reading of books</u> is the proposed meaning. This token was thus marked as the SA-type construal.

267. ....<u>with garden and sea views, and a stone fireplace</u>. *You can lose yourself* <u>in these surroundings</u> as at no other place in Ravello.   (COCA:2001.MAG.TownCountry)

In a similar example, shown in 267, the token alone suggests a LIT (1) or LIT (2) construal; however, the FoA along with the support context contains the reference for the event, 'getting mentally absorbed in the scenery', thus construing an SA Event (i.e., being totally focused on the scenery to the detriment of other perceptions).

These types of tokens were also found in cases that were initially ambiguous between the TSM and SA categories:

268. If *you lose yourself* <u>to rage</u> in the complexity of battle, <u>you are going to be lost</u>...

(COCA:1997.MAG.PsychToday)

In the case of 268, due to the internal emotional state of *rage* along with the meaning of the FoA and support context, an SA categorization seems appropriate here. However, the post-reflexive preposition suggests the TSM-type construal. The difference can be understood by comparing *lose oneself* <u>in rage</u> and *lose oneself* <u>to rage</u>. These are two different conceptions;

the former is one in which the experiencer is completely, mentally involved in his/her own rage to the detriment of any other awareness, i.e., an SA event. The latter is a construal in which one part of the mind is in a psychodynamic opposition to the emotion *rage*. The deeper Self is overpowered by the emotional Self, a TSM-type construal. The support contexts from the expanded context below confirm the TSM-type analysis for example 268.

Expanded context:
Instead, the information you're processing is that an incoming missile is 15 kilometers away, now 10 kilometers away, now 5 kilometers. You have to separate yourself psychologically from the fact that your mortal existence may well end. That is the ancient reality of war. PT: You've been in combat. What did you learn from your experiences? FRIEDMAN: The important thing is that there is an element of rage, but you must remain very distant from it. If *you lose yourself* to rage in the complexity of battle, you are going to be lost. The warrior must continue to make decisions in the face of extreme circumstances. He can not afford to get angry or frightened. (COCA:1997.MAG.PsychToday)

Another example of the subtlety involved when analyzing these kinds of data is the following:

269. ...and comedy is the only way that we can feel present and *lose ourselves*.

(COCA:2014.SPOK.NPR)

Clause final *find x-self* is typically an indicator of TSM because they lack an FoA in which Self-Awareness is to be focused. In the case of 269, however, comedy is the event's FoA for *lose x-self* and thus can be rephrased as *we lose ourselves in comedy*, an SA-type construal because our complete awareness is not on our general perceptions but on *the comedy happening at the moment*. Further evidence of this is the predicate *feel present*, which describes a situation in which one is completely focused on the present moment; the mind does not wander off in ruminations nor is it aware of other perceptions. And when the mental state of totally *feeling present* is achieved, one is completely concentrated on that single moment, in other words, *lost in the moment*, a typical SA Event.

Having laid the groundwork for *lose x-self* and shown examples of some of the challenges involved in analyzing and categorizing the data, the next section discusses the results yielded for *lose x-self* data in the COCA and BNC corpora.

8.3. Results: find and lose

According to the results of the corpora search shown in Table 13 and 14, *lose* is less frequent than *find* and similarly, but on a much greater scale, *lose x-self* is less frequent than *find x-self*.

Table 13. Frequencies and ratios for lose$_v$, find$_v$, lose x-self, and find x-self; COCA and BNC

	[lose]	[find]	lose : find
COCA	44,647	223,828	19.9%
BNC	6,102	40,455	15%
TOTAL	50,749	264,283	19.2%

Table 14. Frequencies and ratios for *lose x-self* and *find x-self* in the COCA and BNC

	[lose] [ppx*]	[find] [ppx*]	lose [ppx*] : find [ppx*]
COCA	1001	27,188	3.7%
BNC	124	5,064	2.4%
TOTAL	1125	32,252	3.5%

In Table 13, in the COCA data, *find* hit 223,828 times and *lose* hit 44,647 times; in the BNC, *find* hit 40,455 times and *lose* hit 6,102 times. When converted into relative ratios, *lose* instantiates 19.9% of *find*, while in the BNC the ratio of *lose:find* is 15%. In other words, things are *lost* almost one-fifth of the time less often than they are *found*, regardless of type of lost object, syntax, metaphorical use, etc.

This inequality is even more pronounced when the verbs are placed within the reflexive construction, shown in Table 14. The relationship [*lose x-self : find x-self*] yields 3.7% in the COCA and 2.4% in the BNC. The Fisher Exact results for *lose:find* (p=0) as well as *lose x-self : find x-self* (p=1.1E-05) are significant for each corpus. In other words, things are *found* much more often than they are *lost*, and this trend is even more pronounced when the verbs occur within the reflexive construction. The reason for this with non-reflexive use is unclear at the present time, but for cases occurring within the reflexive construction, one possible motivation is that it may be more common or 'normal' to become suddenly self-aware during one's daily activities and experiences, i.e., the SA Event-type of *find x-self*. Conversely, being totally focused on one activity or perception to the point of temporarily lacking awareness of general self-perception, i.e., the SA-type *lose x-self*, is a relatively uncommon experience, although desirable on occasion, e.g., being 'in the zone' for activities such as sports, work efficiency, yoga and meditation, etc. A more detailed investigation of all social and pragmatic contexts for

146

find and *lose* is needed for more conclusive results, but the initial results obtained here do establish that *lose* is significantly less common than *find* in both the British and American corpora, and probably for language use in society at large.

Turning attention specifically to the initial search for *lose x-self* (i.e., [lose][ppx*]) in the COCA (sorted by lemma, reciprocals deleted, $n \geq 10$), there were 1001 total tokens instantiating seven reflexive pronouns: *myself, yourself, himself, herself, ourselves, themselves,* and *itself*. In the BNC, there were 124 hits (lemma sorting, no reciprocals, $n \geq 5$) with the same seven pronoun categories. Frequencies are shown in Table 15 (frequency ratios in parentheses). Cross-corpora frequency ratios are comparable for each of the reflexive pronouns except for the feminine third person *herself*. In the BNC, *herself* assumes most frequent position at a 25% hit rate compared to the COCA in which *herself* instantiates 18.6%, yielding a differential of 6.4%. The results for the differential in the masculine *himself* is not nearly as pronounced, at 1.3%; however, this is not significant (p=.2141).

Table 15. Frequencies and frequency ratios (in parentheses) for [lose x-self]; COCA and BNC

[LOSE][ppx*]	COCA	BNC	TOTAL
[LOSE] [HIMSELF]	247 (24.7%)	29 (23.4%)	276 (24.5%)
[LOSE] [HERSELF]	186 (18.6%)	31 (25%)	217 (19.3%)
[LOSE] [MYSELF]	182 (18.2%)	15 (12.1%)	197 (17.5%)
[LOSE] [YOURSELF]	165 (16.5%)	17 (13.7%)	182 (16.2%)
[LOSE] [THEMSELVES]	123 (12.3%)	18 (14.5%)	141 (12.5%)
[LOSE] [ITSELF]	50 (5.0%)	9 (7.3%)	59 (5.2%)
[LOSE] [OURSELVES]	48 (4.8%)	5 (4.0%)	53 (4.7%)
TOTAL	1001	124	1125

There is a noticeable difference between the frequencies of the first person singular *myself* and plural *ourselves*. In a cross corpora ratio comparison, *myself* instantiates 18.2% and 12.1% in the COCA and BNC, respectively, for a cross-corpora average of 15.2%. For *ourselves*, the ratios are 4.8% and 4%, respectively, yielding a 4.4% cross-corpora average. Explanation for the 10.8% frequency differential can be attributed to the conceptions for *lose x-self*. In all three semantic categories, i.e., SA, TSM and LIT (see Figures 13-15), the construal *lose ourselves* seems awkward because it expresses the intimate knowledge of another person's conscious state. Although it is instantiated occasionally in the data, especially for TSM in the COCA (see Fig. 14) and SA in the BNC (see Fig. 15), the low frequency perhaps suggests its awkwardness.

Figure 13. Frequency ratios for [lose][ppx*] by category in the COCA and BNC

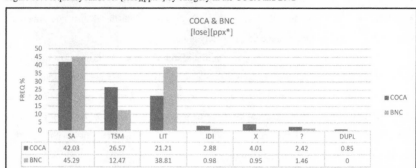

Category abbreviations: SA=Self-Aware Event; TSM=True-Self Metaphor; LIT=literal meaning; IDI=idiomatic meaning; X=non-reflexive use; ?=indeterminate; DUPL=duplicate token in corpus.

Cross-corpora categorizations and frequency profiles for *lose x-self* are shown in Figure 13. Similar to the *find x-self* data, the SA-type had the highest frequency ratio (mean= 43.7%); however, in contrast, the categories TSM (mean=19.5%) and LIT (mean=30%) both yielded relatively high frequencies. Thus, although the data for *find x-self* revealed four metaphorical types and *lose x-self* instantiates only two, SA and TSM frequency ratios are more evenly distributed for *lose x-self*.

Figures 14 and 15 show *lose x-self* frequency comparisons by corpus, according to reflexive pronoun. Cross-corpora frequency similarities are noticeable in the SA category for *herself* (57% and 66.7% in the COCA and BNC, respectively), and *himself* (55% and 44.8%, respectively). As claimed for the 3rd person pronoun *find x-self* data, this is likely due to the narrator/author point of view in which the author and character are one and the same entity (in reality), and thus, the author can assume to know the character's internal perceptions. This is supported by the high number of tokens in the FICTION register (see Figure 19).

270. And his prominent *chin*, the symbol of his force and his will, *was losing itself* among the folds of an indiscreetly fat double chin. (COCA:2011.FIC.Callaloo)

271. Tyres. Just tyres. He stopped the car where *the road lost itself* in sand and got out.
(BNC: C86.W_fict_prose)

Figure 14. COCA frequency ratios for *lose x-self* by pronoun for all semantic categories

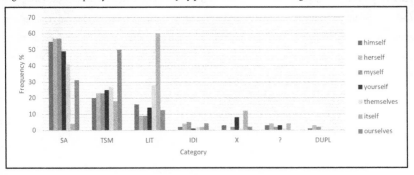

Figure 15. BNC frequency ratios for *lose x-self* by pronoun for all semantic categories

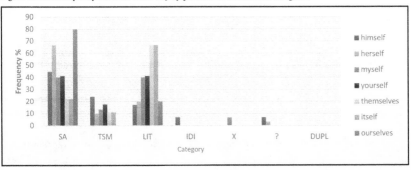

Another noteworthy result is the high frequency of the LIT category occurring with *itself*. This can be explained as a type of Virtual Reflexive Alternation (VRA), where "the subject bears the same semantic relation to the verb as the object does in the typical transitive use of the verb. However…the verb does not change transitivity but instead takes a reflexive pronoun as object" (Levin 1993: 84). Of note is that the verb *lose* does not appear in the list of verbs provided by Levin. The number of tokens instantiated in both corpora here suggests that the VRA may not be as restricted as claimed and that other verbs may also instantiate VRA-type semantics.

One difference between the two corpora pertains to the plural first person reflexive pronoun *ourselves*. In the COCA, usage is spread mostly across three categories, TSM, SA, and LIT, in respective frequency order. However, in the BNC, 80% of the tokens instantiate the SA category, with the remaining 20% instantiating the LIT category. There were no instances of the TSM-type. Similarly, in the COCA, the first person singular pronoun *myself* shows a relatively smooth frequency cline from SA →TSM → LIT. In contrast to this, in the BNC, SA and LIT categories have the same relatively ratio (40%) whereas the TSM-type yields a low frequency (13%). Regional variation is proposed for these differences, where TSM is more common in American English, shown in example 272 below. These occur only rarely in British English, the solitary example provided in 273.

272. *We're all in constant danger of losing ourselves*, losing our identities. It's a daily struggle…

(COCA:2012.MAG.NatGeog)

273. *I lost myself.* I tried to focus on my interior but there was nothing to focus on…

(BNC:FAT.W_fict_prose)

Table 16. Frequencies of clause-final TSM and non-clause-final TSM for *lose x-self*; COCA and BNC

	(a) clause-final TSM	(b) non-clause-final TSM
COCA	46	41
BNC	11	4
TOTAL	57	45

As an example of the benefits of using corpus analysis, it was proposed previously that clause-final position was a general tendency for the TSM construal. In Table 16, the TSM frequencies (bold outline) were used as the input values and the result is not significant (p = .1681). Therefore, clause-final position, although appearing seemingly often, is not a dependent variable for TSM for *lose x-self*. However, although this takes into account collocational evidence, it does not consider the FoA and its semantic function. When the semantic content of the FoA is included and analyzed, it is found to be a nonessential part of the metaphor. For the 45 non-clause-final cases of TSM in the COCA and BNC (n=41 and 4, respectively), all FoAs are adjunctive to the meaning of the main metaphor; i.e., the FoAs can be deleted without change in main construal meaning, as shown below, and supported by the expanded context.

274. But it was definitely dangerous. # " *You* can(sic) *lose yourself* in utterly groundless fantasies, " I sternly cautioned Hideko. (COCA:1996.FIC.LiteraryReview)

Expanded context (abridged):

" I think she has a hard time distinguishing between fantasy and reality. Sometimes you find those types among those who want to be actresses. " # Not that I didn't understand what was going on in her head -in the course of dreaming of the glorious life of an actress, she had come to feel that it had already opened up before her eyes, and ended up lying about it to others. But it was definitely dangerous. # " *You* can (sic) *lose yourself* in utterly groundless fantasies, " I sternly cautioned Hideko. " You've got to spend each day in solid, practical effort. "

And

> 275. *Lucas van Leyden* is an artist of frailer calibre than Drer, and prone to *lose himself* in imitation of stronger men... (BNC:A04.W_ac_humanities)

Expanded context:

In discussing Drer, he treated him as the most versatile artist of a triumvirate, whose other members were Marcantonio Raimondi and Lucas van Leyden. Of the latter he wrote,' *Lucas van Leyden* is an artist of frailer calibre than Drer, and prone to *lose himself* in imitation of stronger men, each of his contemporaries in turn dominating his style.' Another book about the age of Drer, but on a different topic, is The Limewood Sculptors of Renaissance Germany, by Michael Baxandall, published in 1980. The author started his career in the Victoria and Albert Museum, where there is an important group of this sculpture; his book had a double origin in a museum exhibition and a series of lectures.

In all such cases, although the FoAs provide further information about the True-Self Metaphor, they can be deleted without semantic consequence to the main metaphoric conception. This is not so with SA Events, as seen below. The FoAs in SA events are the obligatory object of the experiencer's total and complete awareness, without which the expression is misconstrued as a TSM-type construal.

> 276. The only way *he* could escape from the harsh realities of life was to *lose himself* in books, allowing his imagination to take over... (BNC:B1X.W_fict_prose)

> 277. ...the old horror genre is coming to TV, inviting *us* to *lose ourselves* in evocations of our deepest fears. (COCA:2014.NEWS.Denver)

Methodologically, then, although statistical analyses of collocations are useful in a variety of situations and reveal insights not gleaned easily without their help, broader semantic contexts of metaphorical expressions still need careful inspection for accurate data collection and results.

Table 17. [lose][ppx*] (*n*=500, sorted by lemma), according to register; COCA and BNC

COCA	FREQ	PER MIL	BNC	FREQ	PER MIL
SPOKEN	67	0.61	SPOKEN	6	0.6
FICTION	573	5.46	FICTION	80	5.03
MAGAZINE	220	2	MAGAZINE	13	1.79
NEWSPAPER	96	0.91	NEWSPAPER	0	0
ACADEMIC	92	0.89	ACADEMIC	7	0.46
			NON-ACAD*	10	0.61
			MISC	19	0.91

* The order of NON-ACAD has been changed with ACADEMIC in the BNC to easily visualize cross-corpora comparisons.

Another interesting comparison, although not statistically significant (p-value = 0.1827)), can be drawn for *himself* and *herself*. The masculine pronoun is more frequent in the COCA, yielding an 11% difference between it and the BNC (see Fig. 15 and Table 16), but the feminine reflexive pronoun shows the opposite occurrence at the same frequency differential. Comparisons between feminine and masculine reflexive pronouns within each of the corpora yields a 2% difference between *himself* and *herself* in the COCA, but a 22% difference in the BNC. As with the results for *find x-self* previously discussed, one plausible explanation for this difference may be due to social gender biasing in the British media. However, considering that a large amount of the data collected for *lose x-self* is from the FICTION register, this explanation is more weakly stated here, the values between the FICTION and the non-FICTION amalgamated group not being significant (p-value= 1). Shown in Table 17, the *lose x-self* frequencies yield cross-corpora similarities for most (common) registers (per million). The high ratio of occurrences in the FICTION register is attributed, as it was previously for *find x-self*, to discourse point of view, specifically with regard to the ease with which the narrator/writer can intimately know and convey another person's perceptual awareness, being one and the same person as the character. One frequency difference between the two corpora is the lack of tokens for the NEWSPAPER in the BNC. Reasons for this are difficult to postulate at this time, considering that the COCA results show that NEWSPAPER has a relatively high frequency ratio per million.

A corpus analysis of *lose x-self* revealed interesting results in the data. An investigation is conducted in the next sections to see whether or not the type of antecedent has any bearing on the semantics of this event.

8.4. [p*][lose][ppx*]: pronoun antecedents

In Chapter 7, different collocational patterns were revealed for *find x-self* when antecedent-experiencers are differentiated by noun and pronoun, and so a similar search with the parameter [p*][lose][ppx*] ($n \geq 5$ [56], sort by word) was conducted here as well. Figure 16 shows the combined COCA and BNC frequencies by pronoun, according to conceptual category. Noticeably, the first person singular pronoun *I* is the most frequent for SA events and as discussed above for *find x-self*, this is now to be expected, the first person being a natural point of view from which to describe one's own mental state. The next most frequent are the third person singular pronouns, both masculine and feminine, respectively. Again, the high frequency of tokens in the FICTION register (see Table 18) accounts for this, 3rd person SA Events being easily construed from the narrator/writer's internal point of view of the fictional characters they create.

Figure 16. Frequency results in the COCA and BNC for [p*][lose][ppx*] by pronoun for each category

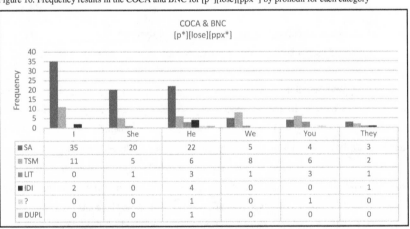

	I	She	He	We	You	They
■ SA	35	20	22	5	4	3
▨ TSM	11	5	6	8	6	2
■ LIT	0	1	3	1	3	1
■ IDI	2	0	4	0	0	1
▨ ?	0	0	1	0	1	0
▨ DUPL	0	0	1	0	0	0

SA=Self-Aware Event; TSM=True-Self Metaphor; LIT= literal use; IDI=idiomatic use; ?=indeterminate; DUPL=duplicate in corpus

Table 18. Frequency and frequency per million of [p*][lose][ppx*] : COCA and BNC

COCA	FREQ	PER MIL	BNC	FREQ	PER MIL
SPOKEN	15	0.14	SPOKEN	1	0.1
FICTION	107	1.02	FICTION	9	0.57

[56] Due to low number of tokens of *lose x-self*, the minimum hit count was set at ≥ 5 and sorted by word for both corpora.

MAGAZINE	35	0.32	MAGAZINE	1	0.14
NEWSPAPER	17	0.16	NEWSPAPER	0	0
ACADEMIC	7	0.07	NON-ACAD	3	0.18
			ACADEMIC	0	0
			MISC	3	0.14

According to conceptual category, SA Events are the most frequent, instantiating at a frequency ratio of 61% for all pronoun experiencer-antecedents (compared to *find x-self* at 42%). However, the TSM construal is also relatively frequent, yielding a cross-corpora frequency ratio of 26% (compared to 2% for *find x-self*). The results for this are significant (p = .0005), lending support to the overall hypothesis of this research that if a construction is *find x-self* or *lose x-self*, it is likely to construe a Self-Aware event. That being said, what is it about *lose x-self* that motivates the 24% higher ratio of the TSM construal compared to *find x-self*?

> 278. I'm afraid I mean that literally. *He's lost himself* - his identity. He has no understanding of who he is. (COCA:1998.FIC.Mov:DarkCity)

> 279. …but as I wondered the subject faded, my mind wandered… *I lost myself.* I tried to focus on my interior but there was nothing to focus on… (BNC:FAT.W_fict_prose)

General anthropo-/sociological support for the high TSM frequency for *lose x-self*, albeit anecdotal, can be seen by the reverence many societies place on people who have *found themselves* (in the TSM sense), i.e., prophets, saints, enlightened beings, whatever their title or religious affiliation. Because of their rarity, societies consider these people special, treasures, jewels, etc. On the other hand, *losing oneself* (in the TSM sense) is so common that many societies have an ever-increasing number of gurus, therapists, cults, hospitals and new-age remedies for 'finding our lost Selves'. In other words, it is proposed here that because the actual number of people who have *lost themselves* is higher than the number of people who have *found themselves*, this is reflected in the data. It is unfortunate that a statistical survey of this is impractical (how would this be confirmed?) Therefore, this tentative explanation should be considered a 'working hypothesis' and not meant as hard evidence.

8.4.1. Fuzzy construals for [p*][lose][ppx*]

There were examples in the data which were able to be construed in multiple ways, with little convincing evidence for determining one type of construal over another. For example, in sentence 280 below, a few interpretations are possible depending upon the context.

> 280. "A man like Lipsky could have lost himself at a hundred tracks." Jamison looked
> back at the colt. (COCA:1995.FIC.Bk:TrueBetray)

Expanded context (abridged):
"Nobody thinks it was suicide? " Jamison shot Gabe a look and stepped out of the box. " Nobody that knew him. " " He could have gotten his hands on some acepromazine, " Matt reminded Jamison. " He'd have known what it would do. Surely he had to know the authorities would catch up with him eventually. " " *A man like Lipsky could have lost himself* at a hundred tracks. " Jamison looked back at the colt. He was dressing the wound himself, as penance for his part in it. " I should have fired him months ago. Everything might've been different then. " And Mick might have been alive. " That part's done, " Gabe said. " But it's not over. Whoever gave Lipsky that last drink is part of it."

One interpretation construes *lose x-self* as a LIT (2)- type, where the experiencer named *Lipsky*, in his attempt to hide from the *authorities*, *loses himself* amongst the populace, i.e., he becomes anonymous among the masses. The FoA at a hundred paces construes a spatial distance, most likely the distance needed from the authorities to make his anonymity successfully. However, looking at other evidence in the expanded context such as the possibility of *suicide* from line one, the expression might be construed to mean that *Lipsky* could have killed himself (*lost himself* = die) quite quickly and efficiently before the authorities could catch him (*at a hundred paces*), in which case the construal would be categorized as an IDI (2)– type. This is not quite convincing either, however, due to line seven in the expanded context, where another character, *Mick*, is introduced for the first time as deceased. Is it possible that *Lipsky* killed himself after being accused of *Mick's* murder? Evidence for this comes in the last sentence in the text, where one of the characters says, *Whoever gave Lipsky that last drink is part of it*. For this type of construal, someone killed *Mick*, and also perhaps *Lipsky*, or perhaps one was a murder and one was a suicide? Either way, that *last drink* has something to do with it. As shown here, a confident decision about construal is difficult to make even given the contextual clues in the expanded context. Because of this ambiguity, the token was marked '? '.

Another ambiguous example and its expanded context is the following:

281. <u>Though she always feels like a tourist and not a traveler,</u> *she can lose*
   herself <u>anyway</u>.   (COCA:1997.FIC.Bk:PassionDreamBook)

Expanded context (abridged):
Her adoration continues uninterrupted, yet somehow, for them, love suffers under such an uneven arrangement. Maybe she is wrong about fate, and love lasting. Her response is to continue to travel. <u>Though she always feels like a tourist and not a traveler,</u> *she can lose herself* <u>anyway</u>. But this unquiet life can not go on indefinitely, so when she reaches London, with its shades of steel, pewter, dove gray, and green, she decides to stay. 6. The first thing Augustine does when he arrives home is to reopen Perfect Fish Photography Studio.

Here as well, because a few plausible interpretations are possible, the token was marked '?'. Under one interpretation, the FoA suggests a TSM-type construal due to both the clause final position (although a sentence-final adverb is present) and the presumption that the woman has psychologically 'given up' on *fate* and *love* and spends her time *travelling* (in order to delude herself into a sense of purpose or happiness?) This creates a psychological dualism, the outer Self traveling and working, while the deeper Self laments a loveless marriage. A different interpretation focuses on the continued *travels* of the woman, from the end of line two, along with the FoA. Throughout these travels, one can be anonymous amongst the new, stimulating surroundings, thus temporarily forgetting one's troubles at home, a LIT (2)-type categorization. Lastly, an SA-type interpretation is also possible in which a paraphrase of the sentence would be, *the woman loses herself in travelling*, where travelling is the only thing in her immediate awareness. This does not set up a psychological dualism like the TSM construal above, but creates a conceptual scenario where the point of focus is a singular awareness (the experience of *travelling*), and this concentrative singularity allows the woman to temporarily forget her despair.

The conceptual resolution of these kinds of examples is theoretically possible if one had the time and resources to locate and interview each of the writers/narrators and obtain complete texts in which further conceptual clues can be searched. Unfortunately, the amount of data being analyzed here is far too numerous to undertake such an in-depth analysis of each and every fuzzy predication. A compromise was made, however, by examining each of the expanded contexts to determine best construal based on contextual evidence. If no resolution was possible, it was marked as such.

8.5. [n*][lose][ppx*]: Nouns as antecedents for lose x-self

Because meaningful differences were found between pronoun and full noun antecedents for *find x-self*, a search was conducted here as well for *lose x-self* in which the antecedents were nouns, i.e., [n*][lose][ppx*]. Total frequency counts were comparatively low, yielding 65 and 11 hits in the COCA and BNC, respectively (reciprocals deleted). The items and frequencies are provided in Appendix 7. Due to the low frequency count, tokens were sorted by word with no minimum frequency imposed.

A few token categorizations needed adjustment due to false experiencer-antecedents occurring in the data. For example, in sentence 282 below, the noun <u>wolves</u> immediately precedes the *lose x-self* construction and thus emerged in the retrieved data as the preverbal noun, but this is not the experiencer-antecedent, only part of its relative clause. There were nine total cases in the COCA, all of which were amended and coded accordingly.

> 282. She said that some who talked to <u>wolves</u> lost themselves, that what was
> human was swallowed up by wolf.   (COCA:1991.FIC.BkSF.DragonReborn)

Total [n* + lose x-self] frequencies, according to conceptual category, are shown in Figure 17. The high frequency of SA Events in the COCA and BNC again supports this type of conceptual categorization for the *lose x-self* construction. The literal use (LIT) was also frequent (n=15), followed by the TSM construal (n=10). There were two idiomatic examples (n=2) and one each of undetermined (?) and non-reflexive (X) categories.

Turning attention now to the types of nouns instantiated in the *lose x-self* construction (see Appendix 7), the use of proper names as antecedents hit at rates of 37.7% and 36.4% in the COCA and BNC, respectively. However, here again (as with the *find x-self* data), only feminine names instantiated (n=4) in the BNC data, whereas in the COCA there were a fairly equal number of each, with 10 feminine (45.5%) and 12 masculine (54.5%) names. Considering that 75% of the examples in the BNC are from the FICTION register (compared to the COCA with 47%, see Table 19), and all feminine names are of the [W_fict_prose] category (although from different source texts), plausible explanations for this discrepancy are: 1) gender biasing within the overall fiction genre in Britain, or 2) the balance of text sources within the fiction register in the BNC. Due to the limited number of examples, however, the conviction for these explanations is weak; a more encompassing investigation along a socio-corpus linguistic framework would be needed to show either of these to be viable explanations.

Figure 17. Frequencies of categories for [n*][lose][ppx*] in the COCA and BNC

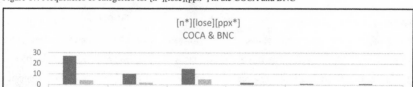

	SA	TSM	LIT	IDI	?	X
■ COCA	27	10	15	2	1	1
▥ BNC	4	2	5	0	0	0

Shown in Table 19, FICTION was the most frequent register, instantiating 47% and 75% in the COCA and BNC, respectively[57]. This was a higher FICTION ratio than *find x-self* (27.7%) in the COCA data. Register variation for *lose x-self* is fairly balanced when all other registers are placed in opposition to the FIC register, calculated as FIC vs. non-FIC (register amalgamation group as with *find x-self*), yielding frequency ratios of 47% vs. 48.5%, respectively. This is quite a different profile from the BNC, with ratios of 75% vs. 25%, respectively. Here as well, media-based gender bias could be proposed as one explanation, but due to the low total frequency count in the BNC data, any generalizations about these frequency ratios must be considered with discretion.

Table 19. Frequency and Per Mil frequency of [n*][lose][ppx*] in the COCA and BNC

BNC	FREQ	PER MIL	% of total	COCA	FREQ	PER MIL	% of total
SPOKEN	0	0	0	SPOKEN	3	0.03	4.5
FICTION	9	0.57	75	FICTION	31	0.3	47
MAGAZINE	0	0	0	MAGAZINE	12	0.11	18.2
NEWSPAPER	0	0	0	NEWSPAPER	9	0.08	13.6
ACADEMIC	1	0.07	8.3	ACADEMIC	11	0.11	16.7
NON-ACAD	0	0	0				
MISC	2	0.1	16.7				
TOTAL	12			TOTAL	66		

The nouns that are used as antecedents as well as their respective frequencies and accompanying verb tenses are shown in Table 20. It can be seen that when a noun is plural it is slightly more

---

[57] This data is from a CHART search for [n*][lose][ppx*] in each of the corpora and includes reciprocals and 'uncorrected' false antecedents.

likely to be in the present tense and vice versa for the singular/past distinction. However, this tendency is not significant (p= 0.1312, integers used as input values).

Table 20. COCA/BNC search [n*][find][ppx]; non-human nouns as antecedents

	singular	plural	present tense	past tense
fingers	-	1	1	-
buildings	-	2	2	-
road	1	-	-	1
planes	1	-	-	1
wind	1	-	-	1
voice	1	-	1	-
tracks	-	1	1	-
sounds	-	1	-	1
song	1	-	1	-
ships	-	1	1	-
ring	1	-	1	-
political parties	-	1	1	-
mind	1	-	-	1
legs	-	1	1	-
Arab community	1	-	1	-
ball	1	-	-	1
TOTAL	9	8	11	6

At the risk of stating the obvious, when an event is construed as SA or TSM, the experiencer is likely to be human, at ratios of 92.6% and 100% respectively. In contrast, the LIT category yielded an experiencer-as-human ratio of 73.7%. This is significant (p=0). In other words, when *lose x-self* is construed metaphorically, the antecedent-experiencer is very likely to be human. When only frequency is taken into account, this is only slightly less true for LIT examples as well, 73% being clearly above the median.

When metonymically construed experiencer-antecedents are analyzed, there is no overlap with the *find x-self* data, although *political parties* and *Arab community* are similar to *Democrats/Republicans* and *group/state/country*, respectively.

There was one metonymic experiencer-antecedent (i.e., *MIND* STANDS FOR *SELF-AWARENESS*) that instantiated the SA-type construal, shown below.

283. From the moment he lost sight of his rude home in the midst of the Forest, *his untutored mind lost itself* in the myriad beauties and forces of nature.

(COCA:2001.ACAD.AmerIndianQ)

Other nouns instantiated cases of the LIT (1) category (*n*=2), and the LIT (2) category (*n*=13). All of these antecedent-experiencers can be categorized as the 'virtual reflexive alternation' (Levin 1993); however, within this set, some of the antecedents can be understood as metonymically construed, specifically, as cases of synecdoche, where a part of something stands for its whole. This metonymic use encourages 'the part' to initiate some action as would 'the whole'. Example above, along with the 284 and 285 below, exemplify this.

> 284. "Did you come here for this? " *the aunt's voice losing itself* in the aunt's marred hand. (COCA:2002.FIC.Bk:Carrying Body)

> 285. …with the voice of the wind and murmuring in the leaves. *My song loses itself* in the ever moving sea. (COCA:1997.SPOK.ABC_Nightline)

The fundamental conceptual question here is, "How can inherently nonconscious and/or inert objects initiate action?" In reality, they cannot. But they can be conceived of as having innate inertia and be construed and predicated as such, metonymically and metaphorically. Especially in cases of synecdoche, the sentient person (i.e., the whole) has conscious control of action, and each part of the whole may be conceived as taking part in that action. In the examples above, a *marred hand* can cover a mouth and muffle a *voice*, but the *voice* can also be conceived of as imbued with its own force inertia and construed and predicated from that perspective, and so, the *voice* can *lose itself* in *the hand*. Similarly, the sound of *the sea* can drown out the sound of a *song*, but *the song* can be conceived of as having action inertia and get *lost*, so that the sound of the *song* does not reach the ear of the hearer. Interestingly, we understand these antecedents as metonymic, but the meaning of the main verb is literal, often the LIT (2) category, i.e., to be unanimous amongst a group of people or objects. In other words, the relationship between the anaphor pair sand their verbs (i.e., the predicate) is literally construed, while the reflexive pronouns themselves are metonymically construed. These kinds of examples are not found in the *find x-self* data. For *find x-self*, all of the non-sentient antecedent-experiencers are typically metonymic for this kind of construal, that is, the nouns are those such as: GROUPS STAND FOR PEOPLE IN THE GROUPS, e.g., *company, government, church*, etc. Although a few of the metonymically-construed nouns for *lose x-self* are directly part of the human whole, e.g., *fingers, voice*, etc., this is not necessarily the case, for example, *buildings, road, wind*, etc. In order for these nouns to be conceived as initiating action and to have these entities acting upon themselves, some cross- or inter-domain mapping is necessary. For example,

286. ...and *the poor buildings lose themselves* in the dim sky... (BNC:H0R.W_fict_prose)

287. To look down along *the tracks losing themselves* in a wilderness of furze.
(COCA:1997.FIC.LiteraryRev)

In the 286 and 287 above, *buildings* ARE *buildings* and *tracks* ARE *tracks*. When analyzing these antecedents individually, there seems to be no cross- or inter-domain mapping. Furthermore, the verb *lose* is literally (LIT 2) construed. So how do *buildings* and *tracks* literally *lose themselves*? The key to this is the proper construal of the antecedents. Since *buildings* and *tracks* cannot act of their own volition, a cognitive device is needed to transmit these volitional qualities onto non-sentient objects. One syntactic technique is the passive voice, i.e., *the buildings were lost in the dim sky* and *the tracks were lost in the wilderness*. Another technique is metaphoric and metonymic construal. Three steps are needed for these types of constructions, only the first of which is inherently metaphoric/metonymic: 1) sentience is mapped onto a non-sentient object, 2) a sentient object is the source of action inertia, and 3) action is performed upon itself. Admittedly, *buildings* or *tracks* are usually not thought of as being sentient in the 'normal' sense, but the construction's form-meaning suggests to the reader a hint of self-initiated action. *Buildings* and *tracks* are thought of *as if* they *lose themselves*. Thus, for non-sentient experiencers in *lose x-self* constructions, metonymy and/or metaphor is hard at work, guiding nuances of meaning.

When understanding and analyzing predications in this way, conceptually difficult data can be accounted for efficiently within the overall data set. As with most hypotheses, however, there are always exceptions. The section below discusses these anomalies.

8.5.1. Fuzzy construals for [n*][lose][ppx*]

The examples below exhibit just how subtle the construal of *lose x-self* can be. Although both tokens construe the general idea of sexual activity, example 288 specifically construes the loss of all awareness except for the sexual act (i.e., SA-event), while in 289, placing oneself physically (and/or emotionally) inside another person during sexual intercourse instantiates the IDI (1)-type.

288. SA: Later *he* would spend the night *losing himself* in mindless sex.

                (COCA:2008.FIC.Bk:BlackSilk)

289. IDI (1): Nothing short of having her, of *losing himself* in her, would satisfy. *He* was afraid the touch of her lips...   (COCA:1994.FIC.Bk:Serendipity)

Other types of ambiguity occurred in examples of media advertisements in which, when examining only the token, *lose x-self* was conceptually 'fuzzy' between SA and LIT (2).

290. SA: *Lose yourself* on an island Seize the day. Grab some containers and head to Sauvie...   (COCA:2006.MAG.Sunset)

291. LIT (2): *Lose yourself* in a tropical jungle on trails flanked by elephant's ear plants with leaves...   (COCA:2006.MAG. SouthernLiv)

By examining only the tokens, it is difficult to determine appropriate construal types. However, examining the surrounding contexts reveals conceptual clues and the construal can then be understood as likely intended.

Expanded contexts: (abridged)

SA: *Lose yourself* on an island Seize the day. Grab some containers and head to Sauvie Island to pick a flat of luscious strawberries at Columbia Farms... or Kruger's Farm Market...The harvest usually peaks on Father's Day weekend... Stroll an island's island. Toss a towel and some snacks into a day pack and...

LIT (2): McKee Botanical Garden. *Lose yourself* in a tropical jungle on trails flanked by elephant's ear plants with leaves almost as big as coffee tables. In clearings, dazzling aquatic flowers dance on the surface of ponds. " We had an explosion of water lilies when we lost some of the tree canopy in Hurricane Frances.

In the first expanded context, the double-underlined parts show the contextual support for the SA construal, i.e., that the tourists to the island should completely focus on the experiences of the *island*. In other words, they should get themselves 'in the zone' so that they can totally absorb the island environment into their awareness without distraction. In the second expanded context, the contextual support conveys a sense of wandering, where one might perhaps go astray, or 'let oneself go astray', encompassed by the densely-foliated environment, this construing the LIT (2) categorization.

For all ambiguous cases, the expanded contexts were consulted. There was one instance in which a final determination could not be made and this was marked '?'. Shown below in 292, the context is a movie review, but insufficient contextual background makes it impossible to confidently determine a single construal.

> 292. *Director Stephen Frears loses himself* in the dazzling dresses.
>
> (COCA:2009.NEWS.Atlanta)

Expanded context:
Based on a novel by the French writer Colette, " Cheri " is a sumptuous but only rarely romantic romance set in France before World War I. Michelle Pfeiffer plays Lea, a fading beauty in all her self-aware glory. *Director Stephen Frears loses himself* in the dazzling dresses. (Roger Moore, McClatchy/Tribune). Rated R (for some sexual content and brief drug use). At Regal Tara. 1 hour, 33 minutes.

Under one interpretation, *lose x-self* conveys the TSM-type construal, where the *Director* is construed as losing his deeper Self (i.e., his innate ability as director). Because he puts so much of his Self into the outward spectacle of *dazzling dresses*, he strays from this deeper "Self-as-director". Another possible interpretation is the SA-type construal, where the *Director* is aware only of the *dazzling dresses* to the detriment of the whole film's intent or quality. Still another (albeit unlikely) scenario construes the LIT (2) sense, where the *Director*, for reasons amusing to imagine, decides to physically hide among *Lea's* numerous *dazzling dresses*, perhaps in her dressing room closet or the movie's costume repository. Therefore, due to these possibilities and the lack of concrete evidence, this was marked '?'.

8.6. Compound Examples of Finding and Losing

There were a few compound examples that conveyed the peculiarity and uniqueness of SA Events, expressing both *find* and *lose* within the same overall conception. Example 293 construes 'awareness of the failure to retain one's composure'.

> 293. Slicing into the chest cavity of the specimen provided by the supply house,
>
> *you find yourself* losing it. (COCA:1991.MAG.Omni)

Notice the continuous tense of the FoA <u>losing it</u>. The experiencer has not yet *lost* it and cannot be in the midst of being *lost*, but can only report on the loss of mental/emotional composure before or after the actual moment of being *lost*. This is the psychological nature of the phenomenon of *losing oneself* under the SA-type construal. Because of the total and complete immersion of the psyche within the object of awareness, no other awareness emerges. In other words, one cannot be reporting an event (in real time) in which there is no other consciousness other than that of the object of awareness, because this reporting necessitates some level of general type of conscious awareness. The writer uses the SA-type [*find x-self* + *lose x-self* FOA] construal to express the surprise and suddenness of the awareness of emotional composure slipping away (but not yet completely gone).

Example 294 shows how both *finding* and *losing oneself* are contrasted within the same sentence for literary effect (note the Poetry sub-register).

> 294. When *I find myself* <u>abstracted</u> or *lose myself* <u>in abstraction</u>, my self blurs at
> its boundaries but nonetheless retains a capacity, an enhanced capacity to
> accept whatever comes across.   (COCA:2015.ACAD.Poetry)

Expanded context:
You want them to have that lovely feeling of being carried away by fame, if only for the first few years. After that, when the chauffeur-driven Mercedes and butlers carrying dry martinis have disappeared, when things become calm in that long inertia of mid-career, they can reap a more mediated harvest of desolately beautiful later poems. # 3707 Section: COMMENT # <u>What is it to go into an abstracted state</u>? <u>When</u> *I find myself* <u>abstracted</u> or *lose myself* <u>in abstraction, my self blurs at its boundaries</u> but nonetheless retains a capacity, an enhanced capacity to accept whatever comes across. <u>Memories, freaks, phrases, and passing thoughts</u> escape judgment as to whether they deserve retaining. Even if they hover and unravel trains of thought, <u>they do not cancel or dislodge anything already contained or passing through this elastic " abstract scene."</u> Contradictions and other dissonance which would become jarring if sentience rose to active reaching, can coexist…

The interplay of the two SA-types reveals the complexity and subtleness of the metaphors and metonymies. The meaning of *find myself abstracted* is interpreted as being aware of an abstracted ego. Similarly, for *lose myself in abstraction*, the meaning is construed as awareness which is completely absorbed in that abstracted ego. This is contrasted with the contextual support (double-underlined) in the expanded context in which the Conceptual Metaphor MIND IS A CONTAINER is construed. This sets up a TSM-type conception not present in the SA Event of the token. Those boundaries, delineated as an abstract scene, set up a dualistic, deeper Self, (one that can *accept whatever comes across*), and another-Self (*Memories, freaks, phrases*, etc..), a.k.a. the Subject and Self (A. Lakoff & Becker 1992; G. Lakoff 1996a), respectively. This creates multi-level metaphorical conceptions in which individual SA Events are working within a larger, discourse-oriented TSM-type construal.

The following example also illustrates the *find-lose x-self* type where the SA-type and TSM-type work together to motivate the conception.

> 295. ...the most rewarding period of his life, when *to lose himself* utterly in God and His Work
> was truly *to find himself.*   (BNC:FRJ.W_fict_prose)

Expanded context:

...relishing settling his mind on sacred thoughts and holy themes in an effort to make himself spiritually equal to the demands of his calling. But that had been all of thirty years ago, and very quickly these demands had multiplied, absorbing more and more time and energy, so that the moments of evening meditation were soon subsumed into the preoccupations and stresses of an active Christianity. Yet the exchange had been all gain, for this became the happiest, the most rewarding period of his life, when *to lose himself* utterly in God and His Work was truly *to find himself.* This was a time of real communion, and it was not long before his parishioners began to think of him, as well as to address him, as Father Brendan rather than as Father McGiff, and he began to look on them as his family, and on Cork, their city, as his only home.

The SA-type *lose x-self* assumes the meaning to be absolutely focused on the task at hand, supported by the FoA *utterly in God and His Work*, along with the double-underlined, supporting context showing the focus on preoccupation and stresses of such concentration and one-pointedness on *His Work*. At this point, the experiencer, due to this extreme focus on *His Work*, *finds himself*, i.e., he finds his True Self, supported by the adverb *truly*, along with the clause-final position of *find x-self*. Thus, within the same sentence, the author sets the SA Event construal as the impetus for the TSM-type construal.

In another example, an SA Event-type *losing oneself* becomes the catalyst for a TSM-type *finding oneself*.

> 296. *Emma* ultimately creates a Leon who is able to fulfill her dreams, for a fleeting moment
> *losing herself* (yet finding herself) in the writing, much as Renee does
>   (COCA:1994.ACAD.Symposium)

Expanded context:

...initially Emma writes to receive letters, to take pleasure in the communication forbidden, impossible on the speech plane, writing subsequently becomes the adjuvant of a waning passion' in the manner of aphrodisiac " (17 18). Here Emma's attitude toward writing resembles Renee's in Part III, when the latter persists in expressing her passion to Max even after he recognizes how little she needs him. For both, writing itself becomes more important than the relationship. Emma ultimately creates a Leon who is able to fulfill her dreams, for a fleeting moment *losing herself* (*yet finding herself*) in the writing, much as Renee does...

In example 296, the SA Event *losing herself in writing* and its resulting mental state provides the stimulus for the TSM-type event *finding herself in writing*; in other words, the total absorption of awareness in writing was the catalyst for a deeper self-realization that resulted in the awareness of her True Self. The syntax here complicates the matter, however, as the two predicates share a prepositional phrase. However, in the SA Event, the PP is not semantically adjunctive (i.e., it is obligatory), whereas for the TSM construal it is truly adjunctive and optional, (the timely use of the parenthesis confirming this). This can be tested by the following originally-created examples;

297. Emma......, for a fleeting moment *losing herself* (in the writing), much as
     Renee does...

298. Emma......, for a fleeting moment *finding herself* (in the writing), much as
     Renee does...

Proposed earlier and evidenced here by numerous corpus examples, the semantic adjunctivity of the FoA is a major factor for the appropriate construal of metaphorically-construed reflexive events. In examples 297 and 298 above, regarding the PP in parentheses (i.e., the FoA) as semantically adjunctive (or not) has ramifications for total conception of the discourse. Although including the FoAs yields either the SA or TSM construal, deleting the FoA yields only the TSM construal. Thus, the FoA is semantically optional for TSM and the opposite holds for SA where the FoA is obligatory for appropriate construal.

Chapter 9: CATCH X-SELF

9.1. Introduction

Semantic variation and collocations of the verbs *find* and *lose* when they occur within the reflexive construction were previously discussed. Continuing this line of research, the construction *catch x-self* will now be investigated. It will be seen that *catch x-self* construes Self-Aware Events that are sudden and contain an added conception of *interruption of one's thought or internally-based action*. This suddenness, occurring with *find x-self* as well, is more pronounced with *catch x-self*, likely due to an entailment from the 'base' meaning of catch, i.e., "to get hold of and stop an object..."(LDOCE 2014). *To stop an object* implies that the object is in motion and the exertion of force to cease that motion is often 'a sudden loss of the object's momentum'. In the case of *catch x-self*, the object is not external but internal, but the same principle applies (metaphorically) to one's own thoughts, emotions, verbalizations and/or bodily functions, as seen in the examples below.

> 299. *He* had been going to say the revulsion of the diners,' but had *caught himself* in time.
> (COCA:1994.FIC.Bk:Recessional)

> 300. *Ari caught himself* nodding again. (COCA:2010.FIC.Analog)

> 301. *Lonie caught herself* feeling sorry that this had to be so. (BNC:GUK.W_fict_prose)

Catch x-self is shown to be complex and subtle in construal and collocation, and here as well, relevant context, predicated as the FoA along with support contexts, are shown to be the linchpins for resolving metaphoric meaning and conceptual ambiguity.

9.2. Method

The method used here follows that of *find x-self* and *lose x-self* and begins with a preliminary corpus search using the parameter [catch][ppx*]. This preliminary search confirms semantic variation and metaphoric use, prompting a more detailed investigation into antecedents that are pronouns and nouns, i.e., [p*][catch][ppx*] and [n*][catch][ppx*], respectively. The results of these investigations are presented below.

9.2.1. Categorization Results

Based on the results of the data for the corpus search [catch][ppx*] in the COCA and BNC (see Appendix 8), four semantic categories are proposed; Self-Aware Event (SA), Divided-Self Causative (DSC), Picture Noun Schema (PNS) and Literal use (LIT). Within the LIT category, four subcategories are proposed:

1) LIT (1): to physically brace or support one's body
2) LIT (2): to get one's body or clothes ensnared on/in something
3) LIT (3): idiom: to catch x-self up (in) smthg = to be in some trouble or problematic situation
4) LIT (4): to be apprehended by some authority, e.g., the police

Explanations and examples of each category are provided below.

SA Event: being suddenly or immediately perceptually aware of one's own action or thought.
    This is semantically similar to *find x-self* but with an intensified temporal entailment (i.e., suddenness).

> 302. *He caught himself* scribbling frantically...   (COCA:1992:NEWS.WashPost)

> 303. Saba feels a tingle of pride each time *she catches herself* thinking in English.
> (COCA: 2012.FIC.SouthernReview)

DSC (Divided-Self Causative): one part of Self exerts force on another part of Self after Self-Awareness of that action or thought emerges.

> 304. After a while Carlos catches himself, laughing along with the tourists. When
>   *he catches himself* he gets quiet and looks to the sea, and then down...
> (COCA:2005.FIC.KenyonRev)

In example 304 above, the first case of *catch x-self* is categorized as SA because only the awareness has emerged without any force to control it. In the second case, however, once this awareness has emerged, a mental force is activated to block or inhibit the action or thought (i.e. *laughing*), thus the DSC designation. Further support for this categorization are tokens in which some speech act is paused or self-interrupted, (marked by a hyphen (-) in the corpus). For example,

305. It's - "*She caught herself* <u>on the edge of a shriek</u>. " It's monstrous."

(COCA: 2010.FIC.Bk:OneMind)

<u>PNS (Picture Noun Schema)</u>: This refers to the outward physical manifestation or representation of the antecedent, typically predicated by examples such as: <u>*one catches oneself*</u> (i.e. sees oneself) in the reflection of a mirror, glass, water, etc.

306. What a sour world Alfred lived in. <u>When</u> *he caught himself* <u>in mirrors it shocked him</u> how young he still looked.　　　(COCA: 2003.FIC.LitCavalcade)

The four Literal senses are delineated below:

<u>LIT 1</u>: to physically brace or support one's body.

307. He runs from the salon and down the back stairs, <u>stumbling down them</u>, *catching himself*, reaching the back door that's standing open. (COCA:2001.FIC.Mov:FromWhereWe)

<u>LIT 2</u>: to get one's body or clothes ensnared on something.

308. …in the fence with Stella sideway easing her way through the hole careful *not to catch herself* <u>on that wire</u>…　　　(COCA:1992.FIC.AntiochRev)

<u>LIT 3</u>: (idiom: <u>to catch x-self up (in) smthg</u>) to be in some trouble or troubling situation.

309. Why lose that opportunity because *you caught yourself up into* something that you hadn't done anything wrong?　　　(COCA: 2011.SPOK.NPR_TellMore)

<u>LIT 4</u>: to be apprehended by some authority, e.g., the police.

310. ...there have been a number of cases in other cities – *they catch themselves*. Take too many risks, think they can play with the cops.   (COCA: 2004.FIC.Movie:Catwoman)

Even though LIT 3 is an idiom and not 'literal' in the strict sense of the meaning, the choice to include it in the LIT category is based on an interpretation of this as a sense extension of LIT 2, where *getting oneself or one's clothing physically ensnared on something* is metaphorically analogous to *getting ensnared in some troubling situation*. Admittedly, this could have been categorized as a separate idiomatic (IDI) category, but for the above reasoning along with the need for systematic economy, these types of examples were labeled LIT 3.

Each of these categories is instantiated in the data at different frequencies and appear along with the formerly described categories non-reflexive (X), indecisive (?), and duplicate (DUPL).

9.2.2. Onset of Awareness

It is notable that for *catch x-self*, SA-UE and TSM categories do not occur in the data. Seen in the non-corpus examples 311 and 312 below, the meanings are dubious except without extreme contextual backgrounding. Whether theoretically possible or not, SA-UE and TSM do not instantiate in the data and are therefore not considered for the purposes of this discussion.

311. SA-UE: $^?$I caught myself in a strange situation.

   $^?$The politicians caught themselves in a war of words.

312. TSM: $^?$I caught myself in a yoga ashram in India.

   $^?$As the poet finished writing her book, she caught herself.

For SA, DSC, and PNS metaphorical categories, a sudden perceptual awareness is entailed, as discussed in the previous section. Even though these display subtle conceptual and collocational differences, they all have this sudden onset of self-perceptual awareness in common. This onset of awareness (Grady & Johnson. 2003) was discussed Section 6.1.5, where Self-Awareness was proposed to be a 'primary scene' for *find/lose x-self* constructions. Although *catch x-self* was not included in that discussion, it is proposed here as additional evidence for the claim made there. The conceptual matrix in Figure 18, (first introduced in section 6.1.5) for *catch x-self* is proposed to be similar to *find x-self* except that the Onset Point (ibid.) is of a more salient, sudden nature. SA Events and PNS both construe the sudden onset of the 'Cognitive Subscene' (i.e., awareness of a perception) as a single event, whereas for Divided-Self Causative events, the construal is a two-step process; the first involves the awareness of the thought or action, and the second involves the force action necessary to impede or discontinue that action. Because the awareness and force action always occur in very close temporal proximity, the event is categorized here as a single event.

Figure 18. Primary Scene: The onset of Self-Awareness (based on Grady and Johnson (2003)

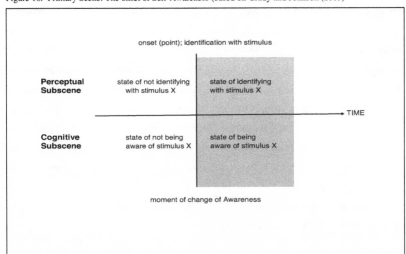

9.2.3. Causative-type Force

Support for the DSC-type category are instances where two FoAs are predicated. In these cases, the first instance conveys the awareness of some thought or action and the second construes some psychodynamic force (Gilquin 2007; Talmy 2000a) that inhibits the thought or action. Three examples were instantiated in the data and are shown below (perceptual awareness is underlined and psychodynamic force is double-underlined).

313. I'm defective. I'm not really a person." *She caught herself* <u>saying the words aloud</u>, <u>and clamped her jaws shut</u>. (COCA:2004.FIC.Analog)

314. …to stop and focus on one thing at a time. As soon as *I catch myself* <u>spinning</u>
<u>around the room, I pause, I breathe in deep and release</u>…

(COCA:2015.ACAD.PhysicalEduc)

315. …girls with EBD, *the young women in this group would often catch themselves* <u>in the act</u>
<u>and self-correct inappropriate behavior</u> independent of redirection from facilitators.

(COCA:2012.ACAD.EducTreatmen.Children)

For examples 313 to 315 above, some internally-initiated thought or action occurs to which an Awareness then emerges. This action or thought is deemed in need of being blocked or inhibited in some way, either mentally or physically. In 313, the woman concluded that the *words* that she was saying were not appropriate, to which she then took action to prevent further similar words from being spoken by *clamping her jaws shut*. In 314, *spinning around the room* is the action deemed in need of being inhibited, and so the action of *pausing and breathing deeply* achieves this. In the most explicit example 315, the *inappropriate behavior* of the young women was *self-corrected*, i.e., changed by themselves. Thus, both the initial thought or action and the counter thought or action are both internally based, the latter being the counter-force to the former.

Having defined and delineated the types of construal that occur with *catch x-self*, the results of the corpus inquiry are discussed below.

9.3. Results

The search parameter [catch][ppx*] (the lemma *catch* followed by any reflexive pronoun) yielded 1204 hits in the COCA ($n \geq 10$) and 59 in the BNC ($n \geq 5$) (reciprocals deleted). For the seven reflexive object pronoun retrieved data sets that had more than 100 tokens, a random sample of 100 was retrieved. The frequency ratios for each of the categories in each corpus are shown in Table 21.

The SA-type construal occurs most frequently in both corpora at a 36.5% mean ratio, followed by the DSC category at a 20.5% mean ratio. Metaphorical expressions (including the PNS category, yielding a 0.7% mean ratio) thus make up more than half of the total data set. Frequencies for individual items, however, show incongruities. For example, in the COCA data, when comparing SA and DSC-type events, the frequency orders for third-person pronouns (i.e., *himself*, *herself*) are the inverse to the overall frequency mean. In other words, for *himself* and *herself*, the DSC construal is more frequent (52% and 51%, respectively) than the SA construal (17% and 33%, respectively), which is incongruent with the results of the total mean where the SA-type is the most frequent category; however, this result is not significant (p=0.0572) and therefore only suggests a weak attraction of the third person pronoun to the DSC construal.

Table 21. Frequency ratios for [catch][ppx*] in the COCA & BNC according to semantic category and reflexive object pronoun

COCA	himself (n=100)	herself (n=100)	myself (n=100)	yourself (n=71)	themselves (n=22)	ourselves (n=19)	itself (n=10)	avg.
SA	17	33	51	50.7	36.4	68.4	10	38.1
DSC	52	51	30	15.5	27.3	15.8	0	26.4
LIT 1	26	10	10	22.5	4.5	5.3	30	15.5
LIT 2	1	1	0	0	4.5	0	30	5.2
LIT 3	0	0	0	2.8	4.5	5.3	10	3.2
LIT 4	0	0	0	0	4.5	0	0	0.6
PNS	1	2	3	2.8	0	0	0	1.3
X	3	0	3	4.2	18.2	5.3	20	7.7
?	1	3	2	0	0	0	0	0.9
DUPL	0	0	0	1.4	0	0	0	0.2

BNC	herself (n=21)	himself (n=19)	themselves (n=0)	myself (n=10)	yourself (n=9)	itself (n=0)	ourselves (n=0)	avg.
SA	47.6	57.9	0	60	77.8	0	0	34.8
DSC	38	21	0	20	22.2	0	0	14.5
LIT 1	4.8	0	0	0	0	0	0	0.7
LIT 2	4.8	5.2	0	0	0	0	0	1.4
LIT 3	0	5.2	0	10	0	0	0	2.2
LIT 4	0	0	0	0	0	0	0	0
PNS	0	0	0	0	0	0	0	0
X	4.8	0	0	0	0	0	0	0.7
?	0	10.5	0	10	0	0	0	2.9
DUPL	0	0	0	0	0	0	0	0

The relatively common occurrence of the PNS category in the COCA (1.3%) is noteworthy. Upon further inspection, this is suggested to be due to the conception of 'seeing one's image in a reflective surface', e.g., *catching oneself in a mirror, pool of water, window*, etc. The lack of instantiations in the BNC is interesting and tentatively suggests either regional variation or corpus data bias as a cause. Due to the low frequency, however, a more concrete statement cannot be made at this time.

One result for which regional variation is determined to be a cause is the lack of tokens for the plural and impersonal pronouns in the BNC. Granted, the frequencies for these in the

COCA are relatively low as well (*themselves* =22, *ourselves* =19, *itself* =10), but the BNC null frequencies are conspicuous.

Detailed analyses will be discussed in the following subsections, but these preliminary results provide strong impetus for a more fine-grained inquiry in which the antecedent types (pronoun vs. noun) are distinguished.

9.3.1. Results for [p*][catch][ppx*]

In a query using the input search parameter [p*][catch][ppx*], there were 347 tokens in the COCA and 19 in the BNC (reciprocals deleted), seen in Table 22. Noticeable in the cross-corpora results column (i.e., COCA+BNC) is the higher frequency of DSC compared to SA (49.5% and 35.5%, respectively), in contrast to the previously discussed higher frequency of SA when the antecedent was not taken into account (see Table 21). When the data is sorted by pronoun, seen in Figure 19, incongruent results appear for the first person singular *myself* (SA=56, DSC=35) compared to *himself* and *herself*, (SA=23,30; DSC=63,59, respectively). A dependent relationship is found between first and third person pronouns when SA and DSC-type construals are considered. Entering each of these frequencies (integers used as input values) into a contingency table (1st person: SA=61, DSC=38; 3rd person: SA=55, DSC=126), the result is significant (p=1E-06). In other words, when the antecedent is a first-person pronoun, the construal is likely to be an SA-type construal in contrast to the third-person pronoun in which the DSC-type construal is more likely. These results again suggest that specifying the type of antecedent can provide unique insights into usage and collocational patterning.

This is corroborated by the results of register type seen in Table 23. Considering the data only for non-fiction register frequencies[58], there is a significant dependent relation (p= .0025) between SA events and the first-person pronoun antecedents (*n*=26) compared to DSC-type events (*n*=15), and vice versa for DSC and third-person pronoun antecedents (*n*=24) and SA events (*n*=9). In other words, for non-fiction registers, SA events are more likely with first person pronoun antecedents and DSC is more likely with third person pronoun antecedents. It is proposed again here that the 'naturalness' of expressing SA events from a first-person point of view is the motivation for these results. That this is significant for the non-fiction register here strengthens this claim made previously for *find* and *lose* described previously.

---

[58] The fiction register was not included in order to analyze 'real-world events', so to speak. Integers were used as input values for significance tests.

Conversely, the propensity for DSC to be more likely for third-person pronoun antecedents is likely due to the FoA being an action that is observable by the speaker/writer. These results contrast with tokens from the FICTION register in which the narrator/author is one and the same entity as the character and can therefore describe internal perceptions from the intimate point of view (i.e., first person) even though the character is a third person entity and the syntax reflects this.

Table 22. Combined frequencies in the COCA and BNC for [p*][catch][ppx*]

COCA	Freq.	BNC	Freq.	COCA+BNC	Freq. (ratio %)
SA	121	SA	9	SA	130 (35.5%)
DSC	172	DSC	9	DSC	181 (49.5%)
PNS	6	PNS	0	PNS	6 (1.6%)
LIT 1	34	LIT 1	0	LIT 1	34 (9.2%)
LIT 2	1	LIT 2	1	LIT 2	2 (0.5%)
LIT 3	1	LIT 3	0	LIT 3	1 (0.3%)
LIT 4	4	LIT 4	0	LIT 4	4 (1.1%)
X	3	X	0	X	3 (0.8%)
?	1	?	0	?	1 (0.3%)
DUPL	4	DUPL	0	DUPL	4 (1.1%)
TOTALS	347		19		366

Figure 19. Frequencies of SA and DSC categories according to pronoun

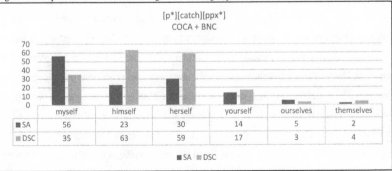

[p*][catch][ppx*]
COCA + BNC

	myself	himself	herself	yourself	ourselves	themselves
SA	56	23	30	14	5	2
DSC	35	63	59	17	3	4

Table 23. Frequencies of [p*][catch][ppx*] by register

COCA	FREQ	PER MIL	BNC	FREQ	PER MIL
SPOKEN	25	0.2	SPOKEN	1	0.1
FICTION	327	3.1	FICTION	14	0.9
MAGAZINE	63	0.6	MAGAZINE	0	0
NEWSPAPER	49	0.5	NEWSPAPER	0	0
ACADEMIC	12	0.1	NON-ACAD	5	0.3
TOTAL	476		ACADEMIC	2	0.1
			MISC	2	0.1
			TOTAL	24	

Figure 20. Cross-corpora frequencies of past and present tense, by pronoun, for [p*][catch][ppx*]

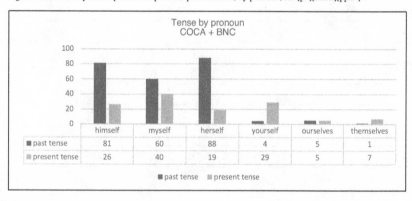

Another collocational trend concerns verb tense. Seen in Figure 20, the high frequency of past tense tokens for the three most common pronouns (i.e., *himself*, *myself* and *herself*) suggests that *catch x-self* is perhaps more 'natural' when the FoA action has already been completed. This can be corroborated by the total frequency counts for past (n=239) and present tense (n=126), a nearly two-fold difference. Upon reflection on the entailed meaning of 'suddenness' discussed earlier for *catch x-self*, the past tense is a logical consequence of that temporal constraint. Due to its speed, along with the entailment for the meaning of *catch*, (i.e., "to get hold of and stop an object" (LDOCE 2014)), the generalized meaning can be construed as *to suddenly hold and stop something*. *To hold something* is a bipolar action, i.e., either an object is held or it isn't. Once an un-held object is held, the action is complete. There is no time duration in which the object is in the process of being held. One can *barely catch* something, but the object is still considered caught; conversely, one can *almost catch* something, in which case the object is not caught. This entailment carries through into the metaphorical construal. Similarly, the emergence of perceptual Self-Awareness can be conceived of as an object that is 'held' in the 'container of the mind' via the MIND IS A CONTAINER conceptual metaphor (G. Lakoff & Johnson 1980).

The past-present tense comparison data also reveal different aspects of the expressions. For example, the present tense is more frequent with the second person (i.e., *you-yourself*; past $n=4$, present $n=29$) and third person plural pronouns (i.e., *they-themselves*; past $n=1$, present $n=7$), contrary to the previous overall results. In the COCA, the ratio for present to past tense for *yourself* is 6:1 and for *themselves* it is 7:1. Why should this be so? Upon closer investigation, shown in the typical examples 316 and 317 below, it is actually not the present tense but the future and conditional tenses that are common, followed by interrogatives, and these together instantiate just over 74% of the cases.

316. Have students begin listening to everything they say to themselves. When *they catch themselves* talking to themselves, whether it is negative or positive…

(COCA:1992.ACAD.InstrPsych)

317. And if *you catch your*self ordering a second cocktail within an hour, slow it down…

(COCA:2011.MAG.Shape)

Thus, for second-person and third-person plural *catch x-self*, it is not a past-present distinction as much as a past-other distinction that can be delineated. Although this data can be analyzed in more detail as to which tense/aspect of the verb with specific antecedent pair is instantiated, due to the lack of applicability to the present topic, this analysis was not conducted. The inquiry would be an interesting one for future research endeavors, however. What is important for the present research is the overall higher ratio of the past tense, likely due to the temporal entailment of the meaning of *catch*.

Other results show a high cross-corpora frequency for the second- and third-person plural pronoun antecedents as general referents (i.e., not specific persons), instantiating at 84%. One motivating factor for this may be the pragmatic function (e.g., speech act) of the tokens. For second-person tokens, 52% of the cases are 'giving advice' to the reader/audience, whereas

17% of the third-person plural tokens were also of this type. This may be due to the type of data used in each corpus, a large amount coming from mainstream media containing articles and media programs that give advice to its readers/listeners. Only a more in-depth and detailed sociolinguistic analysis can reveal to what extent this is instantiated, but for the present inquiry, the above statement is evidentially supported.

The points above all confirm the importance of analyzing metaphors according to type of antecedent as well as 'construal in context', where construal and collocation reveal patterns of use. The next section discusses examples where the antecedents of *catch x-self* are full nouns.

9.4. [n*][catch][ppx*]

A search was conducted with the parameter [n*][catch][ppx*], where the antecedent is a full noun. Due to the limited number of tokens in both corpora, there was no minimum count set for the lemma search (*n*=95 in the COCA, *n*=8 in the BNC, reciprocals deleted). The frequencies for each semantic category are shown in Table 24.

In the COCA, the DSC-type is 1.7 times more frequent than the SA-type, whereas in the BNC, SA is twice as frequent as DSC, although the low frequency warrants caution about positing generalizations. Proper names comprised 84 of the COCA tokens (88%) and six (75%) of the BNC. In the COCA, 48 were masculine and 36 were feminine names, while in the BNC, two were masculine and four were feminine.

Table 24. Category frequencies for [n*][catch][ppx*]

COCA	Freq.		BNC	Freq.
SA	29		SA	4
DSC	51		DSC	2
PNS	2		LIT (2)	1
LIT (1)	8		?	1
LIT (2)	1		Total	8
LIT (3)	1			
?	2			
X	1			
Total	95			

In both corpora, there were six instances of metonymically-construed experiencer-antecedents.

> 318. *Brokers catch themselves* <u>describing an $825,000 house as " sweet</u>...
>
> (COCA:1999.NEWS.NYTimes)

> 319. Do I look like I deliver deliveries? # <u>What you-</u> *The younger barber catches himself* <u>mid-question-a rush to judgment</u>-now that he sees and realizes that Marty and Pop are...
>
> (COCA:2005.FIC.Callaloo)

In examples 318 and 319, *the job title or action* STANDS FOR *the people who work as brokers.* All six metonyms (e.g., *barber, broker, patrolman, researcher, comic, epic poet*) instantiate the ACTION FOR AGENT type (Radden & Kövecses 1999).

By register, 83 (87%) of the COCA and six (75%) of the BNC tokens were of the FICTION register. This high number again supports the claim made previously that the author/narrator assumes the first-person point of view of the character (construing an internal perception) while predicating the third person experiencer-antecedent.

9.5. Fuzzy and other examples

The data for *catch x-self* was not immune to conceptually ambiguous cases. It was sometimes challenging to specify the difference between SA and DSC based on the token alone. In example 320 below, when only the token is considered, the continuous *waving of the fork* suggests an SA construal where *Ken* is perceptually aware of his *fork waving.* However, in the context of the next sentence, once this awareness emerges, *Ken* ceases this action, a DSC-type construal.

> 320. *Ken caught himself* <u>waving his fork around</u> with a piece of steak still attached and shedding bits of batter. <u>He set it on his plate.</u> (COCA:2008.FIC.FantasySciFi)

Another conceptually 'fuzzy' example (below) represents an indecisive ('?') case, which can potentially be construed as SA, PNS, or LIT (4).

> 321. While *President Richard M. Nixon caught himself* <u>on tape using epithets and ripping into</u>

homosexuality, President Obama and the chairman of the Joint Chiefs of Staff have called for gays to be allowed to serve openly in the military.

(COCA:2010.NEWS.WashPost)

Expanded context (abridged)

> The boycott of segregated buses in Montgomery, Ala., began in 1955. California's Supreme Court struck down a ban on interracial marriage in 1948, 18 years before the U.S. Supreme Court did the same. "That all changed in increments, " he said. # Leonard Hirsch, a policy staffer at the Smithsonian Institution, said a symbolic shift has already occurred. While *President Richard M. Nixon caught himself* on tape using epithets and ripping into homosexuality, President Obama and the chairman of the Joint Chiefs of Staff have called for gays to be allowed to serve openly in the military. Still, Obama said during his campaign that he opposed same-sex marriage. (COCA:2010.NEWS.WashPost)

Under the SA-type construal, *Nixon* is aware of both his own attitude and the language he uses concerning the gay community. As such, the main FoA is marked as *using epithets and ripping into homosexuality*. However, if construed as a PNS category, *on tape* is the main FoA, where *Nixon* literally hears an external, physical version of himself *on tape*, similar to if he were to see himself in a film. Finally, under the LIT (4) conception, the agency responsible for enforcing law arrested the president and due to his own carelessness, making it easy for the enforcers to catch *Nixon*. Although historically inaccurate, with enough context this is conceptually possible. All in all, due to the lack of definitive context, this example was marked indecisive '?'.

The argument could be made that the difference between SA and DSC is that the DSC construal contains some negative action that requires cessation. However, positive and negative determinations aren't as clear-cut as they seem and ethical and/or cultural attitudes towards actions are not the sole basis for inhibiting an action. For example, *thinking* is usually considered a positive action, but in the example below it is something to stop and take notice of and perhaps take action to control/inhibit.

> 322. Whenever *you catch yours*elf thinking, say to yourself, That's thinking. No matter how compelling or urgent your thought seems, simply label it and let it go.
>
> (COCA:2005.MAG.Prevention)

In contrast, *greed* is often considered a negative trait, but not always, as in the following example.

323. How does thrift differ from greed? Have *you caught yourself* ever <u>acting in a</u>
<u>greedy fashion</u>? <u>Maybe greed isn't so bad</u>.   (COCA:2004.SPOK.NPR_TalkNation)

Again, these cases show the importance of analyzing sufficient context for the proper
delineation of metaphoric construal and the dangers of basing results only on the specific
metaphoric construction and/or the individual token.

9.6. Compound FIND/CATCH x-self

The examples in this section predicate both *find x-self* and *catch x-self* within the same sentence.
In example 324, a compound SA+DSC-type is construed, where the awareness of *reaching for*
the phone (i.e., SA) is in need of cessation (i.e., DSC).

324. *He* sometimes *finds himself* <u>reaching for the phone</u> to call his father and
then *catching himself* <u>before dialing</u>, remembering that his father is gone.

(COCA: 1991.NEWS.NYTimes)

Example 325 below is an SA+SA complex, where the experiencer is aware of herself being
self-conscious (SA) and in that self-conscious state, further awareness of subsequent thoughts
occurs (SA).

325. *She found herself* <u>self-conscious</u> under Carolyn's exhaustive scrutiny, and *caught herself*
<u>trying to measure and examine the things she said</u> from the girl's point of view.

(BNC: HJH.W_fict_prose)

The relational dynamics of the above conceptions are indeed complex. By delineating the
semantic and collocational subtleties in systematic ways as discussed here, however, it is
possible to describe much of the data and postulate cognitive and other motivations that support
these results.

9.7. Chapter Conclusion

In conclusion to chapter 9, the types of metaphoric construal for *catch x-self* that occur are
similar to that of *find x-self* except for the strengthened entailment of suddenness of action. One

categorical difference is the addition of the Divided-Self Causative (DSC), where two internal actions occur in quick succession. The first is an Awareness of the original action and the second is a force used to impede or block the original action. These sequential actions happen quickly and are thus difficult to identify. Corpus analysis and results for *catch x-self* suggest that conceptual and collocational patterns were able to be distinguished and evidenced by way of context. The contexts for the metaphoric instantiations were explained and justifications suggested. Unresolvable and 'fuzzy' examples were also discussed in detail.

Chapter 10: Conclusions and Discussion

10.1. Introduction

The constructions *find/lose/catch x-self* have been shown to have much semantic variation, and within that variation are collocations that include dependent components. When metaphorically-construed and contained within the reflexive construction, these three verbs construe multiple types of Self-Aware conceptions. Conceptual contexts cannot be ignored when analyzing these types of constructions and often the expanded context is the only recourse for accurate meaning retrieval (Sinclair 1991).

It is claimed that Self-Awareness is an image schema, and as such, it can be utilized as a base conception for metaphoric construal and predication. If this claim is analyzed logically, it stands to reason that the mind cannot be aware of something without an object for its awareness. "The idea that I know is not the same as the idea that I know I know" (Lewis 2006: 21). SA events report on this "knowing-I-know" phenomenon, the latter *knowing* representing the Subject's perceptions and the former *knowing* representing the Awareness of those perceptions. Corpus data has been presented that support this claim.

Table 25. Summary of categorizations and frequency ratios for metaphorically-construed *find/catch/lose x-self*

Categories	find x-self	catch x-self	lose x-self
SA	28.7%	40%	43.5%
SA-UE	65.2%	X	X
TSM	2.1%	X	19.6%
PNS	3.6%	1.1%	X
DSC	X	26.1%	X

Five types of metaphorical events are construed and predicated through the three reflexive constructions, summarized in Table 25. Summarizing typical examples from all metaphoric conceptions found in the data, differences in conception become more transparent.

SA (Self-Aware Events):

326. *Michael Stevinson found himself* afraid to hold his newborn twins, Douglas and Michelle.

(COCA:1998.MAG.Parenting)

327. Then, *she caught herself* smiling:' Feeling pleased with yourself,' she thought immediately...   (BNC:ACB.W_fict_prose)

328. For a time *he lost himself* in the game, his whole self gathered up into the shapes the stones...   (BNC:GUG.W_fict_prose)

SA-UE (Self-Aware Unexpected Event)

329. Wherever you are and in whatever circumstances *you find yourself*, strive always to be a lover...   (BNC:B1F.W_religion)

TSM (True-Self Metaphor):

330. But we have a lot of good *players* that will *find themselves*. It just takes time.

(COCA:1995.NEWS.Houston)

331. In a state of intoxication, *an individual loses himself*. This is the basis of the Dionysiac experience: the collapse of individuation...   (BNC:H0N.W_ac_humanities_arts)

PNS (Picture Noun Schema):

332. *Katie Kauffman* really *finds herself* in the picture with the latest in high-tech animation. (Double entendre with TSM-type)   (COCA.1995.CBS_Morning)

333. *I catch myself* sometimes in the mirror when I'm alone and there it is-my beautiful outside...   (COCA:1998.FIC.ParisRev)

DSC (Divided-Self Causative):

334. I smile because I'm telling this story. And then *I catch myself* and go, "Wait a minute. That's not real.   (COCA:2015.SPOK.CBS)

These different aspects of Self are but the tip of the larger philosophical, psychological and physiological iceberg of what constitutes the Self (Bodhi 2012; Damasio 2010a; Nanamoli 1991; Parker, Mitchell & Boccia 2006; Satchidananda 1984; Stiles 2001). Whatever the perspective, humans have the linguistic capacity to express "knowing what we know", and because these SOURCE concepts of Self are ephemeral and dependent on factors such as biology, age, culture and religion, etc., a more concrete image (i.e., TARGET) is created onto which to map the conception in predication.

One question that has not yet been addressed is: Are there other reflexive constructions that construe Self-Awareness and if so, are they also candidates for SA Events? One category of verbs likely to utilize this image schema is most likely from the Self-Perception category proposed in Chapter 6. The verbs in this category are: *be, catch, check, feel, find, identify, immerse, lose, perceive, regard, see, watch. Catch, find,* and *lose* were already shown to include Self-Aware events, and so a survey of the other verbs is now timely.

Table 26. Verbs from the category 'Perception' and metaphorical construal frequencies in the COCA corpus (*n*=100, random sample of each verb)

verb	Construal Type (frequency)	Total Frequency
be	TSM (25); X (75)	5772
check	DSC (19); lit (37); idi (36); X (8)	446
feel	SA-UE (17) ; lit (77); idi (1); X (5)	2416
identify	lit (39); lit 2 (61)	2622
immerse	lit (5); lit 2 (85); SA (10)	808
perceive	lit (100)	619
regard	lit (78); lit 2 (2); X (20)	431
see	lit (18); met1 (35); met2 (17); X (30)	9049
watch	lit (39); met1 (16); met2 (20); X (22); ? (3)	806

A search with the parameters [v][ppx*] was conducted for the COCA corpus (*n*=100, random sample) for each of the verbs in the category and results are shown in Table 26. The list of verbs, including a corpus example of each metaphorically-construed type, is provided below. Explanations of abbreviated terms from Table 26 are provided when necessary.

<u>be</u>: (TSM=True-Self Metaphor)

335. TSM: "I wanted to feel good *I* wanted to *be myself*," writes Jenner, reflecting on the night…
(COCA:2015.MAG.People)

<u>check</u>: (DSC= to inhibit oneself from doing something; IDI=check in/out of a hotel or clinic)

336. DSC: "Robotically chivalrous", she <u>almost said</u>, but <u>something made her</u> *check herself.*
(COCA:1997.FIC.SouthwestRev)

<u>feel</u>: (SA-UE=to think or know oneself to be in some situation; IDI=to touch one's body, esp. sexually)

337. SA-UE: Dr. Deeb can not picture Saddam acceding to such a term unless *his army feels itself* <u>on the very brink of complete collapse</u>. (COCA:1991.NEWS.CSMonitor)

<u>identify</u>: (LIT 2: affiliate oneself with some group, i.e., "identify oneself as...")

338. Non-metaphoric: lit 2: in 1996, the first time a majority of *voters* -- 51 percent -- *identified themselves* <u>as Republicans</u> in a state once solidly Democratic.
(COCA:1998.NEWS.Atlanta)

<u>immerse</u>: (SA= visceral and total focus on some object or activity, similar to *lose x-self*; LIT 2= to be very involved with some activity)

339. SA: He loves information. He <u>often deals with pain or challenges by</u> *immersing himself* in study... (COCA:2000.NEWS.USAToday)

<u>perceive</u>: (LIT: to think, believe, or understand)

340. Non-metaphoric: <u>How</u> an individual *perceives himself* or herself is key to the achievement of connected knowing. (COCA:2000.ACAD.ReVision)

<u>regard</u>: (LIT= see (in reflective surface); LIT 2= think, believe, understand)

341. LIT: As Lucy closes the door behind them, *he regards himself* sadly <u>in the large silver-framed mirror</u>... (COCA:2008.FIC.Bk:MaryModern)

342. LIT 2: The House of Lords has learned to *regard itself* <u>as a chamber with influence</u>, not with power. (COCA:1999.NEWS.WashPost)

<u>see</u>: (LIT=see; Metaphoric 1=understand, believe; Metaphoric 2=imagine, see in one's mind)

343. Metaphoric 1: *Women* need to *see themselves* <u>as full and active partners</u> in the 21st-century... (COCA:2008.MAG.America)

344. Metaphoric 2: ...we'd both signed the lease. In a terrifying flash *I saw myself* back in my old bedroom... (COCA:2007.FIC.LiteraryRev)

watch: (LIT=watch; Metaphoric 1=imagine, see in mind; Metaphoric 2=be careful)

345. Metaphoric 1: *He watched himself* as if from a distance as he opened the front panel of the chair... (COCA:2006.FIC.Bk:BurningDreams)

346. Metaphoric 2: It's so hard to get good help these days. " " *Watch yourself*, Simon Legree, " Priscilla said, " or I'll tell pop ... (COCA:1992.FIC.Bk:McNallysLuck)

In the search for Self-Awareness and/or other metaphorical events, four have been identified here. There is one construction each that construes SA, SA-UE, TSM, and DSC. The PNS-type construal is absent from the data.

For the verb *feel*, SA-UE events account for 17% of the 100 random sample tokens. The conception of this metaphor is highly fluid, meaning that the demarcation between the literal and metaphorical meanings is 'fuzzy'. In most cases such as 347 below, both physicality and mentality can be attributed to *feel* due to the interconnectedness of thought, emotion, and sensation in human experience. In all of these metaphorical cases (except for the single idiomatic example), however, 'self-perceptual awareness of some externally-initiated situation' (SA-UE) is construed. *Feeling persecuted* can simultaneously be a physical, emotional and mental response sensation, all brought about by some external source, accounting for the difficulty of pinpointing a concrete, compartmentalized conception. That notwithstanding, the focus of the reflexive event is on the awareness of that perception, thus, the attribution of the SA-UE categorization.

347. The religious and traditional *community feels itself* persecuted by the government and by the Supreme Court's decisions. (COCA:1996.ACAD.Church&State)

For *immerse x-self*, shown in 348 below, the SA-type event is construed at a frequency ratio of 10%. Under this construal, *immerse x-self* has a similar meaning to *lose x-self* in which the focus of concentration is so intense that awareness of other perceptions fades into the background of the subconscious.

348. *Antonio* retrieved the model from the pool, laid it out on the grass and *immersed himself* in the task of arranging it in the logical position for a martyr. (COCA:1994.FIC.LiteraryRev)

For *immerse x-self*, the experiencer is aware of and is doing nothing but the task at hand. The metaphor creates a conceptual cross-domain mapping of the SOURCE: *being completely surrounded by liquid*. Here, the surrounding element is *the task* and being completely surrounded by it, there is no other consciousness except for *the task* to the detriment of other kinds of awareness or activity, thus the SA event categorization.

For the verb *be*, TSM accounts for 25% of the tokens. This high ratio was surprising, as was the simple dichotomy of this with non-reflexive examples. However, upon further investigation, it is logical (post-hoc) that this be the case. The copula *be* followed by a reflexive pronoun functions mainly as intensifier, not reflexive:

349. Such facile nihilism is itself dehumanizing to the people who struggle to survive...

(COCA:2010.ACAD.AmerScholar)

Concerning the metaphorical cases, all construe TSM in one degree or another. In other words, there is not one universal True-Self. Depending on the situation, the quality and depth of the True-Self changes. The True-Self is 'the confident Self' in example 350, 'the freedom of speech Self' in 351, and 'the relaxed Self' in 352. The True Self is context-dependent and ephemeral, and as such, reference to what this entails changes with context.

350. ...his body language expressing his own self-confidence and the joy he took in *being himself*. (COCA:2006.NEWS.WashPost)

351. Many students talked about freedom, the chance to *be yourself*.

(COCA:1993.SPOK.ABC_20/20)

352. You can truly relax and *be yourself*, and not worry about where you have to be later...

(COCA:2007.MAG.Ebony)

For *check x-self*, the DSC construal accounts for 19% of the data. *Check x-self* can be a more direct form of causation compared to *catch x-self*, meaning that the second, force-type action is more salient. In general, however, the two constructions are semantically congruent.

353. *Mona* started to laugh, then *checked herself* and said Reid would be back in about an hour.

(COCA:1994.FIC.Commentary)

354. Sometimes *I* have to *check myself* when I'm doing too much for everybody, including you.

(COCA:2013.MAG.Essence)

In conclusion, four perceptual verbs that were categorized in a preliminary corpus analysis were shown to yield the types of metaphorical construal delineated in this research. Specifically, SA, SA-UE, TSM, and DSC are instantiated for the verbs *feel, immerse, be*, and *check*, respectively. Other verbs in the original Self-Perception category, although sometimes construed metaphorically, yielded no instantiations of these kinds of conceptions.

10.2. Comparative analysis of SA verbs + x-self

In this section, SA-type constructions were compared in order to uncover further collocational patterns. The verbs were paired by similarity of meaning: [find ppx : catch ppx], [lose ppx : immerse ppx] and [catch ppx : check ppx]. For each pair, collocations were allowed of up to four places to the right so that nuances in the FoA could be retrieved and analyzed.

In Table 27, the comparison shows the frequency ratios of Word 1 to Word 2. There are 22.16 tokens of the construction *find ppx** for every token of *catch ppx** and so on for the other verb comparisons. *find ppx*- catch ppx** has the largest discrepancy, while *lose ppx* - immerse ppx** has the smallest, suggesting that *lose x-self* and *immerse x-self* contain more similarity in meaning. Interestingly, when the verbs are compared without their reflexive pronouns, the yielded ratios are very different, as shown in Table 28.

Table 27. Ratio comparisons of reflexive *find-catch, lose-immerse*, and *catch-check*

Word 1	Word 2
find ppx* (22.16)	catch ppx* (0.05)
lose ppx* (1.25)	immerse ppx* (0.80)
catch ppx* (2.43)	check ppx* (0.41)

Table 28. Ratio comparisons of *find-catch*, *lose-immerse*, and *catch-check*

Word 1	Word 2
find (5.37)	catch (0.19)
lose (61.11)	immerse (0.02)
catch (0.66)	check (1.53)

Although the complexity of statistically and semantically comparing the intricate contexts for the verbs in Table 28 with their reflexive counterparts in Table 27 is beyond the scope of this investigation, it can be stated tentatively and in general terms that these results represent functional differences between the sets. In other words, each of these verbs acts differently when embedded within the reflexive construction and when not. Comparing the first 20 collocations of *find ppx** and *catch ppx**, seen in Table 29, the FoA profiles are very different. Whereas *find x-self* collocates with adverbs denoting relatively passive, uncontrollable states and verbs of little action (i.e., stative, (Ebeling & Ebeling 2013)) such as *unable*, *standing*, *facing*, *drawn*, *surrounded*, *alone*, etc., *catch x-self* collocates with more active verbs such as *look*, *stop*, *admonish*, *bargain*, etc. This adds support for the claim made above that *find ppx** mainly construes SA-UE events whereas *catch ppx** mainly construes the DSC-type construal.

Table 29. Ratio comparisons of reflexive *find ppx** and *catch ppx** (collocates 4 places to the right)

WORD 1 (W1): FIND PPX* (22.16)						WORD 2 (W2): CATCH PPX* (0.05)				
	WORD	W1	W2	W1/W2	SCORE		WORD	W2	W1	W2/W1	SCORE
1	UNABLE	284	0	568	25.6	1	LOOKS	4	0	8	177.2
2	STANDING	266	0	532	24	2	STOPS	4	0	8	177.2
3	FACING	233	0	466	21	3	)	29	7	4.1	91.8
4	POSITION	178	0	356	16.1	4	REALIZED	4	1	4	88.6
5	WITHOUT	174	0	348	15.7	5	ADMONISHING	2	0	4	88.6
6	DRAWN	166	0	332	15	6	BARRELING	2	0	4	88.6
7	BETWEEN	160	0	320	14.4	7	BARGAINING	2	0	4	88.6
8	SURROUNDED	143	0	286	12.9	8	EXPLAINED	2	0	4	88.6
9	ALONE	278	1	278	12.5	9	FROWNED	2	0	4	88.6
10	WORKING	130	0	260	11.7	10	ID	2	0	4	88.6
11	NEW	129	0	258	11.6	11	LAUGHS	2	0	4	88.6
12	LIVING	128	0	256	11.6	12	MIDSENTENCE	2	0	4	88.6
13	THEMSELVES	5703	23	248	11.2	13	PICKS	2	0	4	88.6
14	SUDDENLY	116	0	232	10.5	14	SMILED	2	0	4	88.6

15	FRONT	114	0	228	10.3	15	STEPPED	2	0	4	88.6
16	INCREASINGLY	109	0	218	9.8	16	STRODE	2	0	4	88.6
17	BEING	211	1	211	9.5	17	TAKES	2	0	4	88.6
18	ONLY	102	0	204	9.2	18	TAPE	2	0	4	88.6
19	UNDER	203	1	203	9.2	19	UNAWARES	2	0	4	88.6
20	TRAPPED	99	0	198	8.9	20	WAITED	2	0	4	88.6

The same comparative investigation was done for *lose x-self* and *immerse x-self*, although the results are not as clear. Shown in Table 30, there is a tendency for *lose x-self* to collocate with mental states (i.e., *thought*) as well as with relations between things, as accounted for by the number of prepositions (e.g., *to*, *at*, *among*, etc.) Contrastively, *immerse x-self* collocates with slightly more concrete things (e.g., *culture*, *study*, *work*, etc.). The collocates *world* and *work* occur with *immerse x-self* at the 8th and 9th positions on the chart, respectively. They also occur with *lose x-self* in positions 38th (0.4) and 39th (0.4), respectively (not shown). Because they share collocations that are part of the FoA, they also likely construe similar metaphorical meanings. This is borne out in the data. The following all construe the SA Event (i.e., SA and/or SA-UE): [immerse][ppx*] in work (*n*=10), [lose][ppx*] in work (*n*=5), [lose][ppx*] in [_at*] world (*n*=8), and [immerse][ppx*] in [_at*] world (*n*=9). These results provisionally suggest that *lose x-self* and *immerse x-self*, although sharing meaning in terms of SA Event construal, mostly maintain independent collocational profiles.

Table 30. Ratio comparisons of reflexive lose ppx* and immerse ppx* (collocates 4 places to the right)

WORD 1 (W1): LOSE PPX* (1.25)					WORD 2 (W2): IMMERSE PPX* (0.80)				
	WORD	W1	W2	W1/W2	SCORE		WORD	W2	W1	W2/W1	SCORE
1	I	32	1	32	25.6	1	CULTURE	20	0	40	50
2	?	10	0	20	16	2	INTO	15	1	15	18.8
3	OTHER	49	3	16.3	13.1	3	STUDY	12	1	12	15
4	YOU	16	1	16	12.8	4	WATER	10	1	10	12.5
5	EACH	45	3	15	12	5	MORE	12	4	3	3.8
6	TO	42	3	14	11.2	6	THEIR	14	6	2.3	2.9
7	AT	13	1	13	10.4	7	'S	15	7	2.1	2.7
8	"	70	6	11.7	9.3	8	WORK	23	12	1.9	2.4
9	AMONG	11	1	11	8.8	9	WORLD	18	10	1.8	2.3
10	THOUGHT	10	1	10	8	10	ALL	10	6	1.7	2.1
11	IF	10	1	10	8	11	THEMSELVES	173	125	1.4	1.7
12	HE	17	3	5.7	4.5	12	IN	772	621	1.2	1.6

13	FOR	28	5	5.6	4.5	13	HIMSELF	285	247	1.2	1.4
14	ITSELF	50	9	5.6	4.4	14	HIS	21	19	1.1	1.4
15	ON	10	2	5	4	15	THIS	17	18	0.9	1.2
16	.	202	44	4.6	3.7	16	THE	294	315	0.9	1.2
17	,	117	52	2.3	1.8	17	HER	16	21	0.8	1
18	AND	65	32	2	1.6	18	THAT	15	20	0.8	0.9
19	OF	18	9	2	1.6	19	YOURSELF	117	163	0.7	0.9
20	OR	10	5	2	1.6	20	IT	17	24	0.7	0.9

The final comparison, shown in Table 31, juxtaposes *catch x-self* and *check x-self*. The differences between these collocational profiles are also considerable. Whereas *catch x-self* collocates with mental verbs (e.g., *thinking*, *wondering*) and action verbs (*saying*, *staring*, *doing*, etc.), supporting the DSC-type analysis for *catch x-self*, *check x-self* often construes the idiomatic meaning of 'checking into or out of a hospital or rehab clinic'. It also construes the DSC-type at a ratio of 19%, as shown above in Table 27, denoting the metaphorical and conceptual similarities with *catch x-self* as described there.

Table 31. Ratio comparisons of reflexive *catch ppx** and *check ppx** (collocates 4 places to the right)

WORD 1 (W1): CATCH PPX* (2.43)						WORD 2 (W2): CHECK PPX* (0.41)					
	WORD	W1	W2	W1/W2	SCORE		WORD	W2	W1	W2/W1	SCORE
1	THINKING	40	0	80	32.9	1	HOSPITAL	27	0	54	131.1
2	SAYING	22	0	44	18.1	2	REHAB	16	0	32	77.7
3	STARING	18	0	36	14.8	3	INTO	104	13	8	19.4
4	WONDERING	18	0	36	14.8	4	OUT	101	13	7.8	18.9
5	EYE	13	0	26	10.7	5	MIRROR	21	6	3.5	8.5
6	UP	20	1	20	8.2	6	EACH	46	39	1.2	2.9
7	HANDS	10	0	20	8.2	7	THEMSELVES	26	23	1.1	2.7
8	'	10	0	20	8.2	8	OTHER	46	41	1.1	2.7
9	OH	10	0	20	8.2	9	ITSELF	11	10	1.1	2.7
10	MY	18	1	18	7.4	10	WHEN	10	10	1	2.4
11	ABOUT	18	1	18	7.4	11	FOR	28	29	1	2.3
12	LOOKING	17	1	17	7	12	OF	11	12	0.9	2.2
13	WHAT	16	1	16	6.6	13	IN	108	121	0.9	2.2

14	AGAINST	15	1	15	6.2	14	YOURSELF	61	71	0.9	2.1
15	DOING	15	1	15	6.2	15	A	68	87	0.8	1.9
16	)	29	2	14.5	6	16	'S	23	32	0.7	1.7
17	JUST	28	2	14	5.8	17	THE	112	167	0.7	1.6
18	HIS	37	3	12.3	5.1	18	I	22	45	0.5	1.2
19	ON	71	6	11.8	4.9	19	AS	10	21	0.5	1.2
20	TIME	29	3	9.7	4	20	TO	15	41	0.4	0.9

These comparisons, although far from exhaustive, reveal various collocational details of Self-Aware Events and help to show that conceptual metaphor and metonymy as well as collocational details can be duly uncovered by way of a corpus analysis.

10.3. Find / Lose x-self: opposites or not?

This section discusses a point made by Lakoff, who writes, "Given that lose and find are opposites, why isn't *I found myself in writing* the opposite of *I lost myself in writing*?" (1996a: 100). To answer this question, he discusses at length the Divided Person conceptual metaphor (1993a, 1996a), which was proposed to account for a great number of metaphors in English. This was discussed theoretically in detail in previous chapters and therefore will not be dealt with again here; however, pragmatic issues related to this will be discussed below.

The first of these issues deals directly with the question proposed by Lakoff above. *find x-self* and *lose x-self* are now known to have various meanings. Knowing this, we need to ask, "Do any of these meanings directly oppose each other, so that *I found myself in writing* does mean the opposite of *I lost myself in writing*?" The following case is taken from the TSM category, originally based on Lakoff's research on the Divided Person Metaphor. (The FoAs in parentheses emphasize their semantically optional role.)

> TSM: *I found myself* (<u>in writing</u>) =
> The act of writing was the impetus for my being aware of my True Self.
>
> *I lost myself* (<u>in writing</u>) =
> The act of writing was the impetus for my being temporarily unaware of my True Self.

Both of these were shown to be instantiated in the corpora. Furthermore, it was seen that the FoAs for TSM-type examples are semantically adjunctive in that they are not necessary for appropriate construal. Thus, if we do not include the FoA in the main metaphoric construal, two opposing meanings can be easily construed, one in which a *deeper Self* is present, and one in which it is not.

Looking at the SA-type construals below, meaning opposition occurs here as well. (The syntax of the semantically obligatory FoAs were adjusted to align with typical usage for SA-type predications.)

SA: *I found myself* writing letters... =
I was perceptually aware that I was writing letters.

I lost myself in letter writing ... =
I had no general perceptual awareness because I was so concentrated on writing letters.

In the first example, the experiencer is perceptually aware of his/her physical and mental state of writing letters in the present moment, while in the second example, general Self-Awareness is not immediately present; one hundred percent of the experiencer's awareness is on *letter-writing*. So, the presence or absence of perceptual Self-Awareness sets these conceptions against each other to form opposing pairs.

This kind of comparison can be done with the PNS category as well, although there is little supporting corpus evidence. The category PNS (Picture Noun Schema) is a construal in which some physical form representing the Self is present, i.e., a picture, video, statue, mannequin, etc. Original (i.e., non-corpus) examples showing this opposition are the following:

PNS: *I found myself* in the cluttered basement. =
I found some representation of myself (a picture, doll, etc.) in the cluttered basement.

I lost myself in the cluttered basement. =
I lost some representation of myself in the cluttered basement.

These examples are not metaphoric in the same sense as previous examples in that the verbs *find* and *lose* are literally construed but the antecedents are metonymic, i.e., they refer to a physical representation of the antecedent and not the antecedent itself (i.e., representation STANDS FOR antecedent.) Admittedly, their low frequency in the corpora constitutes, perhaps, an armchair rebuttal. PNS can be construed to instantiate meaning opposition for *find x-self* and *lose x-self* in the same way many theoretical linguistic examples are proposed, that is, through native speaker intuition and linguistically-based decisions of appropriateness.

It must be stated here that this evidence is not meant to refute Lakoff's claim that *find x-self* and *lose x-self* are not opposites 'in the same way' as non-reflexive uses of *find* and *lose*. However, when explanations of construal have their foundations built upon results of corpus data, a more complete set of information is available to analyze and thus the results are more likely to represent the actual linguistic profile of the population, or at the very least, the sample.

Now that *find x-self, lose x-self and catch x-self* have been analyzed and discussed in detail along various parameters, another metaphorically construed verb that also expresses Self-Awareness as a basic concept, namely, *perceive x-self*, will be taken under investigation.

10.4. Perceive x-self

Although verbs that do not instantiate metaphorical instances described thus far are not discussed at length, a brief comment will be made on one verb's conception that has been vital to this research, namely *perceive*. Self-Aware Events, as claimed here, construe perceptual Self-Awareness. This perception can be extended to include the True-Self Metaphor, the Divided-Self Causative, and the Picture Noun Schema, where some form of self-perceiving is necessary for each type of event to be conceived; for the TSM-type, perception of some deeper Self, perception of two selves for the DSC-type, and perception of one's external representation for the PNS construal. That being said, interestingly, the verb *perceive* does not metaphorically instantiate at all in the data, i.e., it yields 100% literal instantiation. However, it is essential that *perceive* be delineated carefully. Two examples will bear this out.

355. Even when young girls receive high grades, *they may perceive themselves* as
being incompetent in math.   (COCA:1993.ACAD.Bioscience)

356. Here again, *a greater proportion of non-athletes perceived themselves* <u>as</u> <u>overweight</u> when, in fact, no significant differences exist between the two...

(COCA:1991.ACAD.SportBehavior)

According to the LDOCE, *perceive* means, "to understand or think of something or someone in a particular way" (2014) and this seems to cover both examples. However, if example 356 is understood as a more visceral, physiological type of perception, i.e., of the *non-athletes'* physical heaviness, then the following meaning, also considered literal, is appropriate, "to become aware of (something) through the senses, esp the sight; recognize or observe" ("Collins Dictionary Online,"). In an analysis of the expanded contexts of examples 355 and 356 above, there is no evidence as to which interpretation is more appropriate. Due to this, therefore, both of these 'base' meanings were included under the literal category for the verb *perceive*.

A comparison of these dictionary definitions helps reveal the overall difficulties and subtleness of analyzing construal and predication. For example, even though both definitions are not marked metaphoric, should the first definition be considered slightly metaphorical given that the second definition is more physiologically based? In order to address this question and achieve consensus on a large scale, various dictionaries would need to collaborate on definitions and methodological parameters for each entry. For various reasons, this is not likely in the near future, but it is an important issue that needs to be kept in mind for researchers who investigate metaphor, metonymy and collocation.

10.5. Other reflexive constructions

One line of research that has great potential is the following collocation: [v*]_nn* _i* [ppx*], i.e., verb lemma, noun, preposition, reflexive pronoun. For example,

357. When do you *find time for yourself* except when other people are sleeping?

(COCA:1998.NEWS.CSMonitor)

A list of the most frequent 100 entries is shown below (COCA: n=3130, ≥5, reciprocals deleted):

<u>take care of ppx</u>   (n= 2,224, ratio = 67.7%)

<u>draw attention to ppx</u> (n= 157, ratio = 5%)

<u>caught sight of ppx</u>   (n=31, ratio = 0.1%)

find time for ppx	(*n*=15, ratio =0.05%)
lost control of ppx	(*n*=28, ratio =0.09%)
lost track of ppx	(*n*=19, ratio = 0.06%)

[make]__nn*__i* [ppx] (*n*=224, ratio = 7.2%)

make fools of ppx	make fun of ppx	make copy of ppx
make time for ppx	make name for ppx	make money for ppx
make room for ppx	make lives for ppx	make decisions for ppx

From the list above, the three main constructions discussed here, i.e., *find/lose/catch x-self*, are listed below.

[find]_nn* _i* [ppx*], *n*=16 (reciprocals deleted):

find time for ppx	find peace with ppx	find spirituality for ppx
find photographs of ppx	find fault with ppx	find qualities in pps
find similarity between ppx	find room for ppx	find part of ppx
find others like ppx	find strength in ppx	find food for ppx
find pictures on ppx	find confidence in ppx	find places on ppx

[lose]_nn* _i* [ppx*], *n*=23 (reciprocals deleted):

lose touch with ppx	lose control of ppx	lose faith in ppx
lost sight of ppx	lose part of ppx	lose belief in ppx
lose confidence in ppx	lose reality within ppx	
lose power over ppx	lose respect for ppx	
lose consciousness of ppx	lose track of ppx	

[catch]_nn* _i* [ppx*], *n*= 18 (reciprocals deleted):

catch sight of ppx	catch hold of ppx

These types of collocations need to be explored and analyzed at length and there is undoubtedly much to be uncovered. Without analyzing specific contexts, however, meaningful semantic patterning cannot be formally proposed, but at first glance, the results show a wide range of both literal and metaphorical conceptions. Some of these probably instantiate SA Events, Divided Self Phenomena and Picture Noun Schema, such as *find peace with ppx*, *find part of ppx*, *lose touch with ppx*, *lose power over ppx*, *catch sight of ppx* and *catch hold of ppx*, etc.

There seem to be recurrent themes within the overall search parameter [v*]_nn* _i* [ppx*], one example being [make] _nn* _i* [ppx], in which there are nine noun variations and two preposition variations. For this data, along with *find*, *lose* and *catch*, collocations (*find time for x-self*, *lose touch with x-self*, etc.) can be grouped together to form larger, more schematic categories called 'collostructions' (Stefanowitsch & Gries 2003). Collostructions can be thought of as schematic templates onto which lexemes are inserted. Meaning is not only retrievable at the lexeme level; there is meaning at both the abstract schema level and the specific phraseme level, although the nature of that meaning is different. A very abstract collostruction will allow numerous lexemes into its slots and the structure will be more loose or flexible. Its meaning will also be more abstract. At the other end of the spectrum, a very specific idiom will have a very limited number of lexemes possible (without changing the meaning) and have a more rigid collostructure. Collocation schemata are thus a scalable phenomenon, from very abstract (i.e., [v*]_nn* _i* [ppx*]) to more specific (i.e., [p*] found [ppx*] in [n*]), to idiomatic (i.e., [n*] caught sight of [n*]). In other words, depending on the level of schematicity, the flexibility of specific slots of the collocation change (ibid.)

Even in this brief discussion, insights into a type of independence-dependence cline, as it were, can now be gleaned. This cline refers to the level of abstractness of an analysis, i.e., the level of analytical granularity of one's research viewpoint (Sinclair 1991). Depending on this viewpoint, the type of analysis will change because what the researcher is looking for changes. Looking through a simple magnifying glass will reveal different information than an electromagnetic microscope or the Hubble telescope, even if they are all looking in the same direction. This general point will be taken up in the conclusion below.

CHAPTER 11: Conclusions

"Intuitively, we feel that some instances of a word are quite independently chosen, while in other cases we feel that the word combines with others to deliver a single multi-word unit of meaning. We shall call word-meaning independent, and phrase-meaning dependent. In between these two fixed points is collocation, where we see a tendency for words to occur together though they remain largely independent choices" (Sinclair 1991: 71).

The quotation above sums up the overall methodology of the present research, although more generally stated. This corpus analysis has shown that the collostruction [v + pro^refl] contains a variety of collocations, both literal and metaphorical depending upon the verb and the contexts in which they are irrevocably immersed. Within this *construction in context*, the variation of components seems free and independent, but this is only partly so. The present analysis has shown that a limited number of meanings are construed for each of these constructions, some of them literal and some of them metaphorical. Seen in this light, polysemy within the reflexive construction is not as haphazard as it first may have appeared. The collocations display syntactic, semantic and pragmatic patterning, many of which were revealed and described at length, summarized in Table 32.

Table 32. Summary of conceptual variation for perceptually-related verbs when occurring within the reflexive construction (combined totals for the COCA and BNC, excluding categories 'X' and '?')

verb (+ pro^refl)	Construal Type
find x-self	SA ; SA-UE ; TSM ; PNS ; LIT
lose x-self	SA; TSM; IDI (1~3); LIT (1~3)
catch x-self	SA; DSC; PNS; LIT (1~4)
be x-self	TSM
check x-self	DSC; LIT; IDI
feel x-self	SA-UE; LIT; IDI
identify x-self	LIT (1, 2)
immerse x-self	SA; LIT (1,2)
perceive x-self	LIT
regard x-self	LIT (1,2)
see x-self	LIT; MET (1,2)
watch x-self	LIT; MET (1,2)

This research began with three questions, the first of which was "How can metaphoric events be identified and delineated within the reflexive construction?" A unique methodology was implemented for the objective identification of metaphor, based on the foundations of the MIPVU. It demonstrated how specific elements within a construction can be selected and compared to 'base' definitions as well as with other mined corpus data in order to confirm or refute the possibility of metaphoric construal. Due to the restricted nature of the reflexive syntax, this method of metaphor identification proved fairly straightforward to employ and results were conclusive for a variety of contexts. It proved to be a relatively objective method for identifying metaphoric use while at the same time allowing for the flexibility of polysemy and collocational diversification within that limited framework. Thus, the method employed here is evaluated positively for the purpose for which it was intended.

The second question asked, "Do Self-Aware Events (and other identified events) display unique collocational patterning and if so, are these patterns predictable?" Investigated by way of a corpus analysis along various parameters, the answer to this question is undeniably affirmative, with a caveat. This condition is that there will always be some ambiguity when *language in use* is concerned. Even the most well-formed intentions can be misconstrued. This inevitably leads to some 'fuzzy' data, making 100% irrefutable claims unlikely and unrealistic. That being the case, this research has employed metaphor analysis coupled with frequency and likelihood data to show that Self-Aware Events and other identified metaphorical events do display collocational patterning. The analysis revealed two types of Self-Aware Event (i.e., SA and SA-UE), two types of True-Self Metaphor (slightly different senses for *find x-self* and *lose x-self*), and one type each of the Divided-Self Causative (DSC) and Picture Noun Schema (PNS).

The third question posed was "Do the corpus results corroborate or refute the theoretical claims made in Part 1 of the investigation?" This question is a little more difficult to answer concretely due to the different nature of those research aims and methods. As an overall theoretical claim that Self-Aware Events are a predicated reality, then the results here surely evidence that claim. Many examples were analyzed and supported by contextual data and construal and predication of SA Events were shown to be frequently instantiated. However, specific theoretical points are more difficult to corroborate. For example, it can only be suggested that the results of the present data analysis confirm the Cognitive Grammar model of SA Events. Corpus evidence was found that verifies the existence of SA Events, and SA Events were shown to be theoretically plausible from a CG point of view, but whether there is a direct correlation between these is harder to prove. More generally, this means that many theoretical models can be supported by data, but until there is enough independently verifiable data analyzed and tested across the research field, concrete and unwavering theoretical claims are difficult to make (Gibbs 2007, 2016). What can be claimed with certainty here is that corpus evidence supports the existence of Self-Aware Events which have been theoretically demonstrated to be congruent with 'Metonymy within Metaphor', 'Conceptual Metaphor Theory', 'Cognitive Grammar', the 'Awareness Onset Model', as well as a semantically-defined, gradient view of transitivity and reflexivity.

This last point addresses another question posed in the introduction to the Part III, i.e., "do the corpus results analyzed here support the view of perceptual Self-Awareness as an image schema?" A review of the overall results of the research may help to answer this. The *find x-self* construction was examined and it was concluded that there are four types of metaphorical construal for this construction, two of which display Perceptual Self-Awareness. The results of the *lose x-self* construction were shown to display two types of metaphorical construal, one of which construed Perceptual Self-Awareness, and the *catch x-self* construction was found to be metaphorically construed in three ways, two of which construed Perceptual Self-Awareness. Do these results substantiate Self-Awareness as an image schema? According to those results, Perceptual Self-Awareness is an embodied and experiential concept evidenced in the FoAs and supporting contexts. It is not based on any other abstract notion and it can be used as a building block for metaphorical conception, construal, and predication. Because the fundamental definition of image schema is based on these conditions, the answer to the question above must be in the affirmative. This affirmation has the additional consequence of supporting the answer to question three from the previous paragraph in that the theories of CG, Conceptual Metaphor, and indirectly, Metonymy within Metaphor use the concept of image schema (or basic domain) for their theoretical infrastructure. Thus, Self-Awareness is concluded to be an image schema which is employed in a number of metaphorical conceptions predicated mainly by *find*, *lose*, and *catch* when appearing in the verb slot of the reflexive construction.

What are the repercussions of these conclusions? For one thing, it grounds and delineates SA Events in embodied, experiential terms, thus avoiding some of the pitfalls of linguistic-only reasoning often found in Cognitive Linguistics, especially when dealing with conceptual metaphor (Gibbs 2016). Further, because SA Events are based on embodied phenomenon, they should be psychologically, if not physiologically, verifiable. It would be very interesting, indeed, if Cognition and Neurolinguistic studies corroborate the findings presented here. That would certainly help bridge the gap between linguistic and cognitive reality, or at least, provide hard facts to support some theory. One possible experimental scenario I can imagine is for test subjects to read/say/write/hear various SA, SA-UE, TSM, DSC and PNS examples while connected to brain imaging apparatus that show moment-by-moment areas of increased or decreased brain function. This could be compared to other brain imaging results and/or other control tests. One of the control comparisons I have in mind is brain scans taken of meditation practitioners. In some meditation traditions such as Insight Meditation, because Perceptual Self-Awareness is the focus of and is heightened during initial meditative states (personal experience), the idiosyncratic brain activity that occurs can be compared to the test subject's scans. Results (positive correlation or not) could lend scientific validity to the theory of embodied image schemas and metaphor of SA Events by providing evidence from independent fields of research (Gibbs 2007, 2016).

Another avenue that is likely in the near future is the interaction of brain and computer on the neuronal scale, so that the mapping of pre-linguistic ideas onto linguistic structure can be traced all the way from concept to predication. Although still a few years from practicality, being able to see physical cross-domain mapping would be a technological turning point for metaphor studies.

Still another exciting recent trend is the area of translation software, not only from one spoken or written language into another, but to and from sign language as well. All of these advancements and those that haven't even been thought of as yet are soon on their way. It is only a matter of time that Artificial Intelligence is added to corpus data programming. At that time, semantic, syntactic and perhaps even pragmatic analyses can be mined independently by the computer program and the researcher can focus on more theoretical and/or practical use of that data. In this light, the rapid advancements in technology across the spectrum of society will only create new opportunities for researchers willing to embrace them. I look forward to this new era in linguistic research where theories can be tested quickly and efficiently by various kinds of data through various experimental procedures from related and perhaps not-so related fields. The next twenty years will see huge advancements in all these areas as well as some that have not yet been imagined.

Appendix 1

Common verbs appearing in the COCA and BNC for the search parameter [v*][ppx*]

align	allow	ask	assert	attach	avail	be	behave
believe	blame	brace	bring	busy	buy	call	calm
catch	check	commit	compose	concern	consider	control	convince
correct	cover	cross	cut	declare	defend	define	describe
devote	distance	distinguish	do	drag	draw	drive	ease
enjoy	establish	excuse	expose	express	extricate	fancy	feed
feel	find	fling	force	get	give	hang	hate
haul	have	heal	hear	heave	help	hold	hug
hurl	identify	imagine	immerse	introduce	involve	keep	kill
know	launch	lend	let	lock	lose	love	lower
make	manifest	may	organize	perceive	place	position	pour
prepare	present	press	pride	promise	protect	prove	pull
push	put	raise	regard	remind	repeat	resign	resolve
reveal	rid	save	say	seat	see	sell	set
settle	shake	shoot	show	sit	steady	steel	stop
suit	support	surround	take	teach	tell	think	throw
transform	treat	trust	turn	watch	will	work	wrap

Appendix 2

Register and frequency data for [find][ppx*] in the COCA and BNC

COCA	[find][ppx*]			BNC	[find][ppx*]		
	Section Name	# Per Million	# Tokens		Section Name	# Per Million	# Tokens
1	FIC:SciFi/Fant	107.73	2150	1	W_new_arts1	115.65	40
2	MAG:Religion	101.39	433	2	W_fict_prose	114.80	1796
3	ACAD:Misc	91.86	391	3	W_religion	109.45	122
4	FIC:Gen (Jrnl)	91.60	2938	4	W_news_soc	98.81	8
5	FIC:Gen (Book)	79.44	1945	5	W_biography	87.86	307
6	MAG:Women/Men	78.44	765	6	S_lect_arts	80.39	4
7	MAG:News/Opin	74.07	1378	7	W_let_pers	77.16	4
8	MAG:Afric-Amer	72.39	263	8	W_news_sprt	64.88	19
9	MAG:Entertain	68.06	277	9	W_news_misc	63.74	65
10	MAG:Soc/Arts	64.83	496	10	W_nonac_soc	62.19	258
11	FIC:Juvenile	61.74	195	11	S_lect_law	60.27	3
12	MAG:Sports	59.88	648	12	W_news_edit	59.61	6
13	NEWS:Life	59.25	941	13	W_nonac_arts	58.02	216
14	NEWS:Editorial	58.83	260	14	W_essay_schl	55.16	8
15	MAG:Financial	58.59	308	15	S_brdcst_news	55.04	14
16	ACAD:Phil/Rel	55.76	376	16	W_nonac_med	54.46	27
17	ACAD:History	54.39	666	17	W_news_o_sprt	51.49	52
18	ACAD:Humanities	53.08	633	18	W_pop_lore	51.09	371
19	MAG:Children	52.00	85	19	W_news_rprt	47.29	31
20	NEWS:Misc	47.92	1495	20	W_news_o_soc	47.10	53
21	NEWS:News_Intl	47.56	203	21	W_misc	46.84	425
22	SPOK:NPR	45.35	789	22	W_news_o_rep	46.61	125
23	NEWS:News_Local	42.95	259	23	W_fict_drama	44.47	2
24	NEWS:News_Natl	42.84	282	24	W_news_com	43.23	18
25	MAG:Sci/Tech	41.71	527	25	W_ac_hum_arts	38.83	128
26	MAG:Home/Health	40.92	653	26	W_ac_soc_sci	36.45	154
27	ACAD:Law/PolSci	40.11	345	27	W_hansard	35.66	41
28	FIC:Movies	39.14	350	28	W_nonac_law	34.83	155
29	SPOK:NBC	38.91	247	29	S_unclass	34.42	14
30	NEWS:Sports	36.36	510	30	W_news_o_com	34.37	14
31	SPOK:CBS	35.54	458	31	W_news_arts2	33.97	8
32	SPOK:ABC	35.52	551	32	W_news_tabld	32.23	23
33	NEWS:Money	34.87	275	33	S_parliament	31.57	3
34	SPOK:PBS	31.31	207	34	S_sportslive	31.15	1
35	ACAD:Education	30.92	292	35	W_nonac_nat	29.30	73
36	ACAD:Geog/SocSci	29.23	473	36	W_ac_law_edu	28.82	133
37	SPOK:CNN	25.95	536	37	S_pub_debate	28.73	8
38	SPOK:Indep	21.87	95	38	S_apch-script	26.74	12
39	SPOK:MSNBC	20.88	17	39	S_meeting	26.23	35
40	SPOK:FOX	19.20	121	40	W_news_script	24.56	31
41	ACAD:Sci/Tech	13.50	190	41	W_fict_poetry	22.79	5
42	ACAD:Medicine	8.66	58	42	S_interv_oral	20.03	16

Appendix 3

Raw frequencies and frequencies per million for [pro + find + x-self] by register

COCA [p*][find][ppx*]	FREQ	PER MIL
SPOKEN	1,427	13.04
FICTION	4,049	38.6
MAGAZINE	2,526	22.94
NEWSPAPER	1,376	12.99
ACADEMIC	1,041	10.07
1990-1994	1,928	18.54
1995-1999	2,027	19.59
2000-2004	2,036	19.78
2005-2009	1,924	18.86
2010-2015	2,504	20.6
TOTAL	20,838	

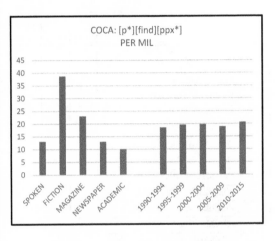

BNC [p*][find][ppx*]	FREQ	PER MIL
SPOKEN	73	7.33
FICTION	805	50.6
MAGAZINE	113	15.56
NEWSPAPER	131	12.52
NON-ACAD	232	14.06
ACADEMIC	121	7.89
MISC	394	18.91
TOTAL	1,869	

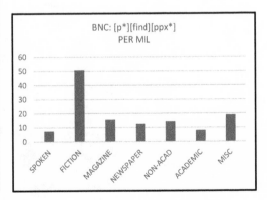

Appendix 4

1) BNC: [n*][find][ppx*] sorted by lemma

BNC	[n*][find][ppx*]; sort by lemma; min=5	FREQ
1	[PEOPLE] [FIND] [THEMSELVES]	22
2	[LINDSEY] [FIND] [HERSELF]	12
3	[MAGGIE] [FIND] [HERSELF]	9
4	[ISABEL] [FIND] [HERSELF]	7
5	[COUNCIL] [FIND] [ITSELF]	6
6	[MEREDITH] [FIND] [HERSELF]	5
7	[WOMAN] [FIND] [THEMSELVES]	5
8	[TEACHER] [FIND] [THEMSELVES]	5
9	[RUTH] [FIND] [HERSELF]	5
10	[RONNI] [FIND] [HERSELF]	5
11	[RACHEL] [FIND] [HERSELF]	5
12	[LUCY] [FIND] [HERSELF]	5
13	[LAURA] [FIND] [HERSELF]	5
14	[JESSAMY] [FIND] [HERSELF]	5
15	[CASSIE] [FIND] [HERSELF]	5
16	[CAROLINE] [FIND] [HERSELF]	5
	TOTAL	111

2) BNC: [n*][find][ppx*] sorted by lemma: per register

	FREQ	SIZE (M)	PER MIL
SPOKEN	16	10	1.61
FICTION	323	15.9	20.3
MAGAZINE	49	7.3	6.75
NEWSPAPER	80	10.5	7.64
NON-ACAD	127	16.5	7.7
ACADEMIC	76	15.3	4.96
MISC	152	20.8	7.3

3) COCA search: [n*][find][ppx*] sorted by lemma

4) COCA search: [n*][find][ppx*] sorted by lemma: per register

1	[PEOPLE] [FIND] [THEMSELVES]	81
2	[WOMAN] [FIND] [THEMSELVES]	44
3	[STATE] [FIND] [ITSELF]	40
4	[GOVERNMENT] [FIND] [ITSELF]	25
5	[MAN] [FIND] [HIMSELF]	23
6	[TEACHER] [FIND] [THEMSELVES]	21
7	[ADMINISTRATION] [FIND] [ITSELF]	21
8	[AMERICAN] [FIND] [THEMSELVES]	21
9	[FAMILY] [FIND] [THEMSELVES]	20
10	[BUSH] [FIND] [HIMSELF]	19
11	[CHILD] [FIND] [THEMSELVES]	18
12	[CHURCH] [FIND] [ITSELF]	18
13	[PRESIDENT] [FIND] [HIMSELF]	18
14	[MAN] [FIND] [THEMSELVES]	17
15	[PARENT] [FIND] [THEMSELVES]	16
16	[COUPLE] [FIND] [THEMSELVES]	16
17	[STUDENT] [FIND] [THEMSELVES]	15
18	[COMPANY] [FIND] [ITSELF]	15
19	[MEMBER] [FIND] [THEMSELVES]	15
20	[INDUSTRY] [FIND] [ITSELF]	15
21	[BOY] [FIND] [HIMSELF]	14
22	[LEADER] [FIND] [THEMSELVES]	14
23	[OFFICIAL] [FIND] [THEMSELVES]	14
24	[WORKER] [FIND] [THEMSELVES]	13
25	[REPUBLICAN] [FIND] [THEMSELVES]	13
26	[WOMAN] [FIND] [HERSELF]	13
27	[MARY] [FIND] [HERSELF]	12
28	[US] [FIND] [ITSELF]	12
29	[CLINTON] [FIND] [HIMSELF]	12
30	[COUNTRY] [FIND] [THEMSELVES]	11
31	[COUNTRY] [FIND] [ITSELF]	11
32	[FRIEND] [FIND] [THEMSELVES]	11
33	[SCROOGE] [FIND] [HIMSELF]	10
34	[KID] [FIND] [THEMSELVES]	10
35	[INDIVIDUAL] [FIND] [THEMSELVES]	10
37	[FORCE] [FIND] [THEMSELVES]	10
37	[FATHER] [FIND] [HIMSELF]	10
	TOTAL	678

CHART	FREQ	SIZE (M)	PER MIL
SPOKEN	575	109.4	5.26
FICTION	1479	104.9	14.1
MAGAZINE	1225	110.1	11.13
NEWSPAPER	1166	106	11
ACADEMIC	976	103.4	9.44
1990-1994	1125	104	10.82
1995-1999	1108	103.4	10.71
2000-2004	1134	102.9	11.02
2005-2009	1005	102	9.85
2010-2015	1049	121.6	8.63
TOTAL	10842		

Appendix 5

FIND X-SELF: Antecedent is a Noun: [n*][find][ppx*], sort by word; COCA&BNC (alphabetical order)

rank	[n*][find][ppx*] COCA	freq	rank	[n*][find][ppx*] BNC	freq
	TOTAL	837		TOTAL	305
11	ADMINISTRATION FINDS ITSELF	13	51	ACE FOUND HERSELF	2
29	ADMINISTRATION FOUND ITSELF	8	23	ADVENTURERS FIND THEMSELVES	3
77	ADMINISTRATORS FIND THEMSELVES	5	46	AJAYI FOUND HERSELF	2
79	ALAN FOUND HIMSELF	5	24	ALEXANDER FOUND HIMSELF	3
78	ALEX FOUND HIMSELF	5	45	ANNE FINDS HERSELF	2
76	ALLIES FOUND THEMSELVES	5	44	ANNE FOUND HERSELF	2
55	AMERICA FINDS ITSELF	6	47	ASHI FOUND HERSELF	2
12	AMERICANS FIND THEMSELVES	13	48	BALDWIN FOUND HIMSELF	2
30	AMERICANS FOUND THEMSELVES	8	49	BBC FOUND ITSELF	2
80	BETH FOUND HERSELF	5	100	BECKENHAM FOUND HIMSELF	1
81	BILL FOUND HIMSELF	5	99	BEESLEY FOUND HIMSELF	1
82	BILLY FOUND HIMSELF	5	52	BENNY FOUND HERSELF	2
31	BOY FINDS HIMSELF	8	50	BRITAIN FOUND ITSELF	2
39	BOY FOUND HIMSELF	7	6	CAROLINE FOUND HERSELF	5
56	BROWN FOUND HIMSELF	6	98	CARRUTHERS FOUND HIMSELF	1
15	BUSH FINDS HIMSELF	11	97	CASE-STUDY FIND THEMSELVES	1
32	BUSH FOUND HIMSELF	8	96	CASEY FOUND HIMSELF	1
83	CARA FOUND HERSELF	5	7	CASSIE FOUND HERSELF	5
84	CATHOLICS FIND THEMSELVES	5	16	CHARLES FOUND HIMSELF	4
57	CHARACTERS FIND THEMSELVES	6	25	CHARLIE FOUND HIMSELF	3
14	CHILDREN FIND THEMSELVES	12	53	CHARLOTTE FOUND HERSELF	2
22	CHILDREN FOUND THEMSELVES	9	54	CHRISTINA FOUND HERSELF	2
19	CHURCH FINDS ITSELF	10	55	CLARE FOUND HERSELF	2
40	CHURCH FOUND ITSELF	7	56	CORNELIUS FOUND HIMSELF	2
85	CITY FINDS ITSELF	5	5	COUNCIL FINDS ITSELF	6
33	CLINTON FOUND HIMSELF	8	57	COUPLE FIND THEMSELVES	2

58	COMPANY FINDS ITSELF	6		58	CRAWFORD FOUND HIMSELF	2
23	COMPANY FOUND ITSELF	9		59	DALGLIESH FOUND HIMSELF	2
41	COUNTRIES FIND THEMSELVES	7		60	ELIZABETH FOUND THEMSELVES	2
42	COUNTRIES FOUND THEMSELVES	7		26	ERIKA FOUND HERSELF	3
24	COUNTRY FINDS ITSELF	9		61	EVA FOUND HERSELF	2
86	COUPLE FIND THEMSELVES	5		62	FAMILY FIND THEMSELVES	2
87	COUPLE FOUND THEMSELVES	5		63	FISH FINDS ITSELF	2
59	COUPLES FIND THEMSELVES	6		64	FRANKIE FOUND HIMSELF	2
88	CREW FOUND THEMSELVES	5		65	GEORGE FOUND HIMSELF	2
89	DAVID FOUND HIMSELF	5		66	GERMANY FOUND ITSELF	2
60	DEMOCRATS FIND THEMSELVES	6		67	HARI FOUND HERSELF	2
61	EDWARD FOUND HIMSELF	6		27	HARRY FOUND HIMSELF	3
43	EMMA FOUND HERSELF	7		68	HELEN FOUND HERSELF	2
90	ERIC FOUND HIMSELF	5		17	HENRY FOUND HIMSELF	4
91	FAMILIES FIND THEMSELVES	5		69	HOUSE FINDS ITSELF	2
92	FAMILIES FOUND THEMSELVES	5		28	HUY FOUND HIMSELF	3
34	FAMILY FOUND THEMSELVES	8		70	IANTHE FOUND HERSELF	2
35	FATHER FOUND HIMSELF	8		29	INDIVIDUALS FIND THEMSELVES	3
93	FORCES FOUND THEMSELVES	5		71	INSTITUTIONS FIND THEMSELVES	2
44	FRIENDS FIND THEMSELVES	7		4	ISABEL FOUND HERSELF	7
94	GIRLS FOUND THEMSELVES	5		30	JACK FOUND HIMSELF	3
16	GOVERNMENT FINDS ITSELF	11		31	JAMES FOUND HIMSELF	3
9	GOVERNMENT FOUND ITSELF	14		18	JENNA FOUND HERSELF	4
95	GROUPS FIND THEMSELVES	5		72	JENNIFER FOUND HERSELF	2
25	INDIVIDUALS FIND THEMSELVES	9		73	JENNY FOUND HERSELF	2
17	INDUSTRY FOUND ITSELF	11		8	JESSAMY FOUND HERSELF	5
96	IRAQ FINDS ITSELF	5		74	JOSEPH FOUND HIMSELF	2
97	JOHN FOUND HIMSELF	5		32	JULIA FOUND HERSELF	3
45	KIDS FIND THEMSELVES	7		75	JULIE FOUND HERSELF	2
98	LAWYERS FIND THEMSELVES	5		76	JULIET FOUND HERSELF	2
26	LEADERS FOUND THEMSELVES	9		33	KATE FOUND HERSELF	3
46	LUCY FOUND HERSELF	7		77	KATHERINE FOUND HERSELF	2
99	MAGGIE FOUND HERSELF	5		34	KELLY FOUND HERSELF	3
10	MAN FINDS HIMSELF	14		78	KOREA FOUND ITSELF	2

36	MAN FOUND HIMSELF	8	9	LAURA FOUND HERSELF	5
100	MANAGERS FOUND THEMSELVES	5	79	LEE FOUND HERSELF	2
62	MARCUS FOUND HIMSELF	6	19	LEWIS FOUND HIMSELF	4
18	MARY FOUND HERSELF	11	2	LINDSEY FOUND HERSELF	12
20	MEMBERS FOUND THEMSELVES	10	35	LISA FOUND HERSELF	3
47	MEN FIND THEMSELVES	7	80	LOUISA FOUND HERSELF	2
37	MEN FOUND THEMSELVES	8	10	LUCY FOUND HERSELF	5
27	OFFICIALS FOUND THEMSELVES	9	3	MAGGIE FOUND HERSELF	9
63	OTHERS FIND THEMSELVES	6	81	MARIA FOUND HERSELF	2
48	OTHERS FOUND THEMSELVES	7	36	MCLEISH FOUND HIMSELF	3
13	PARENTS FIND THEMSELVES	13	82	MELISSA FOUND HERSELF	2
1	PEOPLE FIND THEMSELVES	63	83	MEN FIND THEMSELVES	2
3	PEOPLE FOUND THEMSELVES	17	11	MEREDITH FOUND HERSELF	5
65	PEREGRINE FOUND HIMSELF	6	84	MERRILL FOUND HERSELF	2
66	PLAYERS FIND THEMSELVES	6	37	MUNGO FOUND HIMSELF	3
67	POLICE FOUND THEMSELVES	6	20	PAIGE FOUND HERSELF	4
21	PRESIDENT FINDS HIMSELF	10	85	PARENTS FIND THEMSELVES	2
49	PRESIDENT FOUND HIMSELF	7	1	PEOPLE FIND THEMSELVES	21
68	READERS FIND THEMSELVES	6	86	POLICE FIND THEMSELVES	2
38	REPUBLICANS FIND THEMSELVES	8	12	RACHEL FOUND HERSELF	5
69	RESIDENTS FIND THEMSELVES	6	38	REX FOUND HIMSELF	3
70	ROGER FOUND HIMSELF	6	39	ROBBIE FOUND HERSELF	3
71	SCROOGE FINDS HIMSELF	6	21	ROBYN FOUND HERSELF	4
5	STATES FINDS ITSELF	15	13	RONNI FOUND HERSELF	5
6	STATES FOUND ITSELF	15	14	RUTH FOUND HERSELF	5
7	STUDENTS FIND THEMSELVES	15	87	SAM FOUND HIMSELF	2
72	SUSAN FOUND HERSELF	6	40	SCHOOLS FIND THEMSELVES	3
4	TEACHERS FIND THEMSELVES	17	88	SHAMLOU FOUND HIMSELF	2
50	U.S. FINDS ITSELF	7	89	SMITH FOUND HIMSELF	2
51	UNIVERSITIES FIND THEMSELVES	7	90	STUDENTS FIND THEMSELVES	2
52	VENERA FOUND HERSELF	7	91	SUFFERERS FIND THEMSELVES	2
73	VISITORS FIND THEMSELVES	6	15	TEACHERS FIND THEMSELVES	5
74	WILLIAMS FOUND HIMSELF	6	92	THATCHER FOUND HERSELF	2
75	WOMAN FINDS HERSELF	6	93	THOMAS FOUND HIMSELF	2

53	WOMAN FOUND HERSELF	7		94	TWOFLOWER FOUND HIMSELF	2
2	WOMEN FIND THEMSELVES	27		95	TYSON FOUND HIMSELF	2
8	WOMEN FOUND THEMSELVES	15		41	VIRGINIA FOUND HERSELF	3
28	WORKERS FOUND THEMSELVES	9		42	WILLIE FOUND HIMSELF	3
54	WORLD FINDS ITSELF	7		22	WOMEN FIND THEMSELVES	4
				43	WORKERS FIND THEMSELVES	3

Appendix 6

Modal verbs occurring before [find + x-self]; search parameter = (_vm* [find] [ppx*])

BNC	modals : _vm* [find] [ppx*]	FREQ	COCA	modals : _vm* [find] [ppx*]	FREQ
1	[MAY] [FIND] [YOURSELF]	53	1	[MAY] [FIND] [THEMSELVES]	211
2	[MAY] [FIND] [THEMSELVES]	52	2	[WILL] [FIND] [YOURSELF]	187
3	[WILL] [FIND] [YOURSELF]	48	3	[WILL] [FIND] [THEMSELVES]	164
4	[WILL] [FIND] [THEMSELVES]	48	4	[MAY] [FIND] [YOURSELF]	139
5	[COULD] [FIND] [THEMSELVES]	43	5	[COULD] [FIND] [THEMSELVES]	80
6	[MAY] [FIND] [HIMSELF]	25	6	[WOULD] [FIND] [THEMSELVES]	74
7	[COULD] [FIND] [YOURSELF]	25	7	[WOULD] [FIND] [HIMSELF]	74
8	[WOULD] [FIND] [THEMSELVES]	20	8	[CAN] [FIND] [THEMSELVES]	73
9	[WILL] [FIND] [HIMSELF]	19	9	[MIGHT] [FIND] [YOURSELF]	66
10	[MIGHT] [FIND] [THEMSELVES]	19	10	[WOULD] [FIND] [MYSELF]	63
11	[MAY] [FIND] [ITSELF]	18	11	[MAY] [FIND] [HIMSELF]	59
12	[COULD] [FIND] [HIMSELF]	18	12	[MIGHT] [FIND] [THEMSELVES]	57
13	[CAN] [FIND] [THEMSELVES]	14	13	[WILL] [FIND] [OURSELVES]	52
14	[WILL] [FIND] [ITSELF]	13	14	[WILL] [FIND] [HIMSELF]	52
15	[MIGHT] [FIND] [YOURSELF]	13	15	[COULD] [FIND] [HIMSELF]	45
16	[WOULD] [FIND] [HIMSELF]	13	16	[WILL] [FIND] [ITSELF]	41
17	[MAY] [FIND] [OURSELVES]	11	17	[HAVE] [FIND] [MYSELF]	39
18	[WOULD] [FIND] [HERSELF]	10	18	[WOULD] [FIND] [HERSELF]	36
19	[WOULD] [FIND] [MYSELF]	10	19	[MIGHT] [FIND] [HIMSELF]	34
20	[COULD] [FIND] [ITSELF]	10	20	[COULD] [FIND] [YOURSELF]	34
21	[MIGHT] [FIND] [HIMSELF]	10	21	[MAY] [FIND] [OURSELVES]	33
22	[MIGHT] [FIND] [HERSELF]	9	22	[WILL] [FIND] [MYSELF]	32
23	[MIGHT] [FIND] [ITSELF]	7	23	[COULD] [FIND] [ITSELF]	32
24	[CAN] [FIND] [HIMSELF]	6	24	[MAY] [FIND] [ITSELF]	29
25	[WOULD] [FIND] [ITSELF]	6	25	[CAN] [FIND] [YOURSELF]	28
26	[WILL] [FIND] [OURSELVES]	5	26	[WOULD] [FIND] [ITSELF]	24
27	[MAY] [FIND] [HERSELF]	5	27	[WOULD] [FIND] [OURSELVES]	23
28	[CAN] [FIND] [YOURSELF]	5	28	[MIGHT] [FIND] [ITSELF]	20
	TOTAL	535	29	[COULD] [FIND] [OURSELVES]	16
			30	[HAVE] [FIND] [HIMSELF]	16
			31	[MIGHT] [FIND] [HERSELF]	16
			32	[MIGHT] [FIND] [OURSELVES]	15

				33	[MAY] [FIND] [HERSELF]	14
				34	[HAVE] [FIND] [YOURSELF]	14
				35	[HAVE] [FIND] [HERSELF]	14
				36	[WOULD] [FIND] [YOURSELF]	12
				37	[COULD] [FIND] [HERSELF]	12
				38	[WILL] [FIND] [HERSELF]	12
				39	[WILL] [FIND] [EACH]	10
				40	[CAN] [FIND] [EACH]	10
					TOTAL	1962

Appendix 7

List and frequencies of [n*][lose][ppx*] in the COCA and BNC

BNC		FREQ
1	FINGERS LOSING THEMSELVES	2
2	BUILDINGS LOSE THEMSELVES	1
3	SMYSLOV LOST HERSELF	1
4	ROAD LOST ITSELF	1
5	RACHAELA LOST HERSELF	1
6	PLANES LOSE THEMSELVES	1
7	PEOPLE LOSE EACH	1
8	MEREDITH LOST HERSELF	1
9	LOVER LOSES HIMSELF	1
10	INDIVIDUAL LOSES HIMSELF	1
11	HELEN LOST HERSELF	1
	Sub-TOTAL	12
	TOTAL (minus reciprocals)	11
COCA		FREQ
1	TIME LOSING HIMSELF	2
2	WREN LOST HERSELF	1
3	WOMEN LOSE THEMSELVES	1
4	SOME LOST THEMSELVES	1
5	WIND LOST ITSELF	1
6	WILLIAMS LOST HIMSELF	1
7	VOICE LOSING ITSELF	1
8	VICKERY LOSES HIMSELF	1
9	TRACKS LOSING THEMSELVES	1
10	TIM LOST HIMSELF	1
11	TELL LOSE YOURSELF	1
12	SUFFERER LOSING HIMSELF	1
13	SPIRITS LOSE THEMSELVES	1
14	SOUNDS LOST THEMSELVES	1
15	SONG LOSES ITSELF	1
16	SONG LOSE YOURSELF	1
17	SHIPS LOSE THEMSELVES	1
18	SELF LOSING ITSELF	1
19	SARGIS LOST HIMSELF	1
20	SARAH LOST HERSELF	1
21	CHILDREN LOSE THEMSELVES	1
22	RING LOSES ITSELF	1

23	READER LOSES HIMSELF	1
24	PORTLAND LOSE YOURSELF	1
25	POET LOSES HIMSELF	1
26	PEOPLE LOST THEMSELVES	1
27	PEOPLE LOSE EACH	1
28	POLITICAL PARTIES LOSE THEMSELVES	1
29	NIGHT LOSING HIMSELF	1
30	MOMENT LOSING HERSELF	1
31	MINUTES LOST HIMSELF	1
32	MIND LOST ITSELF	1
33	MEETS LOSES HIMSELF	1
34	MEANS LOSING HIMSELF	1
35	LUCY LOSING HERSELF	1
36	LUCINDA LOST HERSELF	1
37	LEVINE LOSES HIMSELF	1
38	LEGS LOSE THEMSELVES	1
39	LARKEN LOST HIMSELF	1
40	JULIAN LOST HIMSELF	1
41	INDIAN SCOUT LOSING HIMSELF	1
42	OTHERS LOSING THEMSELVES	1
43	GRETA LOSES HERSELF	1
44	GIRL LOSES HERSELF	1
45	GEORGE LOST HIMSELF	1
46	GARDEN LOSE YOURSELF	1
47	FRIENDS LOSE THEMSELVES	1
48	FREARS LOSES HIMSELF	1
49	FATHER LOST HIMSELF	1
50	EUROPE LOST EACH	1
51	DANIEL LOSES HIMSELF	1
52	ARAB COMMUNITY LOSES ITSELF	1
53	CLIENTS LOSE THEMSELVES	1
54	CINNABAR LOSES HERSELF	1
55	CHARACTERS LOSE THEMSELVES	1
56	CAT LOSE YOURSELF	1
57	BUILDINGS LOSE THEMSELVES	1
58	BOY LOSES HIMSELF	1
59	BOBBY LOSES HIMSELF	1
60	BARRIS LOSES HIMSELF	1
61	BALL LOST ITSELF	1
62	ANITA LOST HERSELF	1
63	AGNES LOST HERSELF	1
64	ADAMS LOST HERSELF	1
65	AD LOST HERSELF	1

66	ABIGAIL LOSE HERSELF	1
	Sub-TOTAL	67
	TOTAL (minus reciprocals & false antecedents)	53

Appendix 8

BNC and COCA: frequencies for [catch][ppx*] sorted by lemma

BNC: [catch] [ppx*]		
		FREQ
1	[CATCH] [HERSELF]	21
2	[CATCH] [HIMSELF]	19
3	[CATCH] [MYSELF]	10
4	[CATCH] [YOURSELF]	9
	TOTAL	59
COCA: [catch] [ppx*]		
		FREQ
1	[CATCH] [HIMSELF]	465
2	[CATCH] [HERSELF]	337
3	[CATCH] [MYSELF]	280
4	[CATCH] [YOURSELF]	71
6	[CATCH] [THEMSELVES]	22
7	[CATCH] [OURSELVES]	19
8	[CATCH] [ITSELF]	10
	TOTAL	1204

Appendix 9

COCA: FIND X-SELF: [pp*] [find] [ppx*]

				2015 COCA [pp*] [find] [ppx+] sample 100 (no reciprocals)
1	2005	MAG	WashMonth	39111 # In 1978, while covering California politics, **I found myself** on election night at the Century Plaza Hotel in Los Angeles, which was
2	1995	MAG	Inc.	as large new competitors have entered our market in the last 18 months, **we find ourselves** considering a Big-Team strategy. # " Our industry used to be a bicycle
3	2011	SPOK	NPR_TalkNat	that there's no surprises and there's no - nothing to fear. **I find myself** doing that and I stop. And I ask my wife to tell me
4	2003	ACAD	AmerScholar	Sandel with Mr. Heidelberg in mind, using the word substitution method, soon **I found myself** in deeper waters. In the shower, or when I walked down the
5	1992	FIC	AntiochRev	-- and what is Space/Time if you can't experience it?), **he finds himself** growing agitated, annoyed, if he's forced to listen to the boy
6	2003	SPOK	CNN_KingWknd	totally exhausted and completely wired from all the coffee I'd drunk. And **I found myself** -- in order to get to sleep, I found myself starting to take
7	2002	MAG	MotherJones	me like I had the plague. " Hired as an administrative assistant, **she found herself** being asked to clean the rest room. She got luckier with her next
8	1994	FIC	BkSF.NeptuneCrossing	to ogle trajectories instead of women -- but odder still was the fact that **he found himself** not only following the motions of the balls, but visualizing practically impossible trajectories
9	1996	FIC	NewMoon	; after all, what else would she need? # What indeed? **She found herself** wondering what could possibly be missing the day she smashed three different thoughts against
10	1994	ACAD	ComplntlDev	state-society relations, the state's possibilities for autonomous action were so circumscribed that **it found itself** continuously on the defensive. In effect, it had abandoned a great deal
11	2009	ACAD	PSAJournal	consequences of the digital photography age is that photographers take many more images and **they find themselves** struggling to cope with an ever growing collection of image files that are stored
12	1992	MAG	MotherJones	A to Z "? I didn't press the point.) # **I found myself** wondering whether dealing with old archives was considered a career-path backwater in the KGB
13	2011	FIC	Bk.BeginnersGuide	let -- and in the middle of the night. " # " Perhaps **she found herself** a Prussian duke, " the fourth of their party, Jonathan Sutcliffe,
14	2004	FIC	FantasySciFi	She started talking about the Lord and His place in her life, and **I found myself** feeling nothing. Not angry. Not really even sad. Just empty and
15	2005	MAG	TownCountry	wonder how I'll ever convey what I have seen to the uninitiated. **I find myself** in the unique position of being at a lack for words but simultaneously filled

16	2007	FIC	Analog	led the way there. With Mike's first step onto the bridge, **he found himself** squinting and raising his hand against blinding light in all directions. I knew
17	1995	MAG	Essence	but because of Shimon, I no longer felt that way. Instead, **I found myself** constantly debating Black people who espoused discriminatory beliefs, and I challenged the justification
18	1995	SPOK	PBS_Newshour	through interpreter I was on the fifth floor, and in a second, **I find myself** at ground level with a great slab of concrete hanging over my head.
19	2010	NEWS	SanFranChron	position. # Recently, Phillips realized how much her priorities have changed when **she found herself** in a store buying Merrell hiking shoes rather than a Prada purse as she
20	2006	FIC	Redbook	our entres arrive and the subject is dropped, but as I eat, **I find myself** reliving that first year after the divorce, how friends were always asking me
21	2009	MAG	CountryLiving	scrub away one little dark line. But then my grandmother died, and **I found myself** the owner of an enormous wooden chest containing more than 100 pieces of sterling
22	2003	MAG	WashMonth	trouble with the toilet paper at your workplace? When you tug, do **you find yourself** having difficulty getting more than a sheet or two? If so, you
23	2012	FIC	SouthernRev	1016218039 HE KEEPS YOU. Here in the night about this bed, **you find yourself** thickening down out of dark, gathering in his thoughts, shaped by his
24	2000	FIC	Analog	to bed. As I reached for the handle the door flew open and **I found myself** face to face with the Time Traveller again. Nowadays when he calls on
25	2012	NEWS	Atlanta	took not to get beaten. " # Head, using her experiences after **she found herself** with no home at age 12, is talking to victims who come to
26	2001	FIC	Analog	to which its parent civilization had consented? The geese fell silent, and **she found herself** still speechless. How could it even have been done? The inviolability of
27	1998	MAG	Skiing	far up a ridge into a crown of rocks above the resort. Here **we found ourselves** in a huge bowl beneath towering wooden spires where we spent hours hiking and skiing
28	1994	FIC	LiteraryRev	would be moved to her brother's house in the meantime. At this **she found herself** blessing death, deciding that she too would die. She closed her eyes
29	2000	NEWS	SanFranChron	the first black to play in the American League for the Cleveland Indians, **he found himself** targeted with racial taunts on the playing field. One July evening in a
30	2005	MAG	MotorBoating	uncrowded, if not solitary, anchorages. Shortly after leaving Port Severn, **we found ourselves** in a confusing maze of rocks and low-water buoys, made more puzzling because
31	2012	SPOK	NPR_TalkNat	labor in Britain. It's the liberals in Germany as well. So **they find themselves** at risk of losing support within their own party even though Merkel remains popular

32	1998	ACAD	Monist	pluralist. Berlin, outlining those claims about the unity of values with which **he finds himself** in disagreement, sums them up as follows: # that there exist true
33	1999	MAG	Backpacker	also have stayed in great shape. Despite the drawbacks with the sole, **I find myself** putting on the Solitudes more often than the other boots in my closet.
34	2006	SPOK	NPR_FreshAir	in the early 1930s when he was making the Mickey Mouse cartoons. And **he found himself** unaccountably crying all the time, unable to sleep, desperately unhappy, deep
35	2012	MAG	Skiing	foot of a rolling hill. # Riding up the rusty red double, **I found myself** unable to put my camera down. Instinct drove me to take pictures of
36	1992	SPOK	CBS_SunMorn	: It's just like old times -- that's what friends say when **they find themselves** together again, reminiscing after many years. What's best, of course
37	2005	FIC	Analog	at the time, I'd have never let them do it. Once **I found myself** here, I often thought about pulling the plug on myself. I never
38	1994	NEWS	Atlanta	McKenzie, operating on the premise that no news is good news, said **he finds himself** hoping the telephone doesn't ring. # " You keep telling yourself to
39	2005	ACAD	IndepSchool	leaving campus, not playing with the kids -- nothing. Before long, **I found myself** faking my way through the beginning of the day, trudging to my campus
40	1990	MAG	AmSpect	word is appropriate) until the next issue. For once, also, **I find myself** in agreement with a New Yorker " Talk of the Town " piece:
41	2007	FIC	Analog	last comment almost caused me to break stride. For the first time, **I found myself** really wondering what life looked like from Brittney's perspective. Maybe the little-girl
42	1992	ACAD	AmerEthnicHist	shifting from one set of relations to another; rapidly changing. " # **I found myself** wondering more than once if the other commentators would find more to criticize or
43	2007	FIC	FantasySciFi	: " For your own good, don't go there. And if **you find yourself** wandering the Commons, please do not seek my company. " He extracted
44	2000	MAG	AmerArtist	, Elizabeth O'Reilly is attracted to locations displaying evidence of their history. " **I find myself** curious about abandoned homes, fallow farms, and decaying industrial sites, "
45	2012	FIC	NewStatesman	for May. Since being made redundant from an architectural practice three months ago **she found herself** lingering, loitering even, in places that she would normally have speeded through
46	2007	SPOK	CNN_Newsroom	, ABERCROMBIE: Women are motivated to kill by different circumstances than men. **They find themselves** in fundamentally different circumstances in relationship to their victim. SANCHEZ: Experts will

47	1991	SPOK	PBS_Newshour	have been here and studied and gone into legal practice, yourself, have **you found yourself**, have your expectations about the freedoms enshrined in the Bill of Rights been
48	1992	MAG	Essence	seemed to come looking for me rather than me looking for them. Now **I find myself** wondering where I fit in and what will come next. A top executive
49	2003	MAG	PopMech	patient. A victim of horrific burns suffered in a childhood car accident, **she found herself** caught up in a swirl of unwanted publicity. Her family threatened to sue
50	2009	FIC	Triquarterly	. We stayed in contact. He married Josephine in' 46. And **she found herself** a widow in less than a decade. Her poor sot of a husband
51	2002	FIC	Bk:DarkGuardian	. She never made a sound when she moved. It was eerie. **He found himself** continually glancing at her to assure himself she was with him. Now,
52	1997	SPOK	NBC_Dateline	get paid for deals Lamar had sealed with a handshake. In February, **she found herself** in a financial and emotional free fall. (Cameron-leaving-cl) Ms-ALLEN: Sometimes when you
53	2008	NEWS	SanFranChron	here, a Ray Charles there, a Nat Cole or Sinatra there. **You find yourself** sort of copying the devices they use. And the job is discard as
54	2006	NEWS	Atlanta	. # She exercises four times a week and takes walks, and when **she finds herself** in an elevator with hard floors, she does a little soft-shoe. #
55	2011	FIC	Bk:NaamahsBlessing	I was raised. Now I was not so easily impressed. And yet **I found myself** longing for the familiar. # I wished Jehanne were here. And I
56	1997	SPOK	NPR_Saturday	a level anything like the pictures that the kids were making deserved. And **I found myself** drifting towards wanting to make stuff that was more in that vein, that
57	1992	MAG	RollingStone	glad for the Cotton Club work and enthralled by the black musicians. Soon **he found himself** shooting the likes of Cab Calloway and Louis Armstrong. People had told him
58	2003	SPOK	CBS_Sixty	really something to be proud of? I have to be careful, because **I find myself** telling people that I do n't go to the movies, as if that
59	2006	SPOK	CNN_Zahn	world is what's going to happen to me, doc? And unfortunately **I found myself** reluctant to answer that because I wasn't sure. And I didn't
60	1998	MAG	ChristCentury	your ancient prophets in the Old Testament and the signs foretelling Armageddon, and **I find myself** wondering if we're the generation that is going to see that come about
61	2001	FIC	SatEvenPost	to me that at last my great opportunity had come. At once, **I found myself** burning with zeal, glowing with enthusiasm -- in other words, ardent.
62	1995	MAG	Skiing	" -- lifts us up to the top in about two minutes flat. **I find myself** thinking, " What I wouldn't give for a nice, slow chairlift

63	2006	FIC	Bk:SF:HattieBigSky	myself to hang back--didn't want to be lumped in with someone like Mildred--but **I found myself** running up to him and slipping something in his hand. " For luck
64	2001	FIC	MichiganQRev	Kate would glow. # " You should see where he works, " **she found herself** explaining one night. " It's this complete Tower of Babel, only
65	2002	SPOK	NPR_FreshAir	to carry on performing with somebody you've never acted with before, and **you find yourself** doing the classic thing of talking to one person downstage right and then the
66	2004	FIC	Bk:BlueBlood	drawing my eye to the triple strand of pearls at her throat so that **I found myself** wondering how tightly I'd have to pull them to cut off her oxygen
67	2008	NEWS	Denver	No. Emphatically, no. // I was disheartened, frustrated, angry. **I found myself** wishing that my budget would allow me to order one of the many several-hundred-dollar
68	2003	SPOK	NPR_Saturday	When you think of all the money those rolling bags represent, don't **you find yourself** wondering, Why didn't I think of that?' Well, that
69	2009	NEWS	NYTimes	who wrote the definitive text" A Theology of Liberation,' and **he found himself** deeply moved by the example of Archbishop Romero, a critic of El Salvador
70	1997	ACAD	ArabStudies	. # Kudair, see Khudayyir. # Khudayyir, Dini. " When **I Found Myself.** " Middle East Report. September-October 1987. 27-31. # Khudayyir, Muhammad
71	1997	MAG	Inc.	Honest Bob's AND Ford NOT champagne, " for example. # If **you find yourself** mumbling four-letter words of frustration, sometimes it's best to adopt a low-tech
72	2008	FIC	Bk:GhostRadio	off to sleep, thoughts of the voice and the trip receded, and **he found himself** remembering a recent caller to his radio show. # # Continues...
73	2005	FIC	NewYorker	Paul's Island and having a fair wind both the 18th and the 19th **we found ourselves** in the river on the morning of the 20th and within sight of the
74	1995	ACAD	Mercury	hurts. " # During my first year of graduate school in physics, **I found myself** spending a lot of time with a classmate. Apart from impassioned arguments about
75	2008	MAG	AmericanSpectator	is akin to nothing so much as buying pornography. There's the moment **you find yourself** holding it near your hip and at eye level, there's the
76	2007	MAG	TownCountry	coaster. Just when you were certain your prospects were on the rise, **you found yourself** plunging into a sickening dip. And though your passionate nature usually exalts in
77	1993	SPOK	ABC_20/20	: I hardly like that answer STOSSEL voice-over So what should you do if **you find yourself** in this kind of relationship? Dr. Wetzler says that because the man often
78	2000	FIC	NewEnglandRev	as adding, to company assets by the astuteness of our purchases? # **I find myself**, despite who it was who threw the lion, thinking more about my

79	2001	SPOK	NPR_Sunday	The dog stared back at me in a lonely sort of way and soon **I found myself** talking to her. Hello,' I said. How are you?
80	2000	ACAD	AmerScholar	down at the rows and rows of bald or white-haired heads below me, **I found myself** unable to shake the thought that there would never be a bicentennial celebration for
81	2011	ACAD	SchoolCounsel	. # Time: Time Spent and Time Wasted Time Spent # " Have **you found yourself** spending a lot of time preparing for, engaging in, or recovering from
82	2011	MAG	NatGeog	once thrived atop the High Peaks are now at risk of vanishing. # **I find myself** imagining a time-lapse photo of future changes, imagining, as well, a
83	1995	FIC	FantasySciFi	essentially like every other world. Sad, sad, sad. # Here **I found myself** with four hundred square kilometers of raw stone. How long would it take
84	2002	NEWS	NYTimes	he was able to take a rare break from catering to demanding diners, **he found himself** with that rarest of luxuries in a New York kitchen. He had time
85	2009	NEWS	Houston	travel destinations. # But after a 12-day educational tour of the country, **I find myself** raving about Turkey the way a 6-year-old goes on about her breakfast with Cinderella
86	1991	NEWS	USAToday	cater to ideology, and carry the onerous burden of the arms race, **it found itself** at the breaking point. " # Even the sweeping reforms that accompanied Gorbymania
87	2007	ACAD	SouthwestRev	process that the viewer also undergoes. # It's probably no coincidence that **I find myself** aware of a rhythmic, breath-like quality in these paintings, a movement that
88	2003	FIC	Ploughshares	an attorney in Michigan, had had drive, ambition once, but said **he found himself** standing in front of Lane 4 one afternoon and thinking, What am I
89	2004	NEWS	CSMonitor	, especially if their eyes had lighted on a poor boy: Many of **them found themselves** living with their in-laws, who were not always welcoming. They had to
90	2004	MAG	TodaysParent	were going to react. " Vancouver nurse Zo Schuler understands those feelings. **She found herself** in the unenviable position of having to announce a pregnancy to a supervisor who
91	1990	ACAD	CrossCurrents	beginning of desire. There was a moment in Thomas Merton's life when **he found himself** in the position I have been describing, wanting to be alone with God
92	2007	ACAD	SouthwestRev	generalities. " She points over Ivy's shoulder without looking. " But **I find myself** stuck with the same props. I must have used those moccasins a dozen
93	1996	FIC	KenyonRev	by a lick of moonshine, a very present help in trouble, and **she found herself** now, inwardly quavering before Reba Trelette -- the sophisticated stranger who had inserted
94	2011	FIC	Framework	almost silently through lagoons of such peace and beauty John is entranced... and **he finds himself** filming just the reflection of the sun on the surface of the water...

95	1993	NEWS	NYTimes	Laundromats, Chinese take-out restaurants and video arcades. # Inevitably, though, **he finds himself** out on the streets where he has spent most of his life. Out
96	1993	ACAD	CrossCurrents	nonetheless find our ability to realize and maintain that identity fragile indeed. # **We find ourselves**, I expect, in the same situation as Saint Paul: " I
97	1991	SPOK	ABC_Jennings	BOY Somebody you can look up to BOY Every day I play basketball, **I find myself** daydreaming wishing I can hit all the points just like Michael Jordan hits.
98	2003	FIC	Analog	along for his use when he reached the top. Thus it was that **he found himself** in the sweeping, punishing winds of the mountain top, listening to the
99	2011	FIC	Raritan	have to wait. # Six years later, almost to the day, **I find myself** stepping over rubble into Area D - according to the archeologists' floor plan
100	2007	FIC	FantasySciFi	Sasquatch and D. B. Cooper's lost loot. So, that's how **I found myself** headed back south in a rented van with three guys I'd just met

Appendix 10

BNC: FIND X-SELF: [pp*] [find] [ppx*]

			2015 BNC [pp*] [find] [ppx*] sample 100 (no reciprocals)
1	EA8	W_commerce	but, I learnt the hard way and have been proven in practice. **I find myself** intolerant of management books that seek to prescribe exactly' how it should be
2	B0W	W_non_ac_soc_science	. I said' That's it -- I'm going', and **I found myself** walking out... It's her -- she's very, very difficult.
3	ACW	W_fict_prose	. The sudden change had not come easy to him, and even now **he found himself** muttering' Mam' under his breath because that old name was somehow special
4	KAL	W_letters_personal	of the world in matters of language study and language teaching methodology, so **I found myself**, on one day, giving a rsum of Linguistics in the west over
5	HUA	W_fict_prose	use the service ducts to enter TOP. It was several days later that **he found himself** rising through the complex of dripping wet catwalks and steps that ran around the
6	JXX	W_fict_prose	their parents. Unfortunately, the fragile harmony between them was soon broken when **she found herself** arguing furiously with him in the dress department of Bloomingdales. Due to her
7	HGK	W_fict_prose	disappoint them.' Maggie was still not in any condition to argue and **she found herself** following him to the dark little bar, almost running a gauntlet of greetings
8	F8X	W_fict_prose	black outside: Ace could see the stars and, as she stood, **she found herself** looking down, through one of the side windows, at the reticulated surface
9	H82	W_fict_prose	. Louisa was filled with a terrible wonder at Frere's ignorance. Again **she found herself** astounded that Emilia should have so little feeling for him. His diffidence was
10	K2W	W_newsp_other_report	at 8.30 this morning with a enquiry. The number rang once and then **he found himself** listening to a conversation. The reporter quickly realised the identity of both voices
11	ECG	W_pop_lore	visit than a map and some route descriptions, so thus it was that **we found ourselves** between the Vnon and the Etanons on the campsite at La Brade in August
12	FR3	W_fict_prose	he experimented with his alembic and his aludel. Many were the afternoons when **I found myself** priming the athenor with a set of little bellows, while Mr Broadhurst waved
13	CGE	W_religion	of God's principles for the specific areas of life and experience in which **we find ourselves**. Our need to look more closely at the working relationship is not that
14	ACG	W_religion	the heroics of chapter 22. For Abraham was a hero there. Though **we found ourselves** asking whether the story was about faith or faithlessness, we were left in
15	FR0	W_fict_prose	children were hatched and grew on many different worlds. Many years later, **he found himself** assigned a new First Pilot. A lad with a name that was somehow

16	A77	W_non_ac_soc_science	to write a letter home to his wife. In his late twenties, **he finds himself** having to conduct family business via telephone and letter. The two-month period between
17	CF4	W_non_ac_soc_science	this country perfecting what I call my chameleon act: fitting into whatever environment **I found myself** in; making myself, my Chinese self, invisible in order to avoid
18	HYB	W_ac_polit_law_edu	all other people as persons like oneself; for the total environment in which **we find ourselves**, both natural and cultural; for beauty, delighting in experiencing a sense
19	F9X	W_fict_prose	time since she had had to stop herself simply blowing away an enemy that **she found herself** unable to either maim or restrain.' I've still got the knife
20	A9H	W_newsp_brdsht_nat_sports	to get a 1990 equivalent of Mexico's' Group of death' when **they found themselves** facing Uruguay, West Germany and Denmark. Andrea Arrica, head of the
21	HA0	W_fict_prose	lying in a pool of my own urine. So it was that eventually **I found myself** in a hospital in Swindon close to other victims of Larry Foot. After
22	HHB	W_fict_prose	that it filled her traitorous body with more waves of nerve-tingling sensations. Again **she found herself** responding to the fever of his passionate desire, and as her own need
23	GTC	W_biography	deprived him of the prospect of promotion, and at the age of twenty-five **he found himself** on the retired list, reduced to half pay in 1812. In his
24	FB0	W_ac_soc_science	are not the only ones who perceive the system as unjust, and that **it finds itself** with a crisis of legitimacy on its hands. # Explaining Punishment # Why
25	FU8	W_fict_prose	ease in her seat for more than a few minutes at a time. **She found herself** searching back to her youth for reasons to explain the blind and selfish obsessions
26	JXY	W_fict_prose	large orange ball into the pool before jumping in himself, and within seconds **she found herself** part of a noisy, boisterous game of water hand-ball. The group,
27	H97	W_fict_prose	the sounds coming from the kitchen, of glasses clinking and water splashing, **she found herself** glancing down at his coat. Its rich, soft folds contrasted sharply with
28	C85	W_fict_prose	no more use for them. Meredith's due any time.' And **they found themselves** hurried from the room. Any opportunity for learning more was gone. They
29	HSJ	W_pop_lore	at 50 cents apiece. She started work at 14 and by the time **she found herself** at Vons she'd held a variety of jobs. But by now she
30	B10	W_non_ac_soc_science	can manage the situation, I know how to regulate my anger. If **I find myself** getting upset, I'll know what to do. Try not to take
31	A6X	W_pop_lore	inboard variable race suspension, but it was a dog' -- and also **he found himself** committed by Sir Alfred to building a Le Mans car powered by Rover's

32	GUE	W_fict_prose	his broad shoulders. Fighting down a wave of combined anger and panic, **she found herself** gabbling furiously,' I'm sorry! I was wrong about my mother
33	FTY	W_non_ac_soc_science	through sponsorships, events and appeals of ever more exotic and imaginative kinds. **I find myself** dipping into my pocket and giving to causes that a decade ago I would
34	BN6	W_biography	Anyway, I did some radio interviews and I was quite taken aback when **I found myself** over the front page of the Evening Standard. I can not imagine what
35	CKR	W_biography	worries at Bec; not least during his first year as abbot, when **he found himself** immersed in lawsuits against those who claimed lands and tithes belonging to Bec for
36	FSK	W_fict_prose	asked crossly.' Someone has been playing a stupid game with me. **I found myself** in the kitchen, eating sugar from Lord Pabham's hand. I hate
37	GWB	W_fict_prose	was like trying to recall a dream. Without being aware of getting there **he found himself** outside the printer's shop. Upstairs, Curnow was duty officer.'
38	KDW	S_conv	stuck in on your own all the time! And talking to yourself. **I find myself**, talking to myself! (laugh) (pause) Which is crazy anyway, so I
39	GV6	W_fict_prose	the lobby of her building, waiting for the lift to come down, **she found herself** wondering whether she would bump into Matthew Prescott before next Wednesday. And later
40	JXT	W_fict_prose	done. And so, about a week after their last direct encounter, **she found herself** one evening waiting up for him, sitting with a glass of vodka and
41	H8S	W_fict_prose	had never evoked in her floated through her veins like liquid fire, and **she found herself** responding eagerly, wantonly, to his caresses. And yet, all the
42	AYK	W_misc	there wondering why you can't get to sleep. But, if tonight **you find yourself** yawning at 9.30, why not have an early night? Of course there
43	ASC	W_biography	seat in her car, he asked if he might come too. So **he found himself** unexpectedly spending his holiday in the little port of Cassis. That quickly brightened
44	BP9	W_fict_prose	right and left according to where their jobs were and, following Emil, **I found myself** climbing up not into the dining car but into one of the sleeping cars
45	ACG	W_religion	Eden things get much worse. No sooner was he out of Eden than **we find ourselves** in a field stained with a brother's blood (4.1-16). Abel
46	KA1	W_essay_school	sparkling world of pleasure where he lives' happily ever after', instead **he find himself** in the corrupt, sordid London. G.E. is also a mystery story

47	AB3	W_non_ac_humanities_arts	headfirst into the mainstream -- still exert something verging on hegemony. Me, **I find myself** steadily drifting back to the unfashionable conviction that radical meanings are betrayed by conventional
48	CE7	W_non_ac_humanities_arts	As British diplomats manoeuvred to protect extra-European spheres of influence against foreign rivals, **they found themselves** inexorably drawn into taking sides in the hardening alliance system on the European continent
49	CD9	W_biography	times continued: not for the first or last time in his career, **he found himself** in trouble with the authorities, being disqualified twice, once when he was
50	ANK	W_misc	Chalk greeted them and supplied them with beer but, as they drank, **they found themselves** looking down the barrels of a dozen pistols! The trap had been baited
51	G1X	W_fict_prose	the flesh easily gave way like soft india-rubber before my slightest movement. Suddenly **I found myself** in a sack much larger than my body, but completely dark. I
52	AMU	W_fict_prose	uncontrollable. Now, with the dawn breaking and his death so close, **he found himself** strangely sanguine -- almost as if he were an abstract entity observing, from
53	BMX	W_fict_prose	sent me,' Marian said.' I came...' and suddenly **she found herself** speaking words she had never thought,'... I came to find my
54	HA2	W_fict_prose	. Moreover, he knew and respected Laura Maingay, clearly a recommendation. **She found herself** regretting she'd not been entirely open with him. It was not so
55	C9J	W_pop_lore	overall shape of the guitar gives the memory a bit of a jog and **you find yourself** starting to think Thinline or HM Telecaster, which may not be a good
56	JY3	W_fict_prose	wary smile in return. With confused feelings, she smiled back, but **she found herself** staring in what she realised must seem a nave display of stunned surprise.
57	EWH	W_fict_prose	him glancing at her in a way that held its own silent eloquence. **She found herself** being slowly torn apart in her loyalties: on the one hand she felt
58	FP1	W_fict_prose	likely. London. Extra help for summer." And why do **you find yourself** in Keswick?' She shook her head. It brought to his notice
59	AKB	W_newsp_brdsht_nat_arts	that so often mars his drama. Nor is there a single moment when **you find yourself** wearily wishing that the characters would put a sock into their ceaseless flow of
60	AAE	W_newsp_brdsht_nat_sports	Ireland in Dublin but which both Robson and Jack Charlton agreed to abandon when **they found themselves** paired in the same World Cup group. England, who could meet Brazi
61	EFP	W_fict_prose	have known. Similarly, when they exchanged the names of their schools, **she found herself** immensely relieved when he declared that he was at Winchester, for she had

62	AN8	W_fict_prose	oozed geniality.' Because it is very relevant to the dilemma in which **I find myself**. Now you know -- everyone on the paper knows -- I'm not
63	HRT	W_misc	service at Louth Maltings in January this year. Like many other RAF servicemen **he found himself** stationed in Lincolnshire and after five years service his Lincolnshire bonds were established and
64	HHB	W_fict_prose	minutes,' he told Lucy, then left the room. Later, **she found herself** in the front passenger seat of a comfortable grey Rover, and as the
65	FB2	S_interview_oral_history	you said that you went into a requisition property (SP:PS1N1) Yes, erm, we found ourselves in, rather to go back. After the bombing my wife was housed
66	FAB	W_fict_prose	. The man on the floor who had jacked up grinned at her and **she found herself** grinning back. Then JoJo offered her a tab of LSD. She took
67	A4J	W_newsp_brdsht_nat_misc	wonder what Dignam will make of Claudius?' A year or so back **I found myself** sitting next to him, bearded in his old age and wearing plus fours
68	CB1	W_non_ac_humanities_arts	awareness of everything relevant I find myself moved towards X, overlooking something relevant **I find myself** moved towards Y. Be aware. Therefore let yourself be moved towards X. That
69	G10	W_fict_prose	-- my burden and I must bear it, she had believed -- but **she found herself** discussing it easily and naturally and very trustingly with Raynor.' There is
70	HGN	W_fict_prose	rule is to make eye contact with your interviewers. Not so easy. **I find myself** confronting: # a skull made of Mexican sugarwork; # a tragical grimace
71	G1S	W_fict_prose	and that Johnny had visited the cottage, prowling through the rooms, as **she found herself** doing often enough, but had been unable to reach her. But there
72	HY5	W_ac_humanities_arts	of the eighteenth century claimed that after fourteen years in several highly important posts **he found himself** 20,000 worse off. Nevertheless, the general direction of change is unmistakable.
73	A0T	W_ac_humanities_arts	describe the latter kind of fact. When trying to describe these facts, **we find ourselves** being sucked into the language of phenomenology with its core assumption that our experience
74	HHB	W_fict_prose	vanished as though wiped away with a magic cloth, and -- stupidly -- **she found herself** waiting to be kissed. But it did not happen. Instead he put
75	C9L	W_pop_lore	half an hour of chords, runs and the odd quite musical moment, **I found myself** getting on really well with it. The guitar has a fair amount of

76	HA4	W_fict_prose	be pushed forward into the train, where she stood in a daze until **she found herself** sitting down in a seat offered to her by a small boy.'
77	G2Y	W_pop_lore	tracks # As you drive about the countryside next weekend, and especially if **you find yourself** approaching a town or village once famous for its market days, look out
78	EDP	W_non_ac_humanities_arts	regret having aided Rhee's ambitions to the extent that they had done when **they found themselves** exposed to Rhee's mordant censure. In Washington attention was focused on the
79	JY9	W_fict_prose	my outburst at the time of Simon's death had wrecked our relationship, **I found myself** wondering if there was a chance of rekindling it. As soon as I
80	A77	W_non_ac_soc_science	and besides -- that's cheating. This all sounds well and good until **you find yourself** airborne at night, armed only with a line on a map, and
81	G2F	W_pop_lore	at hand inside that tank and, as you are wearing ear plugs, **you find yourself** floating in a soundless, dark and warm environment. Jacqueline certainly found her
82	CHE	W_biography	her feathers. This means fluffing them out and adapting them to whatever atmosphere **she found herself** in, and is a sure sign of contentment in a lot of birds
83	K5M	W_newsp_other_report	Scottish hierarchy and the Prime Minister on the matter, all without success. **He finds himself** stymied,' unless we go to appeal, which would be the Lands
84	H8Z	W_fict_prose	in a cloud of dust.' Be gone, Emilia Frere,' **she found herself** thinking.' Get you from this parish. Abandon Munding Rectory and your
85	BNL	W_religion	no harm can befall you. The only hazard might be the person who **you find yourself** seated next to. However, the coaches make frequent stops for sightseeing and
86	ADS	W_fict_prose	. She could not stand it another minute. Something snapped inside her and **she found herself** grabbing the mutton and wresting the plate, with what was left of the
87	KS7	S_brdcast_discussn	to come here at some stage. But not this year, but because **we found ourselves** in a very embarrassing situation with the forty point limit and the fact that
88	GVT	W_fict_prose	exciting sense of heightened perception with the wind and rain, as soon as **she found herself** on the pavement outside the house. While everybody else hurried to their destinations
89	K54	W_newsp_other_social	The dogs must also be trained not to be easily distracted by the environment **they find themselves** in. Occasionally, the dogs attract the attention of children, and even
90	HQS	W_fict_prose	prison brought to my notice with a vengeance. But I fancy that if **I found myself** on the field of Waterloo with a foot missing, or in a dentist
91	J3W	S_meeting	larger membership to allow us to speak with strong voice in the many debates **we find ourselves** involved on behalf of our sport whether it be windsurfers, dinghies, offshore

92	CHG	W_fict_prose	everyday articles on the shelves reminded me abruptly of things at home, and **I found myself** thinking of my last night before leaving London. I spent those final few
93	EDE	W_non_ac_soc_science	of Constabulary, 1975 (or almost any other year for that matter) **we find ourselves** assailed within the space of only a few paragraphs with repeated references to The
94	FPU	W_fict_prose	Estella, give him some food. Go, Pip.' And so **I found myself** back in the overgrown garden in the bright daylight. Estella put some bread
95	A91	W_newsp_brdsht_nat_misc	've heard his extraordinary story that you realise this is no ordinary man. **I found myself** surreptitiously studying him. Does he face show courage and conviction -- or does
96	ECT	W_pop_lore	be a really great person living this incredibly interesting and exciting life. They **you find yourself** working in television and you realize you're as much of a wanker as
97	HA4	W_fict_prose	herself for feeling embarrassed. It was with a considerable sense of agitation that **she found herself** opposite room number four. She knocked -- surely too timidly for anybody within
98	HTN	W_fict_prose	, and ran to unfasten the door. The gate swung outwards, and **he found himself** looking up at the massive head of a yawning dragon with creased cheek and
99	FS0	W_biography	n't share the burden of campaigning any more and took a back seat. **I found myself** snowed under from the start. I went to the NUJ to ask them
100	ALN	W_ac_soc_science	recent publicity had brought it all back to her. In her words' **I find myself** blaming this for my self-hate, my lack of confidence, my feeling of

Appendix 11

COCA: LOSE X-SELF: [pp*] [lose] [ppx*]

				2015 COCA [pp*] [lose] [ppx*], sample 100 (no reciprocals!)
1	1990	FIC	Bk:SingingStones	, as usual. She hates to see me have any fun. " **She lost herself** in watching as the road wound through foothills on the way to Charlottesville.
2	2002	MAG	GoodHousekeeping	green tea. Reading these particular books plunges me into an alternate reality. **I lose myself** in against-all-odds exploration, and the present disappears. But before I can lose
3	2008	FIC	Bk:MapMoments	. # Her fingers twine in his hair and she pulls him down. **He loses himself** in the hunger of her kiss, but when they break apart the wrongness
4	1996	MAG	PsychToday	this morning and didn't forget to clean my room.' And then **she loses herself** in the cracks in the ceiling with the first blows to her head.
5	1992	FIC	Atlantic	. Mr. Shimono, some sort of computer genius, apologizes gravely: " **We lose ourselves** on the way. " As a result, Lynne is late getting to
6	1996	FIC	Bk:BeachMusic	sweet-sounding word was merciless and I could not bear to hear it. So **I lost myself** in the oils and condiments of my well-stocked kitchen. I fatted up my
7	2008	FIC	Bk:OrderThings	time that system works. A couple of times it has not. # **I lost myself** the first time when I was only four. I do not recall exactly (* see full quote below)
8	1993	FIC	Bk:Juv:FlightDragonKyn	the birches and then up again into the grazing land above the steading until **it lost itself** in shadow. Orrik ceded the trodden part to me and broke his own
9	2009	FIC	Bk:VanessaAmpVirginia	picture of a crown at the top of her page and without meaning to **I lose myself** in its delicate crenelations. # " Vanessa! This is the second time
10	1996	NEWS	USAToday	Frances Hodgson Burnett. At that time she was an almost forgotten treasure. **I lost myself** in The Secret Garden, The Little Princess, Head of the House of
11	2008	FIC	ContempFic	small bench with lyre-shaped arms and the seat upholstered in very fine kidskin. **I lost myself** in gazing at the grey-blue and grey-green stripes of the wallpaper, or at
12	2005	SPOK	CNN_King	who no matter how skillful they are at their craft, no matter how **they lose themselves** in a character there's some aspect of them that the audience finds appealing
13	1991	FIC	Atlantic	After a moment they are both laughing, and for the rest of the ride **she loses herself** in a conversation about the sixties. At The Palmer House, Anna tips
14	2001	MAG	ChristCentury	where we are, whose we are and what we are doing. Otherwise **we lose ourselves**, and fail to learn with Gandhi that " there is more to life
15	1997	FIC	ArkansasRev	plays and when to sacrifice and should they use the suicide squeeze, and **he lost himself** in the black swirl of ice cubes dancing in his Coke. They talked

16	2008	MAG	PsychToday	flow, " when you are so absorbed in what you're doing that **you lose yourself**. This, in turn, generates feelings of mastery, well-being, and
17	2000	FIC	Esquire	vogue again. It was work -- simple, repetitive, nonintellectual -- and **I lost myself** in it. When I looked up again, it was ten of three
18	2008	FIC	Triquarterly	of wine and literature. Oh, what good fortune that would be! **I lost myself** in thoughts of meeting my kind of people, those with gentle literary mannets
19	1990	FIC	KenyonRev	and being seen, gazing so intently into the soul of the other that **you lose yourself** and become the other. # Carriages gather at the gallery gates. Women
20	2005	FIC	Triquarterly	that another love may push you away, till # lifted by sweet wings **I lost myself** in sleep. # And only then did my tears come to an end
21	2000	FIC	MassachRev	wasn't big enough, let alone fast enough. In my second year **I lost myself** in study instead, an English major of all things. Because, I
22	2007	MAG	People	Davis and I started a floral company, Succulent (www.succulent la.com). **I lose myself** when I'm planting and arranging. Our first paying job was for a
23	1999	SPOK	CBS_Morning	. Mr-ZMUDA: He's amazing. And I got ta tell you, **he lost himself**. He -- we shot 87 days. Jim Carrey was maybe there two
24	2007	FIC	CanadWomStud	She's a huge mountain of warmth, arms embracing the child with breasts **he loses himself** in when he presses his head against her. After Jack died, she
25	1996	SPOK	ABC_Primetime	a mirror that had shattered in a million pieces. In a night, **I lost myself**. NANCY COLLINS: How do you think this incident affected your marriage?
26	1996	SPOK	NPR_TalkNation	the bargaining. But it certainly has changed the job question in Canada. **We lost ourselves** through free trade about 42 operations in Canada, parts, part suppliers.
27	2009	FIC	Bk:StalinEpigram	's apple working against the almost transparently thin skin of his pale throat, **he loses himself** in the thing we call poetry; becomes the poem. When he materializes
28	1999	FIC	Ploughshares	with the thin face and the long hair and big hands. One of **them lost itself** in my hair. " You got soft hair, " he whispered.
29	1994	MAG	HarpersMag	's a bit of a piercing devil himself. He pads about silently as **you lose yourself** in the various exhibits. One moment he's at his desk, the
30	1997	MAG	Ebony	decided to leave me, not only did I lose a lover, but **I lost myself**. I will never allow myself to love another so much that I lose
31	2011	FIC	Bk:BurntMountainNovel	. Allen and to drive the length of Peachtree Road, out to where **it lost itself** in the tangle of Buckhead. There were many fine and even palatial homes

32	1990	FIC	BkSF:AlchymistsJournal	anymore, not after -- my previous experience. Bureaucracy loses you, and **you lose yourself**. I'm hiring on with you. " Lily sighed, looking up
33	1993	FIC	Mov:Arcade	'S ROOM is her haven, a virtual library, filled with books which **she loses herself** in. They're stacked everywhere. And puzzles too. Half-assembled jig-saws.
34	2006	MAG	Prevention	our own star. But sometimes, in considering other people's wishes, **we lose ourselves** and ultimately sell out our own happiness. The decision to be out of
35	1997	ACAD	AmerScholar	perfectly defined something, and so is the necessary. On the contrary, **he lost himself**, owing to the fact that this self was seen fantastically reflected in the
36	2011	NEWS	Denver	his fingers move quickly, and he focuses on something unseen in space: **He loses himself** to the music. # Juele, who usually lives in Nederland or stays
37	2007	FIC	CanadWomStud	She's a huge mountain of warmth, arms embracing the child with breasts **he loses himself** in when he presses his head against her. After Jack died, she
38	2010	MAG	Backpacker	I can stop the aimless circling I've mistaken for progress. Perhaps if **I lose myself** cojnpletely, I'll have a chance to find the way back for real
39	1991	FIC	KansasQ	wheel chair, on the sunporch, Jedediah Leland reminisced about his boss. **I lost myself** in the mystery of what made Mr. Kane tick until I heard noises from
40	1989	MAG	Ms	The second trauma is when the bandages are taken off. That is when **she loses herself**. This is reinforced by comments people make on the streets -- one Bina
41	2004	NEWS	Chicago	sang' God Is Not Sleeping,' and it just took me. **I lost myself**. " # " Have a Little Faith " has re-energized Staples. She
42	2005	FIC	LiteraryRev	, not even anesthesia works like that, where do the senses go? **I lose myself** for a few moments, and manage even to dream, full fledged dreams
43	2004	FIC	Atlantic	don't make a vision you might cling to, or create an idea **you lose yourself** in. Don't look at a map and ponder the depth of the
44	1998	ACAD	CrossCurrents	, we are " the throne of God's glory, " and when **we lose ourselves** in the divine, we become most truly found. We have not wasted
45	2011	FIC	Bk:ZoneOneNovel	that mindless void. Then he felt the fourth skel grab his leg and **he lost himself**. # He woke. He bucked the forbidden thought. # He had
46	2000	MAG	Redbook	my body seemed alive. For as long as I could tolerate it, **I lost myself** in a flow of sensation connecting me to Paul. It wasn't an
47	2003	FIC	NewEnglandRev	, blues, arcs and spirals. Nevertheless they were physical and alive. **She lost herself** in the painting. # Anne, in order to leave Joyce alone with

48	1998	MAG	Ebony	energy trying to attract and hold the attention of a suitable male suitor that **they lose themselves** in the process. Ponder what is important to you -- in life,
49	2002	FIC	Mov:Adaptation	woman typing. It's Susan Orlean: pale, delicate and blond. **We lose ourselves** in her melancholy beauty. # # ORLEAN (V.O.) # I went
50	2011	FIC	Hyphen	I've made and he's stroking hard. He kisses my neck and **I lose myself** in the nuzzling, the radiating tingle. The futon lifts us as if
51	1996	FIC	Bk:BeachMusic	After her funeral, a sadness took over me that seemed permanent, and **I lost myself** in the details and technicalities connected to death in the South. Great sorrow
52	2008	FIC	Bk:KnownWorld	and blame the chains on evenings such as these, and on nights when **he lost himself** completely and fell asleep and didn't come to until morning, covered with
53	1997	MAG	PsychToday	element of rage, but you must remain very distant from it. If **you lose yourself** to rage in the complexity of battle, you are going to be lost
54	2003	FIC	Ploughshares	the train streaked across to the other side and filled the entire span before **it lost itself** around the bend of the hill. At dusk you could see town lights
55	2005	SPOK	CBS_Morning	when you lose the championship it's not like you lost the title, **you lose yourself**, because it's like you're not a man anymore. (Vintage-footage-of) DOW
56	2010	FIC	FantasySciFi	, your queen, has left us. We remember her, but should **we lose ourselves** in mourning? " He pauses and shakes his head, then lifts his
57	2012	MAG	ParentingEarly	Charlie interact with my beautiful fi ance, Jodi. I love to watch **them lose themselves** in each other. # Toughest part of the gig. # The lack
58	1997	MAG	Ebony	lost myself. I will never allow myself to love another so much that **I lose myself**. Halle, thank you for your story. Stay strong. DAE MERRIWETHER
59	1997	FIC	Bk:AfterNight	n't you come out from there and have some fun with us? " **She lost herself** in the delicious daydream of being part of that group of laughing, roughhousing
60	1997	MAG	ChristCentury	models from the past. Some join ultraconservative religious or political movements, or **they lose themselves** in mystics of earlier times as if no cultural distance separated us from the
61	2004	FIC	NewYorker	Des Moines, to the baseball game, that we lost him, or **he lost himself**. One Sunday a few weeks later, the old man, who always
62	1994	FIC	FantasySciFi	fingers kneading the soft flesh under my dress, just above my corset. **I lost myself** in the ecstasy of contact with him. # The dawn glanced red off

63	1994	NEWS	CSMonitor	or ocean of story, just bobbing along together. Close to bliss, **we lose ourselves** in the story. # I've heard that part of the appeal and
64	2002	ACAD	HispanicRev	; he is " el honrado hidalgo del seor Quijana. " But when **he loses himself** in his readings, disdaining financial responsibility to support his fantasy (" vendiendo
65	1999	FIC	Esquire	, where she ravished you, abdomen slapping against abdomen in such fury that **you lost yourself** in her punishing metronome, feeling in that impact the force of the correction
66	2012	SPOK	NBC_Matthews	who have come from other countries, who bring their own cultures. Do **we lose ourselves** in the midst of all this? MATTHEWS: Yeah, Ms-PARKER: I don't
67	1992	FIC	VirginiaQRev	sardonic Lotusland of # # forgetfulness, and guilt. If he lost his daughter **he lost himself**; what became of her was what became of him. He followed her
68	2012	FIC	Analog	she? Where had she been born, what were her goals? Had **she lost herself** as badly as I had? Or perhaps her conscience was clear - nothing
69	2001	ACAD	Symposium	mimetic nature of his novel, declaring that each day as he wrote, **he lost himself** in " la copie exacte et minutieuse de la vie " (9)
70	2008	FIC	Read	: Aye, I do sir. WS: Alas, my apologies. **I lose myself** in ego. I do not intend to sound so pompous! I blame
71	2004	FIC	FantasySciFi	then? Did they return to enshrine themselves in the Bridge, or did **they lose themselves** in the Venetian night? # One always asks oneself those questions too late
72	2003	MAG	Prevention	can emerge when people are so absorbed in a challenging activity they love that **they lose themselves**. Time stops, and they become at one with what they're doing
73	1996	FIC	ParisRev	the well, and she went back to walking around in a loincloth. **I lost myself** between her shiny thighs. # Within her peculiar cosmogony of wide velds,
74	2010	FIC	Bk:ListenerNovel	, caught unawares, and yet also secretly enthralled. At my desk, **I lose myself** in work. It is close to ten o'clock when I realize the rain
75	2002	FIC	Esquire	bullets scattered wildly. He tried to ignore them. You either adjusted or **you lost yourself**. He had heard that, too. He climbed the ridge on his
76	1999	FIC	SouthernRev	to help la princesa, but I watched her lose all regard, watched **her lose herself** to love. Juana la perdida. For her I imagine love was a
77	2010	NEWS	NYTimes	. In the book's finest story," Saving Fats,' **he loses himself** in a stranger's far-fetched tale of the waterborne rescue of Fats Domino from
78	2004	MAG	USCatholic	believe as they believed, we try to think the way they thought. **We lose ourselves** in admiration of these great figures from the past. What these four writers

79	1993	FIC	KenyonRev	and more animated, his voice rising toward indignation and anger and salvation, **I lost myself** staring above the altar at the emaciated peeling figure, crucified for the benefit
80	2008	MAG	USAToday	We were able to intervene before Amber became so embroiled with her friends that **she lost herself**. If you suspect your son or daughter may be an Elite Tormentor,
81	2009	FIC	BkTourDeForce	von Rothbart into a swan, doomed to eternally float on Swan Lake. **She lost herself** in the movement, the longing for humanity, the longing for her prince
82	2004	FIC	MichiganQRev	. So completely absorbed is he in what he sees through the lens that **he loses himself** in cinematic pleasure that seems to him to go beyond the mere fucking taking
83	2008	FIC	LiteraryRev	and die for you, like in a fairytale or a romance magazine. **You lose yourself** in your childhood dreams of noble wild men or brave martyrs, dramatically dead
84	2009	MAG	RollingStone	Who 2.' It's easy, and I catch fire, and **I lose myself** in the music - I've had some of my best moments onstage with
85	2004	FIC	Highlights	alone. Anna pulled her hat down against the rain, pelting now. **She lost herself** in memories of working on the ranch with Papa and Mama. That was
86	1999	FIC	FeministStud	smiles at him. # My eyes search for the horizon again; let **me lose myself** and all these ridiculous thoughts in the endless heaving of the water. It
87	1992	FIC	BkSFMeri	chimney, moss overlaid the crumbling walls. She looked. She searched. **She lost herself** in the tiniest details. Perhaps this year her maturing eyes would find what
88	1991	FIC	SewaneeRev	family, the abiding, comforting rituals of the family's common life. **She lost herself**. # I didn't see it happening, it happened gradually. My
89	1997	FIC	Tikkun	the " woosh, woosh " sound of her mother rolling spices. Often **she lost herself** in the utter serenity of the home, and days slipped by where she
90	2009	FIC	Analog	He drank in the silence of his authence and read it as appreciation. **He lost himself** in the story he had written, saw his authence in there with him
91	1997	FIC	ParisRev	dimensions obtains, Mr. Albemarle felt himself deepening, receding, going in. **He lost himself** in the picture a bit, or altogether, and lost himself in the
92	2002	NEWS	AssocPress	's death. He stopped talking to God. # At Purdue University, **he lost himself** in a haze of drink and drugs. After graduating with a degree in
93	1999	FIC	BkBlackAndBlue	them, to give those women new lives in new places, to help **them lose themselves**, start over in the great expansive anonymous sameness of America. " What
94	2000	FIC	Ploughshares	enormous bell of his body overexposed in white overalls, and for a moment **he loses himself** against the white wall tiles. # He leaves the bucket and mop,

95	2004	FIC	BkSeaTrolls	comfort to his father. Giles Crookleg might grumble like a crow, but **he lost himself** like a bird in the clouds of his own imaginings. He no longer
96	2012	FIC	BkSecondGraveOnLeft	devastated, and yet " # " And yet? " I asked when **he lost himself** in thought again. This was just getting interesting. He couldn't stop
97	2000	FIC	SouthernRev	came back inside and sat on the floor, and it was then that **she lost herself** in dreaming. I kneit next to her. Her hands were no longer
98	2008	FIC	Commentary	gotHelter Skelter, the story of the Manson Family murders. Reading it, **she lost herself** in a world of hippie runaways, swinging Hollywood decadence, and the middleclass
99	2007	ACAD	SouthwestRev	Atlantis: A Journal of Technology and Society, and for a few hours **I lost myself** in full-bore scholarly attacks on egocasters -- those who, with the aid of
100	1994	FIC	HarpersMag	. I was fastidious, careful with things like edges and rocks, and **I lost myself**, always, in the rhythm of the humming machine. When the mowing

Appendix 12

BNC: LOSE X-SELF

		2015 BNC [pp*] [lose] [ppx*]
1	K6Y	S_speech_unscripted	(pause) you know you was good what you were doing but that's where **you lost yourself** didn't you? (SP:PSCMW) Mhm. (SP:PS6MX) And, and er and that
2	FAT	W_fict_prose	why, but as I wondered the subject faded, my mind wandered... **I lost myself.** I tried to focus on my interior but there was nothing to focus
3	FP7	W_fict_prose	as he searched for the missing due. The memory was so strong that **he lost himself** in it. When he emerged, Karen was sitting in an armchair opposite
4	G04	W_fict_prose	, there on the island in the lantern light; how he had watched **her lose herself** in the tune she had been playing; how her voice had seemed the
5	GUG	W_fict_prose	stones to his left, the black to his right. For a time **he lost himself** in the game, his whole self gathered up into the shapes the stones
6	H84	W_fict_prose	Would Reni seek consolation in the arms of his last daughter, or would **he lose himself** in wine? Perhaps there was another route he would choose -- after meeting
7	HGG	W_fict_prose	have a fancy to show myself as far as Newport and Cardiff, while **they lose themselves** in the mountains of Maelienydd and Brecon." And I, my
8	HGV	W_fict_prose	You are mine -- and only mine. I knew it at once when **we lost ourselves** in our mutual passion. And if I had needed proof, it was
9	JY7	W_fict_prose	an intensity that was unnerving. She swung away from him. Why had **she lost herself** that way? She never did; she was always in control, it
10	CK4	W_pop_lore	Crying Game, an experience Jordan understands well.' London's a place **you lose yourself**, isn't it, for Irish people?' he suggests.'
11	A06	W_non_ac_humanities_arts	fucking sincerity. Between your legs the silver comets spiral through the night, **I lose myself**, he says... he says... how beautiful you are Maggie and how
12	OG3	W_non_ac_humanities_arts	are sure you knew it once but now it is so hazy. Will **you lose yourself**? What will you discover? You need a map. Make a map
13	EG0	W_non_ac_soc_science	's independence. # THE LANDSCAPE # As you walk through the industrial towns **you lose yourself** in labyrinths of little brick houses blackened by smoke, festering in planless chaos
14	B1F	W_religion	ridiculous airs and pomposities, and it is even valuable in the transcendent lest **we lose ourselves** in arrogance and pride and stray far from the real beauty of life.
15	CBN	W_biography	is a passion just like that of a sailor for the sea'. **He lost himself** in its possibilities, its immensity, he went far out, and came
16	CDG	W_biography	he was a wonderful, sweet, charming man. But when he drank **he lost himself** somehow.' By 1953 the name of James Dean was being bandied about

References

Abraham, W. (1995). Diathesis: The Middle, Particularly. *Discourse, Grammar and Typology: Papers in honor of John WM Verhaar, 27*, 3.

Ackema, P., & Schoorlemmer, M. (1994). The middle construction and the syntax-semantics interface. *Lingua, 93*(1), 59-90.

Alighieri, D. (2008). Divine Comedy, Inferno. Retrieved from https://justcheckingonall.wordpress.com/2008/02/28/complete-dante-alighieris-divine-comedy-in-pdf-3-books/

Allerton, D. (2006). 7 Verbs and their Satellites. *The Handbook of English Linguistics, 36*, 146.

Barcelona, A. (2000). Metaphor and Metonymy at the Crossroads: A Cognitive Perspective [Topics in English Linguistics 30]. *Berlin and New York: Mouton de Gruyter.*

Barcelona, A. (2002). Clarifying and applying the notions of metaphor and metonymy within cognitive linguistics: An update. *Dirven, René, and Ralf Pörings, eds. Metaphor and metonymy in comparison and contrast. Vol. 20. Walter de Gruyter, 2002.*, 207-277.

Barlow, M. (1996). Corpora for theory and practice. *International Journal of Corpus Linguistics, 1*(1), 1-37.

Barlow, M., & Kemmer, S. (1994). A Schema-Based Approach to Grammatical Description. *The Reality of Linguistic Rules, 26*, 19.

Bartsch, R. (2002). Generating polysemy: Metaphor and metonymy *Metaphor and metonymy in comparison and contrast* (Vol. 20, pp. 49).

Biber, D., Longman, & Co. (1999). *Longman Grammar of Spoken and Written English.* Harlow, England ; [New York]: Longman.

Bodhi, B. (2012). *Comprehensive Manual of Abhidhamma: The Abhidhammattha Sangaha*: Pariyatti Publishing.

Bowers, J. (2002). Transitivity. *Linguistic inquiry, 33*(2), 183-224.

The British National Corpus (BNC XML Edition). (2007). from Distributed by Bodleian Libraries, University od Oxford on behalf of the BNC Consortium URL: http://www.natcorp.ox.ac.uk/

Calude, A. S. (2007). Light and heavy reflexive marking: The Middle Domain in Romanian. *Annual Review of Cognitive Linguistics, 5*(1), 239-269.

Cameron, L. (2008). Metaphor and talk *The Cambridge handbook of metaphor and thought* (pp. 197-211). Cambridge: Cambridge University Press.

Collins Cobuild English Grammar. (2011). (J. Sinclair Ed.). Great Britain: HarperCollins.

Collins Dictionary Online. Glasgow, Scotland: HarperCollins Publishers Limited.

Collins English Dictionary online. (2014). Retrieved from
http://www.collinsdictionary.com/dictionary/english/find-oneself#find-oneself_1

Comrie, B. (1989). *Language Universals and Linguistic Typology: Syntax and Morphology*:
University of Chicago press.

Crisp, P. (2002). Metaphorical propositions: a rationale. *Language and Literature, 11*(1), 7-
16.

Croft, W. (1993). The role of domains in the interpretation of metaphors and metonymies.
Cognitive Linguistics, 4(4), 335-370.

Croft, W., & Cruse, D. A. (2004). *Cognitive Linguistics*: Cambridge University Press.

Damasio, A. (2010a). *Self Comes to Mind: Constructing the Conscious Mind*. New York:
Pantheon.

Damasio, A. (2010b). Self comes to mind: constructing the conscious mind. *New York:
Pantheon.*

Davies, M. (2008). The Corpus of Contemporary American English. from Brigham Young
University http://corpus.byu.edu/coca/

Davies, M. (2016, Sept. 4, 2016). [Personal communication].

de Swart, P. (2006). Case markedness. *Case, Valency and Transitivity*, 249-267.

Deignan, A. (2005). *Metaphor and Corpus Linguistics* (Vol. 6): John Benjamins Publishing.

Deignan, A. (2007). The grammar of linguistic metaphors. In A. Stefanowitsch & S. Gries
(Eds.), *Corpus-based approaches to metaphor and metonymy*: Walter de Gruyter.

Deignan, A. (2007). The grammar of linguistic metaphors. In A. Stefanowitsch & S. Gries
(Eds.), *Corpus-based Approaches to Metaphor and Metonymy* (pp. 106-122). Berlin:
Walter de Gruyter.

Deignan, A. (2008). Corpus linguistics and metaphor *The Cambridge handbook of metaphor
and thought* (Vol. 280, pp. 290). Cambridge: Cambridge University Press.

Dirven, R. (2002). Metonymy and metaphor: different mental strategies of conceptualisation.
Metaphor and metonymy in comparison and contrast, 112.

Dixon, R. M. (2005). *A semantic approach to English grammar*: Oxford University Press.

Dixon, R. M., & Aĭkhenval'd, A. I. U. r. (2000). *Changing Valency: Case Studies in
Transitivity*: Cambridge University Press.

Dowty, D. (1991). Thematic proto-roles and argument selection. *Language*, 547-619.

Doyle, A. (2007). Passives, middles, and reflexives in Irish. *Folia Linguistica Historica, 41*(Historica vol. 28, 1-2), 115-144.

Ebeling, J., & Ebeling, S. O. (2013). *Patterns in Contrast* (Vol. 58): John Benjamins Publishing.

Faltz, L. M. (1985). *Reflexivization : A Study in Universal Syntax*. New York: Garland Publishing.

Fauconnier, G. (1985). *Mental Spaces : Aspects of Meaning Construction in Natural Language*. Cambridge, Mass ; London: MIT Press.

Feldman, J. (2008). From molecule to metaphor: a neural theory of language. Cambridge, MA: The MIT Pess, Cambridge MA.

Feyaerts, K. (2000). Refining the Inheritance Hypothesis: Interaction between metaphoric and metonymic hierarchies. In A. Barcelona (Ed.), *Metaphor and metonymy at the crossroads. A cognitive perspective* (pp. 59-78). Berlin and New York: Mouton de Gruyter.

Frajzyngier, Z. (2000). Domains of point of view and coreferentiality. *Reflexives: Forms and functions*, 125-152.

Frajzyngier, Z., & Curl, T. S. (2000). *Reflexives : forms and functions*. Amsterdam ; Philadelphia: J. Benjamins.

Fukaya, T. (2002). On Viewing Reflexives in the Bank of English: Their Distribution and Function. *English Corpus Linguistics in Japan*(38).

Gärdenfors, P., & Löhndorf, S. (2013). What is a domain? Dimensional structures versus meronomic relations. *Cognitive Linguistics, 24*(3), 437-456.

Gast, V., & Siemund, P. (2006). Rethinking the relationship between SELF-intensifiers and reflexives. *Linguistics, 44*(2), 343-381.

Geniusiene, E. (1987). *The typology of reflexives* (Vol. 2): Walter de Gruyter.

Gibbs Jr, R. W. (2008). *The Cambridge handbook of metaphor and thought*. Cambridge: Cambridge University Press.

Gibbs, R. W. (1994). The poetics of mind: Cambridge: Cambridge University Press.

Gibbs, R. W. (2002). Psycholinguistic comments on metaphor identification. *Langauge and Literature, 11*(1), 78-84.

Gibbs, R. W. (2007). Why cognitive linguists should care more about empirical methods. In M. Gonzalez-Marquez (Ed.), *Methods in Cognitive Linguistics* (pp. 2-18). Amsterdam: John Benjamins Publishing.

Gibbs, R. W. (2016). Seven Empirical Challenges for Cognitive Linguistics. *Journal of Cognitive Linguistics, 2*(March 2017), 13.

Gilquin, G. (2007). Causing oneself to do something: The psychodynamics of causative constructions. In E. M. a. M. Bermúdez, Leonel Ruiz (Ed.), *Linguistics in the Twenty First Century* (pp. 37-46). Newcastle, UK: Cambridge Scholars Press.

Gilquin, G. (2010a). *Corpus, Cognition and Causative Constructions.* Amsterdam ; Philadelphia: John Benjamins Publishing.

Gilquin, G. (2010b). *Corpus, cognition and causative constructions [electronic resource].* Amsterdam ; Philadelphia: John Benjamins Pub. Co.

Goatly, A. (2002). Text-linguistic comments on metaphor identification. *Language and Literature, 11*(1), 70-74.

Goossens, L. (2002). Metaphtonymy: The interaction of metaphor and metonymy in expressions for linguistic action *Metaphor and metonymy in comparison and contrast* (pp. 349-378). Berlin and New York: Mouton de Gruyter.

Goossens, L., Pauwels, P., Rudzka-Ostyn, B., Simon-Vandenbergen, A.-M., & Vanparys, J. (1995). *By Word of Mouth: Metaphor, Metonymy and Linguistic Action in a Cognitive Perspective* (Vol. 33): John Benjamins Publishing.

Grady, & Johnson. (2003). Converging evidence for the notions of subscene and primary scene. In R. P. Dirven, R. (Ed.), *Metaphor and Metonymy in Contrast* (pp. 533-554). Berlin: Mouton de Gruyter.

Grady, J., & C., J. (2003). Converging evidence for the notions of subscene and primary scene. In R. P. Dirven, R. (Ed.), *Metaphor and Metonymy in Contrast* (pp. 533-554). Berlin: Mouton de Gruyter.

Grady, J., & Johnson, C. (2012). *Converging evidence for the notions of subscene and primary scene.* Paper presented at the Proceedings of the Annual Meeting of the Berkeley Linguistics Society.

Grady, J. E. (2005). Image schemas and perception: Refining a definition. *From Perception to Meaning: Image Schemas in Cognitive Linguistics, 29*, 35.

Group, P. (2007). MIP: A method for identifying metaphorically used words in discourse. *Metaphor and symbol, 22*(1), 1-39.

Helke, M. (1979). *The Grammar of English Reflexives.* New York: Garland Publishing.

Herbst, T. (2007). Valency complements or valency patterns? *Trends in Linguistics Studies and Monographs, 187*, 15.

Herbst, T., & Götz-Votteler, K. (2007). *Valency: theoretical, descriptive and cognitive issues* (Vol. 187): Walter de Gruyter.

Herbst, T., Heath, D., Roe, I. F., & Götz, D. (2004). *A Valency Dictionary of English: A Corpus-based Analysis of the Complementation Patterns of English Verbs, Nouns and Adjectives* (Vol. 40): Walter de Gruyter.

Heywood, J., Semino, E., & Short, M. (2002). Linguistic Metaphor Identification in Two Extracts from Novels. *Language and Literature, 11*(1), 35-54.

Hopper, P. J., & Thompson, S. A. (1980). Transitivity in grammar and discourse. *Language*, 251-299.

Hunston, S., & Francis, G. (2000). *Pattern Grammar: A Corpus-driven Approach to the Lexical Grammar of English*: John Benjamins Publishing.

Hunt, A. (2016). Left Hand Problems. *The Round Table*. Retrieved from http://shsroundtable.com/uncategorized/2016/01/15/left-handed-problems/

Ismael, J. (2006). *The Situated Self*. Oxford: Oxford University Press.

Janzen, G. (2008). *The reflexive nature of consciousness* (Vol. 72): John Benjamins Publishing, Amsterdam.

Johnson, M. (2005). The philosophical significance of image schemas. In B. Hampe (Ed.), *From Perception to Meaning: Image Schemas in Cognitive Linguistics* (pp. 15-33). Berlin and New York: Mouton de Gruyter.

Johnson, M. (2013). *The Body in the Mind: The Bodily Basis of Meaning, Imagination, and Reason*. Chicago: University of Chicago Press.

Kalinina, E., Kolomatsky, D., & Sudobina, A. (2006). Transitivity increase markers interacting with verb semantics. *Case, Valency and Transitivity*, 441-463.

Kemmer, S. (1993). *The Middle Voice*. Amsterdam ; Philadelphia: John Benjamins Publishing.

Klaiman, M. H. (1991). *Grammatical Voice* (Vol. 59): Cambridge University Press.

König, E., & Gast, V. (2002). Reflexive pronouns and other uses of self-forms in English. *Zeitschrift für Anglistik und Amerikanistik, 50*(3), 1-14.

König, E., & Gast, V. (2008). *Reciprocals and reflexives : theoretical and typological explorations*. Berlin ; New York: Mouton de Gruyter.

Konig, E., & Siemund, P. (2000). Intensifiers and reflexives: a typological perspective. *Z: Frajzyngier and T. Curl, eds, Reflexives.'Forms and Functions. Benjamins, Amsterdam*, 41-74.

Kovecses, Z. (2002). *Metaphor: A Practical Introduction*. Oxford: Oxford University Press.

Kovecses, Z. (2006). Language, mind, and culture. Z. *Kovecses.-Oxford: Oxford University Press.*

Kövecses, Z. (2002). Cognitive-linguistic comments on metaphor identification. *Language and Literature, 11*(1), 74-78.

Kövecses, Z. (2003). *Metaphor and Emotion: Language, Culture, and Body in Human Feeling*: Cambridge University Press.

Kövecses, Z. (2010). A new look at metaphorical creativity in cognitive linguistics. *Cognitive Linguistics, 21*(4), 663-697.

Kulikov, L., Malchukov, A., & de Swart, P. (2006). *Case, valency and transitivity* (Vol. 77): John Benjamins Publishing.

Kuno, S. (1987). *Functional syntax : anaphora, discourse and empathy.* Chicago ; London: University of Chicago Press.

Lakoff, A., & Becker, M. (1992). Me, Myself, and I. *Manuscript, University of California, Berkeley.*

Lakoff, G. (1990a). The invariance hypothesis: Is abstract reason based on image-schemas? *Cognitive Linguistics (includes Cognitive Linguistic Bibliography), 1*(1), 39-74.

Lakoff, G. (1990b). *Women, fire, and dangerous things: What categories reveal about the mind.* Cambridge: Cambridge Univ Press.

Lakoff, G. (1992). Multiple selves: the metaphorical models of the self inherent in our conceptual system. Retrieved from https://escholarship.org/uc/item/53g1n5b2

Lakoff, G. (1993a). The contemporary theory of metaphor. In A. Ortony (Ed.), *Metaphor and thought* (pp. 202-251). Cambridge: Cambridge University Press.

Lakoff, G. (1993b). The contemporary theory of metaphor. *Metaphor and thought, 2,* 202-251.

Lakoff, G. (1996a). Sorry, I'm not myself today: The metaphor system for conceptualizing the self. In G. F. E. Sweetser (Ed.), *Spaces, worlds, and grammar* (pp. 91-123). Chicago, Illinois. USA: University of Chicago Press.

Lakoff, G. (1996b). Sorry, I'm not myself today: The metaphor system for conceptualizing the self. *Spaces, worlds, and grammar,* 91-123.

Lakoff, G., & Johnson, M. (1980). The metaphorical structure of the human conceptual system. *Cognitive science, 4*(2), 195-208.

Lakoff, G., & Johnson, M. (1999). *Philosophy in the Flesh: The Embodied Mind and its Challenge to Western Thought.* New York: Basic books.

Lakoff, G., & Johnson, M. (2003). *Metaphors we live by. 1980*. Chicago: University of Chicago Press.

Lakoff, G., & Johnson, M. (2008). *Metaphors We Live By*. Chicago: University of Chicago Press.

Lakoff, G., & Kövecses, Z. (1987). The cognitive model of anger inherent in American English. *Cultural Models in Language and Thought*, 195-221.

Lakoff, G., & Turner, M. (2009). *More Than Cool Reason: A Field Guide to Poetic Metaphor*. Chicago: University of Chicago Press.

Langacker, R. W. (1985). Observations and speculations on subjectivity. *Iconicity in Syntax, 1*(985), 109.

Langacker, R. W. (1987a). Foundations of Cognitive Grammar, vol. 1, Theoretical Prerequisites, vol. 2, Descriptive Application: Stanford, CA: Stanford University Press.

Langacker, R. W. (1987b). *Foundations of Cognitive Grammar: Theoretical Prerequisites* (Vol. 1). Stanford, California: Stanford university press.

Langacker, R. W. (1990). Subjectification. *Cognitive Linguistics, 1*(1), 5-38.

Langacker, R. W. (2002). *Concept, Image, and Symbol*. Berlin and New York: Mouton de Gruyter Inc.

Langacker, R. W. (2006). *Descriptive Application, Vol. II*. Stanford, California: Stanford University Press.

Langacker, R. W. (2008). *Cognitive Grammar: A Basic Introduction*. Oxford: Oxford University Press.

Langacker, R. W. (2009). Metonymic grammar. In K.-U. Panther, L. L. Thornburg, & A. Barcelona (Eds.), *Metonymy and metaphor in grammar* (Vol. 25, pp. 45-71). Amsterdam / Philadelphia: John Benjamins Publishing Company.

Lange, C. (2007). *Reflexivity and Intensification in English : A Study of Texts and Contexts*. Frankfurt am Main ; Oxford: Peter Lang.

LaPolla, R. J. (1996). *Middle voice marking in Tibeto-Burman*. Paper presented at the Proceedings of the fourth international symposium on languages and linguistics: Pan-Asiatic linguistics.

LDOCE. (2014). Longman Dictionary of Contemporary English Online. Available from Pearson Education Limited, from Pearson Education Limited http://www.ldoceonline.com/search/?q=find

Lederer, J. (2013). Understanding the Self: How spatial parameters influence the distribution of anaphora within prepositional phrases. *Cognitive Linguistics, 24*(3), 483-529.

Lekakou, M. (2002). Middle semantics and its realization in English and Greek. *UCLA Working Papers in Linguistics, 14*, 399-416.

Levin, B. (1993). *English verb classes and alternations: A preliminary investigation*: University of Chicago press.

Levin, B., & Hovav, M. R. (2005). *Argument realization*: Cambridge University Press.

Lewis, M. (2006). Myself and me. In R. W. M. Sue Taylor Parker, Maria L. Boccia (Ed.), *Self-awareness in animals and humans: Developmental perspectives* (pp. 20). Cambridge: Cambridge University Press.

Littlemore, J. (2015). *Metonymy*: Cambridge University Press.

Longman Dictionary of Contemporary English. (2014). Retrieved from http://www.ldoceonline.com/search/?q=find

Maldonado, R. (2000). Conceptual distance and transitivity increase in Spanish reflexives. *TYPOLOGICAL STUDIES IN LANGUAGE, 40*, 153-186.

Martin, J. B. (2000). 12 Creek voice: beyond valency. *Changing Valency: Case studies in transitivity*, 375.

Matsuki, K. (1995). Metaphors of anger in Japanese. *Language and the Cognitive Construal of the World, 82*, 137.

Matthews, P. (2007). The scope of valency in grammar. *Trends in Linguistics Studies and Monographs, 187*, 3.

McGraw-Hill. (2002). kick oneself. *Dictionary of American Idioms and Phrasal Verbs*. Retrieved from http://idioms.thefreedictionary.com/kick+oneself

Milne, A. A. (1926). *Winnie-The-Pooh*. New York: Dutton Children's Books.

Næss, Å. (2007). *Prototypical transitivity* (Vol. 72): John Benjamins Publishing.

Nanamoli, B. (1991). *The Path of Purification: Visuddhimagga*: Buddhist Publication Society.

Nida-Rümelin, M. (2011). The conceptual origin of subject body dualism. In A. Coliva (Ed.), *The Self and Self-Knowledge*. Oxford: Oxford University Press.

OEDO, O. E. D. (2008). *Oxford English dictionary online*: Oxford University Press, Oxford, UK http://www. oed. com.

Onishi, M. (2000). Transitivity and valency-changing derivations in Motuna. *Changing Valency: Case studies in transitivity*, 115-143.

Oxford University, P. (2015). Oxford Dictionaries Online. [Find].

Panther, K.-U., Thornburg, L. L., & Barcelona, A. (2009). *Metonymy and metaphor in grammar* (Vol. 25). Amsterdam / Philadelphia: John Benjamins Publishing.

Parker, S. T., Mitchell, R. W., & Boccia, M. L. (Eds.). (2006). *Self-awareness in Animals and Humans: Developmental Perspectives*: Cambridge University Press.

Peitsara, K. (1997). The development of reflexive strategies in English. *Grammaticalization at Work: Studies of Long-term Developments in English, 24*, 277.

Quirk, R., Greenbaum, S., Leech, G., & Svartvik, J. (1985). *A Comprehensive Grammar of the English Language* (Vol. 397). New York, USA: Longman Group, Ltd.

Radden, G. (2002). How metonymic are metaphors. In R. P. Dirven, R. (Ed.), *Metaphor and metonymy in comparison and contrast* (pp. 407-434). Berlin and New York: Mouton de Gruyter.

Radden, G., & Kövecses, Z. (1999). Towards a theory of metonymy. In A. Ortony (Ed.), *Metonymy in language and thought* (pp. 17-60). Cambridge: Cambridge University Press.

Rice, S. (2011). *Towards a transitive prototype: Evidence from some atypical English passives*. Paper presented at the Proceedings of the annual meeting of the Berkeley Linguistics Society.

Rozas, V. V. (2007). A usage-based approach to prototypical transitivity. *Trends in Linguistics Studies and Monographs, 198*, 17.

Ruiz de Mendoza, F. J., & Díez, O. (2002). Patterns of conceptual interaction. In R. P. Dirven, R. (Ed.), *Metaphor and metonymy in comparison and contrast* (Vol. 532). Berlin and New York: Mouton de Gruyter.

Safir, K. J. (2004). *The Syntax of Anaphora*. Oxford ; New York: Oxford University Press.

Satchidananda, S. (1984). *The Yoga Sutras of Patanjali: Translation and Commentary by Sri Swami Satchidananda*. Yogaville, Virginia: Integral Yoga Publications.

Sinclair, J. (1991). *Corpus, concordance, collocation*: Oxford University Press.

Sinclair, J. (1991). *Corpus, Concordance, Collocation*: Oxford University Press.

Smith, M. (2004). Light and heavy reflexives1. *Linguistics, 42*(3), 573-615.

Stangroom, J. (2017). Social Sciences Statistics. Retrieved from http://www.socscistatistics.com/Default.aspx

Steen, G. (2002). Towards a procedure for metaphor identification. *Language and Literature, 11*(1), 17-33.

Steen, G., Dorst, A. G., Hermann, J., Kaal, A. A., Krennmayr, T., & Pasma, T. (2010). *A Method for Linguistic Metaphor Identification* (Vol. 14). Amsterdam: John Benjamins Publishing.

Stefanowitsch, A., & Gries, S. T. (2003). Collostructions: Investigating the interaction of words and constructions. *International journal of corpus linguistics, 8*(2), 209-243.

Stefanowitsch, A., & Gries, S. T. (Eds.). (2007). *Corpus-based Approaches to Metaphor and Metonymy*. Berlin: Mouton de Gruyter.

Stephens, N. (2006). Agentivity and the virtual reflexive construction. *Demoting the agent: Passive, middle and other voice phenomena. Amsterdam*, 275-300.

Stiles, M. (2001). *Yoga Sutras of Patanjali*: Weiser Books.

Talmy, L. (2000a). Toward a cognitive semantics. Volume 1: Concept structuring systems. Volume 2: Typology and process in concept structuring: Cambridge, MA: MIT Press.

Talmy, L. (2000b). Toward a cognitive semantics. Volume II: Typology and process in concept structuring: Cambridge, MA: The MIT Press.

Talmy, L. (2001a). *Toward a cognitive semantics*. Cambridge, Mass. ; London: MIT.

Talmy, L. (2001b). *Toward a Cognitive Semantics* (Vol. 1). Cambridge, Mass. ; London: MIT.

Talmy, L. (2003). *Toward a cognitive semantics*. Cambridge, Mass. ; London: MIT.

Taoka, I. (1999). Find Oneself+ C 構文の意味論 (Find Oneself+ C Koubunn-no Imiron). *英語語法文法研究 (Eigo-Gouhou-Bunpou-Kenkyu)*(6), 129-140.

Taoka, I. (2009). Find+ Oneself+ Complement no Tokusei to Dentatsu-kouka (Find+ Oneself+ Complement の特性と伝達効果). *Osaka Kougyou Daigaku Kiyou (大阪工業大学紀要. 人文社会篇), 53*, 1-10.

Taylor, J. R. (2003). *Linguistic Categorization*. Oxford: Oxford University Press.

Thomas Herbst, P. U., Thomas Proisl, Sebastian Rettig. (2014). Erlangen Valency Patternbank. Retrieved from www.patternbank.uni-erlangen.de/cgi-bin/patternbank.cgi?do=wsq&shw=find&search=Search

Tuggy, D. (2007). Schematicity. In D. C. Geeraerts, Hubert (Ed.), *The Oxford Handbook of Cognitive Linguistics. Oxford*. Oxford: Oxford University Press.

Van Hoek, K. (1997). *Anaphora and conceptual structure*. Chicago ; London: University of Chicago Press.

Warren, B. (2002). An alternative account of the interpretation of referential metonymy and
metaphor. In R. P. Dirven, R. (Ed.), *Metaphor and metonymy in comparison and
contrast* (pp. 113-130). Berlin and New York: Walter de Gruyter.

Watson, J. S. (2006). Detection of self: The perfect algorithm. In S. T. Parker, R. W. Mitchell,
& M. L. Boccia (Eds.), *Self-awareness in animals and humans: Developmental
perspectives* (pp. 131). Cambridge: Cambridge University Press.

Williams, P. (2000). *The Reflexive Nature of Awareness: A Tibetan Madhyamaka Defence.*
New Delhi: Motilal Banarsidass Publishers.

Yu, N. (2008). Metaphor from body and culture. In R. W. Gibbs Jr (Ed.), *The Cambridge
Handbook of Metaphor and Thought* (pp. 247-261). New York: Cambridge University
Press.

Printed in the USA
CPSIA information can be obtained
at www.ICGtesting.com
LVHW090746060923
757286LV00004BA/527